Exquisite Slaves

In *Exquisite Slaves*, Tamara J. Walker examines how slaves used elegant clothing as a language for expressing attitudes about gender and status in the wealthy urban center of eighteenth- and nineteenth-century Lima, Peru. Drawing on traditional historical research methods, visual studies, feminist theory, and material culture scholarship, Walker argues that clothing was an emblem of not only the reach but also the limits of slaveholders' power and racial domination. Even as it acknowledges the significant limits imposed on slaves' access to elegant clothing, *Exquisite Slaves* also showcases the insistence and ingenuity with which slaves dressed to convey their own sense of humanity and dignity. Building on other scholars' work on slaves' agency and subjectivity in examining how they made use of myriad legal discourses and forums, *Exquisite Slaves* argues for the importance of understanding the body itself as a site of claims-making.

TAMARA J. WALKER earned her PhD in history from the University of Michigan. Her previous work has appeared in *Slavery & Abolition*, *Safundi*, *Gender & History*, and *The Journal of Family History*.

Exquisite Slaves
Race, Clothing, and Status in Colonial Lima

TAMARA J. WALKER

CAMBRIDGE
UNIVERSITY PRESS

University Printing House, Cambridge CB2 8BS, United Kingdom

One Liberty Plaza, 20th Floor, New York, NY 10006, USA

477 Williamstown Road, Port Melbourne, VIC 3207, Australia

314-321, 3rd Floor, Plot 3, Splendor Forum, Jasola District Centre, New Delhi - 110025, India

79 Anson Road, #06-04/06, Singapore 079906

Cambridge University Press is part of the University of Cambridge.

It furthers the University's mission by disseminating knowledge in the pursuit of education, learning and research at the highest international levels of excellence.

www.cambridge.org
Information on this title: www.cambridge.org/9781107445956
DOI: 10.1017/9781316018781

© Tamara J. Walker 2017

This publication is in copyright. Subject to statutory exception and to the provisions of relevant collective licensing agreements, no reproduction of any part may take place without the written permission of Cambridge University Press.

First published 2017
First paperback edition 2019

A catalogue record for this publication is available from the British Library

Library of Congress Cataloging in Publication data
Names: Walker, Tamara J., 1978- author.
Title: Exquisite slaves : race, clothing, and status in colonial Lima / Tamara J. Walker.
Description: New York : Cambridge University Press, 2017. | Includes bibliographical references and index.
Identifiers: LCCN 2016056215 | ISBN 9781107084032 (Hardback : alk. paper)
Subjects: LCSH: Lima (Peru)–Social life and customs–18th century. | Clothing and dress–Social aspects–Peru–Lima–History–18th century. | Blacks–Clothing–Peru–Lima–History–18th century. | Slaves–Clothing–Peru–Lima–History–18th century. | Blacks–Race identity–Peru–Lima–History.
Classification: LCC F3601.9.B55 W35 2017 | DDC 985/.25500496009033–dc23
LC record available at https://lccn.loc.gov/2016056215

ISBN 978-1-107-08403-2 Hardback
ISBN 978-1-107-44595-6 Paperback

Cambridge University Press has no responsibility for the persistence or accuracy of URLs for external or third-party internet websites referred to in this publication, and does not guarantee that any content on such websites is, or will remain, accurate or appropriate.

Contents

	Acknowledgments	*page* vi
	Introduction	1
1	Slavery and the Aesthetic of Mastery	20
2	Legal Status, Gender, and Self-Fashioning	43
3	Black Bodies and Boundary Trouble	78
4	*Casta* Painting and Colonial Ideation	97
5	Print Culture and the Problem of Slavery	128
6	Ladies, Gentlemen, Slaves, and Citizens	145
	Epilogue	165
	Endnotes	174
	Bibliography	209
	Index	226

Acknowledgments

This book has benefited from the support of several institutions and individuals who played instrumental roles at crucial stages. During my PhD studies, the Rackham School of Graduate Studies, the Department of History, and the Latin American and Caribbean Studies Program at the University of Michigan funded exploratory archival trips and regularly subsidized my travel expenses thereafter; the US Department of Education for the Fulbright-Hays DDRA Award funded dissertation research in Peru; and the Ford Foundation not only provided financial assistance during the dissertation writing process but also made me part of a supportive and enduring network of fellows.

While in graduate school, I also had the immense fortune of finding guidance and community at my home institution and when I traveled beyond its borders. To my dissertation chair, Rebecca J. Scott, I am thankful for her example, patience, encouragement, and eye for all manner of contextual, linguistic, logical, and mechanical detail. I also owe profound thanks to Sueann Caulfield, Michele Mitchell, Ifeoma Nwankwo, and Richard Turits, who helped shape the dissertation from conception to completion, and to Rachel O'Toole, whose arrival in Ann Arbor during the final stages of the writing process proved immeasurably fortuitous. I am also grateful to several readers and colleagues from near and far, including Carlos Aguirre, Herman Bennett, Carlos Contreras, Aisha Finch, Tanji Gilliam, Jean Hébrard, Jessica M. Johnson, Brandy Jones, Brooke Jones, Martha Jones, Silvia Lara, Johonna McCants, Stephanie McNulty, Jeremy Mumford, Scarlett O'Phelan Godoy, Julia Paulson, Rebekah Pite, Vincent Peloso, Karen Spalding, and Ben Vinson, for their feedback on various components and drafts of the dissertation.

Throughout my time in Lima I have encountered only the most generous souls, including program coordinators, archivists, and researchers. I am especially grateful to Henry Harman, Marcela Harth, and Illa Quintanilla at the Peru Fulbright Commission, as well as to the staff at the the Archivo Arzobispal de Lima (AAL), the Archivo General de la Nación (AGN), the Biblioteca Nacional del Perú (BNP), the Insituto Riva-Agüero (IRA), and the Instituto de Estudios Peruanos (IEP) for their knowledge of the rich collections and their thoughtful guidance as I worked through them. Special thanks go to Yolanda Auquí and "Don Manuel" at the AGN; to Laura Gutiérrez and Melecio Tineo Morón at the AAL; to Greta Manrique Mondolfo at the IRA; and to Jesús Lopez at LUNDU.

After finishing graduate school and beginning my career at The University of Pennsylvania, I received early support in the form of a Mellon Postdoctoral Teaching Fellowship, a Trustees Council of Penn Women summer research stipend, and a School of Arts & Sciences Research Opportunity Grant, which enabled me to travel to Peru and Spain for additional research. I owe Ann Matter special thanks for showing stunning generosity when she replenished my research fund with a portion of her own. A Career Enhancement Fellowship from the Woodrow Wilson National Fellowship Foundation provided support for me to take leave from teaching, and the opportunity to join another dynamic community of scholars. The departments of History and Africana Studies, along with the program in Latin American and Latino Studies at Penn, were also sources of both fiscal and scholarly generosity. I am particularly grateful to the History Department for organizing a manuscript workshop on my behalf, and to Kathleen Brown, Susan Deans-Smith, Ann Farnsworth-Alvear, Steve Hahn, Kris Lane, Daniel Richter, and Eve Troutt-Powell for providing close readings of my work. I am also thankful to the Annenberg Seminar in History and the English Department's Latitudes Reading Group for the opportunity to present chapter drafts, and to the members of the Race and Empire Faculty Working Group at Penn for providing the kind of intellectual home we scholars always want to be part of but rarely encounter. I am particularly grateful to David Eng, Jed Esty, Tsitsi Jaji, Suvir Kaul, David Kazanjian, Ania Loomba, Christopher McKnight-Nichols, Deborah Thomas, and Chi-Ming Yang for their critiques, advice, and friendship over the years.

As was true when I was a graduate student, I have been lucky to find a diverse scholarly community that transcends institutional walls. I would have been totally unmoored as I embarked on revising my dissertation had it not been for the members of my various writing groups, including Michelle Chase, Marcela Echeverri, Anne Eller, Mikaela Luttrell-Rowland, Yuko Miki, Okezi Otovo, Rebekah Pite, Sarah Sarzynski, and Zeb Tortorici, to whom I give thanks for their well-read and thoughtful critiques of my drafts and for the pleasure of their company (in person, via Skype, over the phone, and in spirit) as we all climbed our respective mountains. In addition, I thank the following people and programs for the opportunity to present work in progress: Lee Ann Fujii, Susan Sell, and the IGIS Research Seminar Series at the George Washington University; Rebecca J. Scott and the "'Leap on Shore Accompanied by your Scribe ...': Cultural Approaches to the History of the Iberian Atlantic and the Caribbean" Collaborative Workshop at the University of Michigan; Frank Guridy and the Department of History at the University of Texas at Austin; Ramnarayan Rawat and the History Workshop at the University of Delaware; Jenny Hirsh and the Maryland Institute College of Art; Daina Berry and the Sexuality and Slavery Workshop at the University of Texas at Austin; Sinclair Thomson and the New York City Latin American History Workshop; Larissa Brewer Garcia, Ashley Cohen, Matthew Goldmark, María Elena Martínez, Yolanda Martínez-San Miguel, Jocelyn Olcott, Shana Redmond, David Sartorius, Adam Warren, and the Tepoztlán Institute for the Transnational History of the Americas; and Ademide Adelusi-Adeluyi, Michael Gomez, and the African Diaspora Workshop at New York University.

It has been a genuine privilege and pleasure to work with Deborah Gershenowitz and Kristina Deusch at Cambridge University

Press. Debbie's early enthusiasm for the project has meant the world to me, as has her encouragement and kind support along the way. I owe additional thanks to the two anonymous readers for Cambridge University Press for their tremendously erudite, constructive, and animating suggestions. I also thank Herman Bennett and Herbert Klein for carefully critiquing drafts of the manuscript, and Kate Epstein, Lyman Johnson, Jennifer Morgan, and Ben Vinson for their generous advice, feedback, and support.

I owe my family more than I can ever repay, and give thanks to my mom, Phyllis, for all that I am and want to be. My sister Tanisha, the most curious and clever of us all, is the reader I considered most often as I wrote. I also thank my grandparents, the late John and Willie Mae, for giving me so much of their love for so much of my life, as well as for the children, grandchildren, and great-grandchildren who are their best legacy. That Uncle Buddy, Joyce, and Jackie are no longer around to read these words breaks my heart all over again. To my husband, Aaron Gabow, I owe my entire sense of balance and contentment, and I will forever hold dear the patient nurturing (and kind bullying) that pushed me to the finish. And to the rest of my chosen family – Niki Mandler Acosta, Sivonne Davis, Autumn François, Lee Ann Fujii, Patricia and Hal Gabow, Anna Holland Edwards, Brooke Jones, Mikaela Luttrell-Rowland, Stephanie McNulty, Angela Moore, Tenaya and Scott Newkirk, Julia Paulson, and Ellen Scott – thanks for always making me enjoy the world of the living as much as that of the long-dead.

Introduction

Upon arriving in the viceregal capital of Lima as part of a clandestine mission that took him to various parts of South America between 1712 and 1714, French engineer Amedée Frézier described a lavish setting. "Lima," he wrote, "is the depot for the treasures of Peru," where stunning architecture, gilded carriages, and luxury goods abounded.[1] The Frenchman was particularly taken during his visit by the costumes of the city's inhabitants:

> Men and women are equally inclined toward magnificence in dress: the women, not content to just wear rich and beautiful fabrics, adorn themselves with a prodigious quantity of laces, and are insatiable in their desire for pearls, precious stones, bracelets, earrings, and other paraphernalia, the costs of which ruin many husbands and gentlemen.[2]

Frézier was not alone in these impressions. Travelers from around the world wrote similar descriptions upon paying a visit to the city in the early part of the eighteenth century, and their references to *limeños'* sartorial splendor were so frequent as to cohere into an informal kind of visitors' script.

When British naval captain William Betagh took his turn to write about Lima upon his arrival in the 1720s, he observed that "of all parts of the world, the people are most expensive in their habit," before going on to note that "the pride of both sexes appears chiefly in *Maclin* and *Brussels* lace, with which they trim their linen in a most extravagant manner, not omitting their sheets and pillows."[3] For their part, Spanish travelers Jorge Juan and Antonio de Ulloa described a city with wide-open possibilities for luxurious consumption:

> The usual dress of the men differs very little from that worn in Spain, nor is there much variation among the different hierarchies; because there is a variety of fabrics that is widely available, everyone wears what they can purchase. So it is not uncommon to see a *mulato*, or any other working man, dressed in rich fabrics, equal to anything that can be worn by a man of superior *calidad*.[4]

Even locals joined in on these effusive descriptions. The writer Pedro de Peralta y Barnuevo proudly praised his hometown as "not only one of the greatest cities in the world for the number of its inhabitants (who are among the best in terms of temperament and circumstance), and one the most opulent for its abundance and riches, but it presides with grandeur over an entire Empire."[5]

Taken together, these accounts paint a vivid picture of Lima's eighteenth-century opulence. But they also flatten the terrain of the city's social and sartorial landscape. They depict an environment in which Spaniards (defined here as Iberian-born *peninsulares* and American-born *criollos*), Indians, Africans, and their mixed-race offspring (a group collectively known as *castas*) largely enjoyed equal access to finery. Regardless of their ancestry, legal condition, socioeconomic status, or even sex, it seemed that for *limeños*, money was the only barrier – as well as the only key – to experiencing all the material riches the city had the offer. Moreover, the authors give the impression that all of Lima's inhabitants shared and expressed the same aesthetic sensibilities.

Exquisite Slaves takes the world at the margins of these descriptions – the Lima that Frézier, Betagh, Juan, Ulloa, Peralta y Barnuevo, and others could not or would not describe – as its primary focus. In broad terms, the book examines the relationship between clothing and status in an ethnically diverse, urban slaveholding society. It does so by focusing on the varying forms of access *limeños* had to elegant dress and the diversity and meanings of their fashions. As its title suggests, the book gives particular attention to the city's population of

African slaves, who not only figured prominently in Spaniards' sartorial displays but developed their own methods and modes of elegant self-presentation as well. As a result, they were also the primary subjects of various writings about dress and deportment, from sumptuary laws, travel accounts, as well as contemporary discourses surrounding who should wear what and why.

The book opens in the early eighteenth century, when Lima was capital of the Viceroyalty of Peru, gateway to the silver-mining center at Potosí, nexus of trade between East and West, home to a thriving urban economy, and a city of superlatives. It was one of Spain's most significant imperial footholds, its premier engine of wealth, and a site of unparalleled luxurious consumption. The period also marked the height of slaves' demographic visibility in Lima. By 1700, Lima's population totaled around 37,000 souls, including roughly 18,000 Spaniards, 13,000 slaves, and 6,000 free people of African, Indian, and mixed racial ancestry.[6] In other words, slaves comprised more than a third of the city's population and were almost equal in number to American- and Iberian-born Spaniards. Moreover, slaves operated at nearly every point on the city's public spectrum – accompanying their owners through city streets, selling wares for daily wages, performing work for hire, participating in royal and religious festivals, as well as taking part in the city's dynamic social life. Setting the book in this period, therefore, allows for the consideration of how Lima's eminence, wealth, ethnic diversity, and status as a slaveholding society shaped the relationship between clothing and status in the region. In taking the analysis into the latter decades of the eighteenth century and through the abolition of slavery in Peru in 1854, the book also shows how the discourse and behavior surrounding dress evolved over the course of profound economic, social, and demographic transformations.

HISTORIOGRAPHIC FOUNDATION

This book is informed by, engages with, and seeks to contribute to several fields of inquiry. To begin, it owes an enormous debt to the work of Frederick Bowser, whose foundational study of Peruvian slavery traced how the holding of slaves went from a fifteenth-century rarity to a ubiquity by the sixteenth century, when the institution constituted the very backbone of the region's coastal economy. Bowser explores the variety of experiences of African slaves in the region, observing that in Peru they were primarily employed in urban service and – particularly in Lima – across a spectrum of household and extra-domestic occupations, with female slaves working in the domestic sector and as street vendors and men finding employment as day laborers known as *jornaleros*, who paid a large portion of their wages to their owners and saved any remaining portions for their own purposes. More recently, scholars of Peru's long seventeenth and eighteenth centuries – including Carlos Aguirre, Peter Blanchard, Christine Hünefeldt, Rachel O'Toole, and Jean-Pierre Tardieu – have shown that the urban character of slavery in the region (not only in Lima but in Trujillo and Cuzco as well) helped equip slaves with a remarkable degree of social and economic mobility.[7] I situate my own project within this discourse, and see in clothing the potential not only to examine challenges to slavery but also to explore how slaves shaped and negotiated ideas about beauty, status, and selfhood.

I am not the first student of slavery to pursue such an interest. In recent years, several historians have offered compelling snapshots of the significance of clothing and self-fashioning in slaveholding and post-abolition societies throughout the Americas. In his study of slavery and absolutism in colonial Mexico, Herman Bennett has noted the extent to which slaveholders in Mexico City outfitted their slaves in finery in order to lay claim to a civilized status. For them, the public and ostentatious display of mastery over African bodies was integral to their identity as Spaniards.[8] However, the proliferation of sumptuary laws in the region made clear that owners could never fully confine luxury to their own spheres and modes of self-expression. This was a widespread phenomenon: as Ira Berlin has observed, urban slaves in the North American colonies frequently aroused the ire of white planters for making their way about town in elegant costumes, complete with pocket watches and powdered wigs. The problem, as slave owners saw it, was that these urban slaves were posing a threat to "their exclusive claim to the symbols of civilization."[9]

Beyond simply appropriating their owners' tools of self-presentation, slaves also incorporated their own creativity and cultural sensibilities into their dress. This was often a matter of necessity: Stephanie M.H. Camp, for instance, has shown how enslaved men and women in the US South went to great lengths – often risking their personal safety – to attend what were known as "outlaw parties," which, in addition to serving as dance venues, provided rare but meaningful opportunities to wear stylish clothing. These events held particular appeal to enslaved women, who took time between laboring for their owners and families to fashion hoop skirts out of grapevines or tree limbs, and dye dresses vibrant colors. Not only did these costumes showcase the women's ingenuity and creativity in procuring and designing festive attire, but they also facilitated escape from the forced androgyny of slavery.[10] Slaves' creativity was also a matter of taste, for even when they stole or purchased their own clothing, or accepted their owners' castoffs, slaves would appropriate the dominant culture's clothing practices and adapt them to their own conventions. Shane White and Graham White refer to this as a kind of "cultural *bricolage*" that gave shape and meaning to a uniquely African-American aesthetic.[11] As Sidney Mintz and Richard Price have argued, slaves saw in clothing the opportunity to express or assert their individuality in the context of slavery's "relentless assault on personal identity."[12]

Taken together, this scholarship (along with the work of Steeve O. Buckridge, Sylvia Lara, Dylan Penningroth, Sophie White, and others) hints at just how much dress mattered to masters and slaves, to men and women, as well as to both urbanites and rural dwellers throughout the centuries-long history of slavery in the Americas.[13] But no scholar has produced a comprehensive examination of the layered, gendered, and at times conflicting meanings clothing contained for slaves and for those who presumed to control them. Such an examination faces a lack of a single source base or methodology that could adequately address this question in a way that captures the overlapping experiences of diverse social groups, a problem *Exquisite Slaves* addresses with a novel approach that makes use of diverse strands of inquiry, evidentiary fragments, and interpretive methods in order to examine the evolving and often contentious relationship between color, status, and self-presentation.

SOURCE BASE AND METHODOLOGY

Slavery was so integral to economic, social, and religious life in Peru that scholars have been able to rely on a wealth of civil and ecclesiastical sources to produce histories of the institution from its emergence in the sixteenth century through its abolition in 1854. But while abundant evidence reflects slaves' ethnic origins, numerical representation, geographic distribution, as well as their contributions to Peru's urban, plantation, and highland economies, documentation related to their clothing practices and the responses they provoked is scattered and incomplete. Addressing the question of slaves' material lives and circumstances, therefore, is less a matter of managing a "mound of documentation,"[14] as Frederick Bowser described his experience writing about the beginnings of slavery in Peru, than it is a twin exercise in the close reading of core documents and the careful piecing together of evidentiary fragments.

The core documents for this study include the following materials: nearly 100 criminal and civil cases in which slaves stood accused of stealing clothing or other valuable material goods; hundreds of pages of manumission letters, bills of sale, wills, and inventories recorded by 10 notaries; Spanish-, French-, and English-language travel accounts of visits to Peru; and more than 30 drawings and paintings. Why and how do I use these sources? To begin, court records provide as close to a 360-degree view of slaves and their orbits as an historian is likely to find in Peruvian archives. Although few in number, the cases I have chosen for this study are filled with scores of people: they appear on the record as claimants, alleged accomplices, witnesses, and even as third parties in witness testimonies. As the enslaved and free relatives, friends, acquaintances, neighbors, owners, and hirers of the accused, they represent a broad spectrum of colors and classes. Their presence thus makes the cases about more than the solitary, sealed-off actions of a handful of alleged thieves. Instead, they give us an understanding of how slaves behaved in ways that were shaped by and caused reverberations throughout the communities and culture in which they lived.

Court cases also contain details that are not available in other records. Although Peru did not have a tradition of slave narration, the rote questions notaries posed to claimants, alleged perpetrators, and witnesses in criminal cases yield answers that, while at times paraphrased, provide a rare first-person accounting of slaves' occupations, living situations, marital status, family composition, and personal relationships. In building my analysis of the rich, lively, and often-entertaining narratives contained within these criminal investigations, I used several guides. Chief among them were the works of scholars who have done skillful analyses of small or singular databases. For example, Sandra Lauderdale Graham's careful explorations of wills, annulment petitions, and divorce proceedings from nineteenth-century Brazil show how important it is to linger on cases in order to extract as many details as possible about the public and private lives of the actors named therein, and to embrace what she calls "the uncertain process of piecing together historically grounded but more ambiguous possibilities" when it is not possible to draw absolute conclusions.[15] Similarly, Joanne Rappaport has highlighted the value of using archival records as "ethnographic scenarios" that can yield insights into the texture of an individual's experience of particular social contexts and dynamics.[16] Heeding these lessons, I have mined the cases at the center of my study for more than just the hard facts they contain; in taking the time to also ask questions about and ponder the actors' motivations, silences, and elisions, I seek to make room for their complicated subjectivities.

Part of this process also involves acknowledging the power dynamics encountered by witnesses and accused perpetrators when they recorded their testimonies. Natalie Zemon Davis's examination of royal letters of pardon or remission in sixteenth-century France is particularly instructive, given how attuned it is to the impact of social structures on the substance and composition of court documents.[17] With that in mind, I give close attention to the circumstances under which witnesses and alleged perpetrators contributed to theft investigations. To be sure, as João José Reis has shown in his work on slave rebellion in Brazil, criminal cases have a way of rendering testimony as conversational even though it was often extracted under physical or emotional duress, particularly when slaves were called upon to share any information or knowledge they had, whether they wanted to offer it or not.[18] The harshness of the legal system can thus be easily mistaken for witnesses' candor and complicity in proving a suspect's guilt, or for a slave's eager confession of wrongdoing. Even absent threats or the direct administration of violence, the repetition or rewording of questions to witnesses and suspects on part of notaries in criminal theft investigations often served to intimidate or even confuse them. Here, Kathryn Burns's insights into the motivations guiding these scribes are particularly helpful given how much power notaries wielded in shaping what historians consider to be "the record."[19] In this regard, the work of historians of the US South who have grappled with similar challenges posed by WPA slave testimonies also informs my analysis. Considering the racial and status gulfs separating the mostly white WPA employees (many of whom belonged to old slaveholding families) from their formerly enslaved interview subjects, the documents are rife with omissions and other noticeable forms of self-censorship.[20] Thus, even though criminal theft investigations are somewhat unwieldy analogues in format and content to WPA narratives, they nonetheless share many similar tensions between interviewer and subject.

At the same time, there are some key differences between WPA interviews and criminal theft investigations. For one, WPA interviews took place well after the abolition of slavery, and while the interviewers came from backgrounds and adopted interrogative styles that may have reminded formerly enslaved interviewees of their old masters, interviewees also understood that they were not being asked questions because they were in trouble with the law. Rather, they were being asked questions about their life experiences. In contrast, interviewees in criminal theft investigations (or, more specifically, slaves accused of clothing theft, along with their alleged accomplices and beneficiaries) knew that they were, or could be, in trouble. Thus, their evasions and vague replies must be read in light of their specific and constraining circumstances.

Ultimately, like Arlette Farge, I devote space to the details of these cases "not for the love of drawing (or the picture itself), nor for the sake of description, but because it is through these that one is able to follow men and women as they grapple with the whole of the social scene."[21] But criminal records do not tell us everything, and using them as the sole window onto slaves' material circumstances may implicitly reproduce accusers' and colonial officials' notions that slaves mainly gained access to elegant clothing and other valuable resources through theft. For this reason, as well as to deepen my analysis of criminal cases, I have also drawn on notary records produced by Orencio de Ascarrunz, Silvestre Bravo, Andrés Calero, José Cardenas, Juan Casio, Juan de Dios Moreno, Fernando J. de la Hermosa, Jose Simeon Ayllon Salazar, Teodoro Ayllón Salazar, and Gerónimo de Villafuerte. These men were among dozens of active notaries during the period under study; I narrowed down the list to these men in order to have a consistent sampling across my periodization and a core group of notaries (Orencio de Ascarurunz, Fernando J. de la Hermosa, and Teodoro Ayllón Salazar chief among them) who were regularly visited by slaveholders and by clients of African descent.

My approach with these sources – in particular the manumission records, wills, and inventories contained within the notebooks – was to tease out the ways in which slaves gained access to freedom, money, clothing, and other valuables. Examining the records in this way means examining the world of social and transactional relationships that yielded slaves meaningful material rewards. Among other things, this approach shows how an enslaved mother's ties to a free African woman could position her to borrow money to purchase her son's freedom, and how an enslaved woman could come into possession of her owner's vast wardrobe.[22] This approach necessarily relies on examining wills left by slaveholders who made provisions for slaves' freedom and inheritances. In some cases, they even detailed the affective ties that led them to make such arrangements.

Reading wills alongside criminal cases helps address the question of why some slaves resorted to – or got accused of – stealing, while others did not. Some simply lacked the social ties that could result in gifts of cash to use however they wished, or bequests of elegant clothing and other valuable material goods. The wills also show that enslaved women were the primary beneficiaries of gifts and bequests from free people (whether those free people were male or female, of Spanish, African, Indian, or mixed racial ancestry), which left enslaved men in need and in pursuit of other, often-illicit, means of gaining access to finery. This disparity raises additional questions: Did slaves perceive the difference between inheritance, purchase, and theft to be a meaningful one? Put another way, did the matter of *how* a man got his hands on elegant clothing mean as much as what he did with it when he got it? Further, is it possible that some slaves preferred the act of stealing to the act of purchasing, particularly when it involved owners or hirers against whom they may have held ill will or contempt? Again, I cannot always answer these questions with certainty, but asking them is crucial to making sense of how slaves understood and navigated the system that held them in bondage.

Another question that arose from my reading of the documents for this study was what the clothing – and even the people – in question may have looked like. This was driven by a desire to examine the outcomes of slaves' actions and the reasons for observers' reactions. Travel accounts are particularly useful to this enterprise.

Given Lima's popularity among European merchants in the eighteenth and nineteenth centuries, the city's inhabitants make frequent appearances in the travel literature of the era. So too did their outfits, which visitors recorded down to the cut, color, fit, design detail, and geographic origins. Yet visitors' observations also reflected their own biases and motivations. During a period when "the slave trade and slavery were the hottest issues in Western debate," eighteenth- and nineteenth-century European travelers to South America, as Magnus Mörner has argued, "had already made up their mind for or against when setting out for Latin America. What was their frame of reference? Did the actual observation change or even modify their preconceived views? If we are unable to answer these questions, the value of their testimony necessarily becomes uncertain."[23] Further, to ask Mörner's questions in a different way, how did their ideas about slavery shape their ideas about dress? To what extent did those ideas mold or shape how visitors made sense of the clothing practices and sartorial displays they observed? Asking these questions means striking a balance between not taking visitors' accounts literally and still giving them full and serious consideration.

In addition to travel accounts, I have drawn on diverse visual records from the period. Some of these appeared in the pages of popular narratives – such as the monochrome engraving by a Spanish artist named Diego de Villanueva that accompanied Jorge Juan and Antonio de Ulloa's description of their 1747 visit to Lima – while others – like a collection of 20 full-color *casta* paintings completed in late eighteenth-century Peru, as well as a selection from the nearly 200 watercolors produced by an African-descent artist in nineteenth-century Lima named Francisco "Pancho" Fierro – were created to stand on their own. My approach to these images was twofold. First, I examined the content within the four corners: What is in the foreground or background of the image, and why? Who are the central figures, what are they wearing, and how are they positioned in relation to one other? Second, I treated them as documents in their own right, and therefore subjected them to similar questions asked of other records: What were the circumstances of their creation, their intended purposes, and presumed audiences? How do the images compare to one another and to contemporaneous records? What would explain the tensions between them?

Built around this corpus of court cases, notarial records, travel accounts, and images are an assortment of juridical ordinances, census data, annulment petitions, newspaper editorials, and runaway notices. I call these records fragments. That is because, in some cases, there is just one extant example of its kind – like a lone 1798 wardrobe order recorded by a tailor instructed to make several uniforms for five slaves belonging to Viceroy Ambrosio O'Higgins – rather than a series thereof. In other cases, there may be a series of records but just for a relatively short period. One such source is newspaper content; I characterize it as fragmentary because a newspaper could be published in colonial Lima for a relatively short window of time, or with frequent publication interruptions, owing to lack of either resources or subscribers, or both. Their content, too, could vary over time, as in the case of the monthly *Gaceta de Lima* (1743–94). When it first appeared, it included a mixture of "Noticias de Europa," or news about Europe, and "Noticias de Lima," or local news. But in its final three decades it began to focus more on global events, with extant issues showing that the publication gave increasingly minimal attention to local matters. Other publications include the *Diario de Lima*, Spanish America's first daily paper, which was founded in 1790 and printed its last issue in 1793. While other publications began and halted in fits and starts in the early nineteenth century, Lima would not see another consistent publication of a daily newspaper until *El Comercio* was founded in 1839.

Using these types of sources, then, to track changes over time or draw general conclusions is difficult given the sporadic and short bursts in which they appeared. But neither is the task impossible: indeed, the very emergence of print culture in Lima changed how *limeños* went about the business of buying and selling human property, the kinds of resources they could make use of when their slaves ran away, and how they talked about the institution of slavery itself.

Together, these diverse sources provide various vantage points from which to analyze the activities of colonial officials, slaveholders, slaves, and free people of African descent during a period marked by tremendous economic, social, and political change. They also help illustrate the multiple ways in which clothing took on meaning: through processes of writing (into legal code), acquiring (through theft, craft, inheritance, and purchase), selling (in legal and informal markets), and wearing. In analyzing the documentary traces left by each of these processes, and drawing upon a rich and diverse body of scholarship, this book shows how, through clothing, slaves expressed ideas about their status and, in the process, challenged the social, economic, and – most importantly – legal boundaries of slavery.

WRITING, RACE, AND SLAVERY

Like others before me, I have chosen to retain the color classifications that appear in my sources. This is primarily a decision of necessity, given the proliferation of cumbersome and difficult-to-translate categories that emerged to describe people of variously mixed European, African, and Indian ancestry, particularly in the eighteenth century. Terms like *quinterona* and *quinterona de mestizo* not only have no immediate cognates but also suggest mathematical impossibilities. Further, retaining Spanish-language color classifications is also a decision of conviction. In this sense I share Ada Ferrer's belief in the need for historians to "avoid projecting onto their subjects categories derived from other times and other places."[24] While a term like *quarterón(a)* has a cognate in the English language (to use a somewhat familiar terminological example), the word "quadroon" is weighted with meanings rooted in a specifically North American social and racial history, with an accretion of myths and fantasies peculiar to such contexts as colonial New Orleans and Philadelphia.[25] There are also false cognates, like *sambo*, a word whose orthography in Spanish and English are the same. The Spanish word *sambo* (sometimes written *zambo/a*) refers to an individual of mixed African and Indian ancestry.[26] In contrast, the term "sambo" in the United States derisively referred to an African-American behavioral archetype and had no specific ancestral significance.[27] Similarly, a term like *chino* is bereft of meaning when translated into English. While the precise origins of the term are unknown, it appeared in Quechua dictionaries as early as 1553, to refer to an Indian or *mestiza* woman of low status.[28] Given Lima's geographic position on the Pacific coast and its trade links with Asia, the term might also have referred to individuals whose phenotype resembled that of Chinese arrivals via the Manila galleon. By the last half of the nineteenth century, however, the term literally referred to individuals of Chinese descent, who began to arrive in Peru beginning in the 1840s to support the guano export industry. There are additional terms, such as *quarterón(a) de mestizo/a*, whose genesis and meanings are highly specific in terms of time and place. The first recorded mention of the term *quarterón(a) de mestizo* appeared in a 1770 collection of Peruvian casta paintings to describe individuals descended from successive generations of mixing between Spaniards and Indians. By 1771, the term (along with several other neologisms) appeared in official census records in the region, during a period when Bourbon officials sought to determine tribute and conscription obligations based on Indian or African ancestry. Such labels thus stand as a testament to both the keen interest in ordering and classification that took hold of colonial Spanish America during the era of the enlightenment, as well as the relationship between ideas about race and Bourbon-era reformism.

In short, to translate the Spanish-language color terms by using the words English provides not only endows them with social meanings that they did not necessarily contain but also obscures the ones that they did. Moreover, in this case, translating the Spanish-language color terms into English carries with it the risk of teleology, which might finish this story before I have had a chance to tell it. To suggest through translation that a *mulato/a* or *negro/a* in eighteenth-century Peru occupied a similar position in the region's social or racial hierarchy as a "mulatto" or a "Negro" in North America's racial regime is to effectively remove clothing from the equation. Presumed ancestry alone does not explain social status across geographic boundaries.

With these cautions in mind, I will use certain terms for the sake of linguistic economy. The term "Spaniards" here collectively describes Iberian-born *peninsulares* and American-born *criollos*. It is a straightforward translation of the term *españoles*, which appeared as a census category throughout the eighteenth century and partially functioned as a color category alongside other terms such as *indios* and *pardos* (a catch-all category that generally included free people of African descent), since it referred to both *peninsulares* and *criollos*. Colonial records not only marked people of African, Indian, and mixed-racial ancestry with color terms but also marked some subjects by omitting color terms. While the lack of a racial modifier did not necessarily indicate that a given subject was "white" – the absence of color terms means only that a person had escaped classification – I do use the term "Spaniard" to bring into focus the racial dimensions of a given situation or encounter.

NARRATIVE STRUCTURE

The multidirectional and multidimensional nature of the struggle over the boundaries of African-descent people's access to dress emerges from the very beginning of this book and prevails throughout. To bring this struggle into focus, each of the book's chapters takes a different thematic approach that roughly coheres around a specific source base. The first chapter opens with a 1723 sumptuary law that sought to regulate the dress of *negros, mulatos, indios,* and *mestizos*. The law was intended to be absolute in its directives, broad in its application, and effective immediately. Yet it was an outright failure, thanks largely to the behavior of other colonial officials and elite Spanish slaveholders. Their commitment to incorporating slaves into elegant sartorial displays was a peninsular inheritance and a consequence of Lima's administrative importance to Spain, its tremendous wealth, as well as its racial and ethnic diversity.

However, as Chapter 2 makes clear, slaves were more than mere canvasses for the expression of their owners' identities. Although we cannot know what was in the hearts and minds of the slaves whose limited access to literacy left their thoughts and feelings about their bodies largely unrecorded, many did take actions that demonstrated just how strong was their own commitment to elegant self-presentation. They had their own ways and reasons to acquire elegant dress. In addition to outfitting themselves in finery, they provided clothing to social intimates as well. For these men and women, clothing was a key tool with which they laid claim to their humanity and challenged the limits of their condition.

Chapter 3 builds on this discussion to show how clothing functioned to blur boundaries, not only between slavery and freedom but also along the lines of racial identity and racial privilege. It signaled the extent to which slaves and free castas' sartorial displays had overwhelmed legislative efforts to restrict access to elegant clothing, and as Chapter 4 shows, prompted other measures to keep them in place. This chapter opens in 1770, when Peru's Viceroy Manuel de Amat y Junyient commissioned a series of twenty *casta* paintings from the workshop of Cristobal Lozano to be sent to Spain's Prince of Asturias (Charles III), in the hopes that the young monarch would include them in his new *Gabinete de Historia Natural*, or natural history museum. Unlike the Mexican genre of casta painting, which features "scenes" of daily life – in kitchens, at markets, and elsewhere – the Peruvian images place their focus squarely on the individuals and their dress. In addition to briefly analyzing Mexican and Peruvian casta painting in comparison, this chapter deciphers the Peruvian paintings' message about the relationship between clothing, color, and status, particularly in light of their intended audience. Since Amat intended them to be displayed in a museum in Spain, the images positively reflected the influence of Spanish colonialism. They suggested a fixed racial hierarchy in Peru, with (American- and Iberian-born) Spaniards comfortably occupying the top tiers and wielding control over everyone else's material conditions. How did these images map onto colonial reality? To answer this question, the chapter weaves a discussion of the casta paintings alongside diverse records that detail the ways in which families headed by enslaved and free people of African, Indian, and mixed-racial ancestry challenged the idea that Spanish men were the gatekeepers to status and material comfort. In other words, the chapter argues that casta paintings depicted the world as Amat wished it could be rather than how it in fact was.

Chapter 5 further illustrates the tension between colonial fantasy and reality by focusing on confused status distinctions the *Diario de Lima* and *Mercurio Peruano*, two newspapers published between 1790 and 1795, which contained runaway notices as well as arguments about slaves as obstacles to familial productivity, moral rectitude, and racial purity. The papers cited examples of practices – such as the ownership of multiple household slaves, the outfitting of them in finery, and the releasing of elite Spanish mothers and daughters from domestic responsibilities – that were popular throughout the city during this period. But the papers' passionate pleas for readers to rid their homes of slaves and to cease outfitting them in luxurious clothing – all "in honor of the Nation and the Patria" – suggested that the practices persisted.

Chapter 6 opens in the early part of the nineteenth century, with the declaration of Peruvian independence. It focuses on how enslaved and free people of African descent helped shape and give meaning to the ideas of freedom, liberty, and citizenship that circulated during the era. Chief among them were the men forced to enlist in the army by their owners, or who joined of their own accord, recognizing the potential in military service for freedom and upward mobility. For these men, the uniforms they wore not only communicated their political allegiances (whether they were forged by force or in earnest) but also helped them lay claim to a certain pride and sense of self.

One observer of the period captured these men and their social worlds in vibrant detail. The grandson of slaves, Francisco "Pancho" Fierro was a self-taught watercolorist who became a pioneer in the artistic tradition of *costumbrismo*. Fierro took special interest in uniformed soldiers and other African-descent men and women who populated Lima's streetscapes; they appear in his watercolors at work, play, and everywhere in between. They cut fine figures in market scenes and in the company of companions and made their way to and through public processions, festive dances, and religious ceremonies while wearing colorful costumes. By focusing on the kinds of men and women other artists of the period confined to the margins, Fierro conveys a more complex image of their humanity and aesthetic practices. His work reveals a compelling story about the early years of independence and the final decades of the institution of slavery. For men and women of African descent in this story, stepping outside of the roles cast for them in the past and endorsed by slave owners and observers allowed them to lay claim to dynamic social identities. Yet, as the book's Epilogue makes clear, they would continue to face many cruel reminders that no matter how much they improved their condition – because they had attained freedom, because they had fought in the independence armies, and because they had worked hard to carve a place for themselves and their families – they would continue to encounter rancorous assumptions about their deficiencies.

In the process of contextualizing and comparing the myriad ways in which *limeños* acquired, used, and assigned meaning to clothing, this book weaves two primary claims into a central argument. The first claim is that, for elite Spaniards in Lima, control over dress (which included both restricting access to elegant finery as well as, somewhat ironically, outfitting their slaves in it) was central to their assertion of wealth, status, and racial dominance in the region. The second claim is that elegant clothing was also a tool that enslaved men and women used to negotiate their status, express ideas about masculinity and femininity, and attend to conceptions of belonging in ways that not only reflected but also challenged the dominant norms. In connecting these claims, *Exquisite Slaves* shows that dress was an emblem of both the reach as well as the limits of slavery, racial domination, and socioeconomic exclusion in Lima.

1 Slavery and the Aesthetic of Mastery

In September 1725, Peru's Viceroy, José de Armendaríz (the Marqués de Castelfuerte), introduced a sumptuary regulation that sought to "moderate the scandalous excess" of the clothes worn by *negros, mulatos, indios,* and *mestizos* of both sexes and to limit the "frequent thefts" they allegedly committed "to maintain such costly finery."[1] The law represented an attempt to shore up the boundaries of luxury in this colonial society and to ensure that people of African, Indian, and mixed-racial ancestry – regardless of their legal or socioeconomic status – did not get to wear the Dutch wools, Chinese laces, silver jewelry, and other sumptuous fashions that abounded in the region.

The viceroy also acknowledged the fact that this was not a new problem. An earlier law, passed on April 2, 1723 by Pedro Antonio de Echave y Roxas, an *oidor* (judge) at Lima's *Real Audiencia*, had called for similar restrictions but was an immediate failure. As Armendaríz put it:

> The same abuses continued with even greater disorder, thanks to the shelter and protection the transgressors received from government ministers. According to one account, two *negras* belonging to [José Zevallos Guerra] the Conde de las Torres – an *oidor* of this very *Audiencia* – violated the conditions of the law within twenty-four hours of its publication, setting an example for the abuses to continue without punishment.[2]

The viceroy did not elaborate on the accusations against the judge's slaves.[3] He failed to specify what exactly the women had done to break the law, how their act of disobedience was discovered, or why the two were not punished. Nor did the viceroy indicate whether the judge himself had played a role in the incident. But even with these vague allegations, the reference to Zevallos Guerra made clear that despite whatever truth there may have been to the earlier law on the issue of stealing, there were problems that ran much deeper.

This fact was on full display later in the month of April 1723, when Lima played host to a series of celebrations in honor of the marriage of Spain's Prince of Asturias. The festivities formed part of a long tradition of putting on royal ceremonies that – as one observer put it on his visit to Lima in the 1720s – were "made with more show and pageantry than those in Europe."[4] As was customary for such occasions, an official chronicler was present to record the proceedings, which unfolded between the twelfth and twenty-third of the month. In this case, the chronicler detailed bullfights and sermons that took place throughout the city, as well as a rousing parade in which judges, *alcaldes*, and *ministros* wore maroon-colored uniforms bordered in a fringe made of silver, rode horses fitted with ornate saddles, and were accompanied by a procession of "lucidly adorned" slaves.[5] In other words, by dressing their slaves in finery and incorporating them into public pageantry, some officials in Lima were openly flouting the 1723 law within just days of its publication. Instead of falling in line with their colleagues to present a united front and lead by example, they were pursuing their own desires. In this regard the men were hardly alone. Other Spaniards in Lima were similarly invested in putting their slaves on elegant display, not just for royal ceremonies but also during religious festivals, as part of their own rites of passage, as well as in everyday rituals. These practices, which converged to create what I have chosen to call an "aesthetic of mastery," traced their origins to early modern Spain, took on their distinctive local shapes and meanings during Lima's early formation, and, by the eighteenth century, constituted such a cornerstone of urban life in the region that they seemed capable of weathering even the most aggressive attempts to stop them.

THE CITY OF THE KINGS: BACKGROUND AND EARLY FORMATION

When Francisco Pizarro founded Lima in 1535, he named it the City of the Kings to commemorate the arrival of the three wise men in Bethlehem. In addition to its spiritual meaning, the name came to possess an earthly significance with the help of several sixteenth-century occurrences. The first was the 1542 naming of the city as capital of the Viceroyalty of Peru. Along with Mexico City to the north (which served as capital to the Viceroyalty of New Spain), Lima was home to the Crown's most important representatives, including viceroys, judges, and other officials, and a site where Spain's presence would be felt more strongly than anywhere else in the Americas. Accordingly, the cities were designed with Spanish models in mind. In Lima (a roughly triangular metropolis with the Rimac River defining the northeastern border and a rural hinterland, known as the Lima Valley, stretching to the southwest and to the east), not only had churches been erected on indigenous ceremonial grounds and religious sites to supplant the authority of local religions but also they were intentionally grandiose and awesome structures designed to fortify the place of Christianity in colonial society.[6] These buildings, along with others housing educational institutions and administrative offices, were also modeled after the opulent and extravagantly detailed baroque architectural traditions popular in Europe.[7] Moreover, Lima's public squares – chief among them the Plaza Mayor, framed as it was by the viceregal palace looming large on the north side, arcades housing fine shops to the south, a grandiose cathedral to the east, and the *cabildo*, or city hall, to the west – were literally surrounded on all sides by evidence of Spain's political, economic, intellectual, religious, and administrative power in the region.[8]

In addition to its status as a center of imperial power, Lima was also linked to one of the premier engines of wealth in the New World: the mining center housed at the *Cerro Rico* (Rich Hill) of Potosí. After commencing production in 1545, Potosí saw immediate profits thanks to the skillful smelting techniques of the indigenous miners employed in forced labor rotations. Furthering the early success of the industry was the advent of amalgamation (an innovative refining process involving the use of mercury extracted from mines at Huancavelica to reduce the silver ore) in the 1570s. By the end of the sixteenth century, the mining industry was a staggering success.[9] And though Lima stood thousands of kilometers away from Potosí and other mining towns, it was a close neighbor to Callao, the port from which silver made its way along the Pacific coast to Spain and other points around the globe.[10] Together with its administrative status and geographic positioning, Lima made an ideal home base for the mine owners, operators, and intermediaries who drew their wealth from the mountains.

The success of the mining industry saw Callao become a dynamic trade hub, and Lima a rich market for the consumption of luxury goods. Following the inauguration of Philippine-Spanish American commerce in the latter part of the sixteenth century, transpacific trading ships known as Manila Galleons sailed to Acapulco stocked with porcelain, silk, spices, iron, wax, and other precious merchandise from the East (once docked at Acapulco, these goods made their way via merchant ships to points south, including to the port of Callao).[11] The galleon voyages operated in concert with a Spanish fleet system that moved between the Americas and Spain, ferrying American silver and gold across the Atlantic and unloading European agricultural products and textiles in the colonies.[12]

The silver that financed the luxury trade would also become Peru's greatest bargaining chip in the slave trade. While small numbers of African slaves had been in the region since the conquest, the mid-sixteenth century would see their numbers rise. With the Indian population being increasingly drained to suit the demands of mining operations, and with the Spanish Crown drawing heightened criticism for the abuses it was heaping on natives in Peru and elsewhere, African labor held particular appeal. The expense of importing labor to the highlands of Peru, coupled with concerns about Africans' presumed incapacity to survive at altitudes exceeding 11,000 feet (which conveniently ignored how the dangers of the work itself succeeded in taking the lives of even native highland Indians) led the Crown to purchase slaves not for mining at Potosí, but instead for dispatch to lower-altitude gold mines at Carabaya in south-eastern Peru and at Chachapoyas in the North.[13]

It soon became clear, however, that slaves lacked Indians' mining expertise and efficiency, and the Crown's efforts proved less lucrative than expected.[14] Spain ultimately settled on continuing to extract most of its mining labor from the large Indian population (though African slaves nonetheless remained important fixtures in the mining sector and other highland industries) to assure the most robust profit margins possible, while employing African slaves in other capacities elsewhere. Some worked as muleteers who crossed treacherous rivers and mountains to transport silver and other merchandise to and from the mines or as seamen who moved and traded goods along the Pacific coast.[15] African slaves also held tremendous appeal to coastal colonists who needed laborers on *haciendas* in Lima's agricultural valleys where they could produce fruit, wine, corn, wheat, barley, and sugar and in the urban center where their labor could facilitate the maintenance and operation of the private residencies, monasteries, churches, taverns, and streets.[16]

Thus began in earnest the beginnings of a coastal slaveholding enterprise, which by the 1580s saw Lima-based traders sending ships stocked with silver to Cartagena (the primary point of distribution for slaves bound for the pacific coast of South America), and returning to Callao having skimmed off "the cream of the Cartagena supply" and filled their holds with slaves from West and West-Central Africa.[17] The vast majority of them were destined for Lima's urban center, where they were purchased by owners with varying household sizes and labor needs. In addition to slaves who performed household or domestic duties (such as tending to rooms and grounds, preparing meals, and washing clothes) were those who were hired out so their owners could live on the resulting income. In fact, the widespread practice of hiring out slaves – who were known as *jornaleros* and found employ in a range of skilled and manual capacities so their owners could live on the resulting income – held particular appeal to what Frederick Bowser has described as the "gentlewoman of little means," or the single and widowed woman for whom slave ownership was not an extravagance so much as an important "difference between a degree of comfort and ruin."[18] Meanwhile, wealthier and higher-status *limeños* purchased as many slaves as they could afford (sometimes as many as thirty), to perform specialized, gender-specific tasks: women typically performed duties as either laundresses, seamstresses, wet-nurses, and chambermaids or public escorts (about which I shall say more later in this chapter), while men were generally tasked with driving carriages, leading horses, and gardening, as well as with some cooking and washing duties.[19] Together, these enslaved men and women operated in private and public realms, on behalf of male and female owners across the socioeconomic spectrum.

Thus, from its earliest years, Lima had taken on its most defining and enduring features. It was one of Spain's most important administrative centers, one of the wealthiest cities in the Americas, a destination for global commodities, and a major center of urban slavery. The simultaneity of eminence, wealth, luxury, and slavery helped create a lively public culture that consisted of ceremonies in honor of the Spanish Crown, festivities marking the arrivals of viceroys, religious liturgies, secular celebrations, public promenades, and other activities, nearly all of which featured elegantly dressed Spaniards in the equally sumptuous company of their African slaves.[20]

THE CITY OF PAGEANTRY: OLD WORLD ANTECEDENTS AND NEW WORLD ADAPTATIONS

Lima's early colonial public culture, along with Spaniards and slaves' joint participation in it, had antecedents in the Old World. Beginning in the last half of the fifteenth century, when the Portuguese gained a monopoly over the African slave trade, enslaved Africans were increasingly common fixtures in households, workshops, and streetscapes across the Iberian Peninsula.[21] And while slaveholding was within fairly wide reach in Spain, it was most prevalent among those claiming pure Spanish blood, "Old Christian" ancestry, and noble lineage. For them, the desire to fill their households with as many "squires, ladies, male and female slaves, and beasts of burden" as possible was particularly strong.[22] In addition to enlisting Africans to work as domestic servants, these slaveholders also used their human property as public escorts. In fifteenth-century Valencia, for instance, noblemen frequently made their way around town surrounded by armed slaves who, beyond providing protection from enemies, served as symbols of the masculine power and authority wielded by their owners. As Debra Blumenthal has suggested, in a region where no figure was considered to be more base or vile than an African slave, an owner might even "seek the enhancement of his honour by entrusting the maiming, injuring, and dishonouring of his enemies to his slave."[23] Put another way, it was not enough for a man to simply bear his own arms and use his own might against his enemies; the mark of a truly honorable man was the ability to have his slave (or slaves) fight his battles for him. That way, whatever physical harm his opponent suffered would be accompanied by a grievous injury to his status as well.

Beyond arming their slaves, nobles in Spain also incorporated them into stunning public spectacles. Toward the end of Philip III's reign in the seventeenth century, for example, the Duke of Osuna made a famed entrance at a joust in Madrid's Plaza Mayor in the company of one hundred footmen adorned in livery identical to his own blue and gold uniform.[24] In addition to showcasing the Duke's ability to wield command over such a large assemblage of male subordinates, the scene signaled the reach of his socioeconomic power. In a highly honorific culture such as that of early modern Spain, where a man's status derived from his ability to provide for the members of his household, administer to the resources and property contained therein, and make distributions to dependents as necessary, the scene at the joust made clear that the Duke was more than just an effective patriarch and family steward. So successful was he in his duties, in fact, that he could even acquire large numbers of slaves and outfit every single one of them in impressive finery.

The Duke's spectacle was certainly remarkable in size, but it was hardly unusual in substance. Noblewomen in sixteenth- and seventeenth-century Seville, for their part, regularly surrounded themselves during street parades and festivals with female slaves dressed *á la Turque* (a local version of masquerade that featured brightly colored, ornately detailed, and flowing fabrics from Turkey).[25] As was true of arming slaves and dressing them in livery, these practices were heavily rooted in gendered notions of honor. Thanks to their status as the wives and daughters of noblemen, these women and their slaves were outfitted in ways that signaled the wealth and honorable status of the men to whom they were bound. During a period of widespread fascination with the Ottoman Empire, the costumes were especially compelling evidence of men's abilities to gain access to some of the most valuable material treasures the world had to offer.

But while the sight of a male slaveholder surrounded by a retinue of male slaves evidenced the former's masculine authority, the sight of a female slaveholder surrounded by female slaves conveyed a different sort of message. Because noblewomen in Spain derived their reputational status from their husbands and fathers, they were obliged to maintain their virtue to preserve the purity of their bloodlines and protect their familial honor.[26] Consequently, they lived their lives largely cloistered inside their homes, where they would "at all times be well attended and served," and where they could safely avoid any potential threats to their and their families' honor.[27] But when it was time to leave those spaces in pursuit of social diversion and in fulfillment of religious obligations, they did so with a profound sense of responsibility for how others would perceive them and, by extension, their families. Attending festivals in the company of female slaves thus provided Spanish noblewomen with a way of appearing in public while remaining safely removed from public interactions and the temptations, dangers, and suspicions that could accompany them.

Spaniards' use of slaves in public pageantry raises compelling questions. If, by arming slaves, owners could dishonor their enemies by subjecting them to injury at the hands of Africans, could dressing slaves in finery likewise serve as an attack on someone else's honor, albeit for a different set of reasons? Could a Duke's liveried footmen or a noblewoman's retinue of turned-out escorts serve as a source of shame or embarrassment to the owners' rivals by putting the latter groups' own material shortcomings into sharper relief? The available records make it impossible to answer such questions with any certainty, but asking them nonetheless makes room for a consideration of how the sight of richly attired Africans may have resonated among Spaniards who could not afford to outfit their own bodies or their families' so impressively. Perhaps, for them, the sight of African slaves – who by definition were subordinate in every way – dressed in elegance served as an additional heap of insult on their own inability to do the same. And, more than that, such a sight could also have undermined their own claims to noble status and superiority over Africans.

In any case, by incorporating their male and female slaves into spectacles both large and small, which featured weaponry as well as luxurious finery, Spanish slaveholders of both sexes gave shape to an increasingly coherent concept: beyond being well suited to various forms of manual, skilled, and household labor, Africans could also serve as powerful status symbols. They provided owners with the means to express their masculine authority and feminine vulnerability, their access to the world of goods, and their sense of honor, in ways that were easily and widely understood by diverse audiences.

In her work on race in early modern England, Kim Hall describes a similar practice of incorporating black bodies into the region's "symbolic economy of elite culture."[28] By this, Hall is referring to the use of Africans as concubines, servants, portrait subjects, and other "curiosities who represented the riches that could be obtained by European travelers, traders, and collectors in the Atlantic enterprise."[29] The parallels between these and the previously discussed Iberian customs not only hint at a broader tradition in which Africans served as both physical and symbolic laborers in Europe but also highlight the need for further and comparative scholarly inquiry into the impact of such a tradition on Europe's overseas imperial projects and slaveholding regimes.

In the case of the Spanish empire, the notion of Africans' dual functionality found particularly firm footing in Lima. As capital of the Viceroyalty of Peru and seat of imperial authority in South America, the city was the perfect setting in which to recreate Spanish society and traditions in the New World. Therefore, it was hardly surprising that, as early as the 1530s, the viceroy, *audiencia* judges, city council members, government ministers, and other local officials were arming their slaves with swords and firearms while out in public.[30] Certainly, as was the case in the Iberian context, the practice of arming slaves conveyed a message of masculine power in that it signaled an owner's ability to exercise command over Africans. However, at the same time that the practice of arming slaves drew clear inspiration and meaning from the Old World, it also resonated in ways that were specific to the New World context in which it took shape. Because Lima's colonial officials represented the Crown and its interests – indeed, absent Spanish monarchs, who would never set foot in the Americas for the duration of colonial rule, they were the most important figures in the region – appearing in public with armed slaves underscored their unique authority, which metaphorically extended beyond the bodies of their human property to include the rest of colonial society. The act thus functioned alongside the usurpation of indigenous land and customs, and the imposition of Spanish institutions and systems, as a manifestation of Spanish imperial dominance in the New World. It reminded everyone crossing the officials' paths that they were the very embodiment of law and order: they were deserving of respect and deference and willing to deploy violence to enforce it.

So impressive were these practices, and effective in their messaging, that they could not be contained within the sphere of colonial officials. In fact, they quickly reverberated throughout colonial society. With slaveholding so widely accessible in Lima by the latter part of the sixteenth century, the practice of arming slaves found favor across the spectrum of Spanish slaveholders, from wealthy elites in possession of multiple slaves to lower-status and aspirational sorts who owned just one or two. The practice also took hold among unaccompanied slaves and free people of African descent. In fact, in 1538, Lima's city council saw the need to prohibit all persons of African descent from carrying weapons, except in the cases of those accompanying council members and judges.[31] But because the law made room for exceptions – namely, in cases of slaveholders willing to pay fees for the privilege of arming their slaves – it inadvertently encouraged continued abuses. To begin, it led slaveholders to behave as though they were exceptions to the rules, regardless of whether their basis for doing so was legitimate or not. Further, the examples set by these individuals helped contribute to a climate of generalized disregard for the law. Just over a decade later, in 1549, lawmakers attempted to correct their earlier mistake by enacting more restrictive measures, with even stiffer and more far-reaching penalties. By then, all slaves, no matter their owners' status, were prohibited from carrying arms, as were all free persons of African descent. Anyone found in violation of the law faced lashings, castration, and even death.[32]

While it was clear that slaveholders themselves counted among the primary violators, the language of these laws targeted the city's African-descent population for punishment. Put another way, even if an owner provided the weapon and the order to carry it, his slave would face direct punishment should it ever be meted out. This imbalance, between who was ultimately responsible for breaking the law and who would suffer consequences for it, points to the tension lying at the heart of slaves' dual functionality as both property and status symbols. By law, slaves were beholden to the will of their owners. Yet even though slaves could no more refuse to carry arms for their owners than they could refuse to cook or clean for them, laws like the one passed in 1549 (along with others, which will be discussed later) nonetheless forced slaves to endure the consequences of following orders. That being said, there was still a certain way in which these punishments were very clearly directed at owners themselves, given that a male slave's castration would remove his reproductive capability and, therefore, his ability to add to his owner's roster of human property. In addition, the act of sentencing a slave to death represented a direct financial loss for his owner.

Nevertheless, because so many slaveholding officials in Lima remained convinced of their exceptionalism, or at least seemed unconcerned with the risks of being held (directly or indirectly) accountable in any case, they continued to arm their slaves well into the seventeenth century.[33] So, too, did other Spanish slaveholders in the region, which in turn led to additional legislation on the subject that was likewise quickly and roundly ignored.[34] Along with colonial officials, and to the degree that their resources allowed them, Spanish slaveholders from across the socioeconomic spectrum also began incorporating their slaves into other kinds of status displays. For elite Spaniards, in particular, this included traveling around town in the comfort of gilded, richly appointed, and heavily curtained *calesas*, or carriages, which were drawn by horses and guided by elegantly liveried slave coachmen. These *cocheros* and *caleseros*, as the coachmen were variously known, guided their passengers to theater performances, bullfights, church masses, and other occasions, where their arrivals announced the wealth, prestige, and importance of the men and women who were ensconced inside.[35] And it soon became common practice for a merchant, silversmith, or milliner to begin "prefacing his name with 'Don,' buckling a rapier, and dressing his slaves in livery" for walks down city streets,[36] and for those same types to join other slaveholders in outfitting their human property in "colorful and luxurious clothing" during royal ceremonies in honor of the Spanish Crown.[37]

Together these practices formed part of a local aesthetic of mastery that served to showcase Spaniards' dominion over both luxury goods and human beings. To be sure, some elements of the aesthetic had obvious parallels in early modern Spain where, as we have seen, noblemen and women attended public festivals in the company of richly attired slave escorts to signal their wealth and gender-based status. But it was increasingly clear that, for Spaniards in Lima, incorporating slaves into public spectacles had become not just a status marker – it was a significant component of their cultural identity in the region as well. It meant that, no matter the distance, they could still maintain meaningful and tangible connections to the Iberian world.

That similar practices were visible in the viceregal capital of Mexico City suggests the existence of a broader tradition within the Spanish diaspora that was built around the public display of African bodies. Upon his visit to Mexico City in the seventeenth century Thomas Gage observed:

> Two thousand coaches, full of gallants, ladies and citizens, to see and to be seen ... the gentlemen have their train of blackamoor slaves, some a dozen, some half a dozen, waiting on them in brave and gallant liveries, heavy with gold and silver lace, with silk stockings on their black legs, and roses on their feet, and swords by their side; the ladies also carry their train by their coach's side of such jet-like damsels ... who with their bravery and white mantles over them seem to be, as the Spaniard saith [sic], *"mosca en leche,"* a fly in milk.[38]

According to Herman Bennett, these "spectacles of ostentation" were as natural to Spaniards in Mexico City as engaging in other Old World customs like drinking wine and eating olives.[39]

At the same time, however, once they took root in the New World, these practices could no longer belong to Spaniards alone. As surely as arming slaves and dressing them in finery for daily promenades and royal ceremonies had moved beyond the realm of colonial officials to spread among Spanish slaveholders of various classes in Lima, the desire to distinguish oneself through elegant self-presentation had spread among unaccompanied slaves and free *castas* (who collectively outnumbered Spaniards by a ratio of 1.5 to 1).[40] They, too, were finding ways to arm themselves, acquire their own finery, and do the same for their families, social intimates, and dependents. Subsequent chapters will address these groups and their sartorial practices more fully, but for now it suffices to note that together, Lima's diverse population helped create the atmosphere described by Jesuit missionary Bernabé Cobo in the early part of the seventeenth century:

> The pomp and splendor of its citizens' manners and attire are so great and widespread that at festivals it is impossible to tell them apart from the way they look; everyone, including those who are nobles and those who are not, dresses extravagantly and richly in silk and all manner of finery.[41]

For certain officials in Lima, these practices represented an unacceptable state of affairs. Because the ubiquity of elegant clothing was blurring status distinctions, it was therefore imperative to impose limits on who could enjoy access to certain luxury goods so that they would, in turn, function as material markers of status.

RACE, GENDER, AND THE ALLURE OF DISPLAY

To advance this agenda, lawmakers zeroed in on specific populations that they viewed as in need of particular control. And so, in 1631, Lima's city council renewed a years-old ban prohibiting enslaved and free women of African descent from wearing silk, gold, silver, and slippers adorned with silver bells. The law specifically indicated that even the African-descent wives of Spaniards (regardless of whether the women were enslaved or free) should adhere to its constraints and restrict themselves to the wearing of woolen clothing only.[42]

Nevertheless, despite their pointed language on the subject, officials were confronting the same problems years later. A 1665 law ordered that "no mulatto woman, nor Negro woman, free or slave, wear woolen cloth, nor any cloth of silk, nor lace of gold, silver, black or white" on pain of exile and "severe punishment." And a similar law was passed yet again in 1667, with the added threat that all violators in the first instance would face confiscation of their goods and those in the second instance a fifty-peso fine, and third-time offenders would be subject to 200 lashes and an eight-year period of exile.[43]

The language of these laws revealed the extent to which enslaved and free women of African descent were an early and enduringly nettlesome target of lawmakers' efforts to restrict access to finery. Yet despite the fact that these women had myriad opportunities and resources with which to gain access to elegant clothing (as we shall see in detail later), it was clear that lawmakers were first and foremost concerned with how Spaniards contributed to the women's importunate sartorial displays. From lawmakers' perspectives, by dressing their female slaves in finery, slaveholders were setting examples for the rest of colonial society to follow and helping to blur the boundaries of status. (Meanwhile, they seemed to have no problem at this point with owners dressing their male slaves in livery for carriage rides, walks around town, and public ceremonies.) Spanish men who were married to African-descent women were also part of the problem, in that they were providing their wives with elegant clothing (or at the very least encouraging their wearing of it), just as they would have done had they been married to Spanish women.[44] Thus, by explicitly calling out the African-descent wives of Spaniards, and making clear that they would suffer punishments along with other offenders, lawmakers were sending the message that no matter their choice in husbands, these women would never be equal to Spaniards in the eyes of the law.

Moreover, even though the proposed punishments were directed at enslaved and free women of African-descent, the laws sent clear messages to Spaniards as well. For slaveholders, of course, the possibility of an enslaved woman's exile would mean the loss of valuable human property. But for the Spanish men married to African-descent women, the message had a decidedly more personal edge. It said that in marrying African-descent women, these men were forfeiting certain rights and privileges of their own. Unlike their counterparts who were married to Spanish women, they could not expect to outfit their wives in finery as a way of showcasing their own wealth and status as providers and heads of household. And while these men would not face direct consequences should they fail to follow the rules, the indignities and punishments that awaited their wives would further undermine their own sense of patriarchal authority.

As had happened with earlier laws governing slaves' access to arms, these seventeenth-century sumptuary regulations ultimately failed to effect any visible or tangible changes. By the eighteenth century, to return to the period that opened this chapter, Spaniards were still the chief agents of and the major barriers to the enforcement of sumptuary legislation in the region. Recall that in 1723, a local judge had prohibited all *negros, mulatos, indios,* and *mestizos* – regardless of their legal status or sex – from dressing in what he vaguely referred to as "scandalous excess" and "costly finery." The references were likely intentionally vague so that they could encompass more than the woolen cloths, laces, silks, and gold that had been prohibited in earlier laws. This time, the list of forbidden items could include other luxury goods such as damask, pearls, and diamonds, or anything else that might emerge as a problem item down the line. Once again, though, slaveholders were among the most egregious in their display of disregard for the law's provisions. There was the *audiencia* judge, José Zevallos Guerra, whose two female slaves had allegedly violated the law within two hours of its publication (likely with clothing the he supplied), and the numerous officials who were marching with their liveried slaves in a parade held later that month.

There were still other instances unfolding on a daily basis that stoked additional concerns. A particularly compelling illustration comes from February 1725, when Lima played host to ceremonies on behalf of deceased Spanish monarch Luis I. On this occasion, Viceroy José de Armendaríz presided over an official performance of a *saynete*, or a one-act comedic play, at the viceregal palace.[45] Titled *El Amor Duende*, the piece was written by Jerónimo Monforte y Vera and features five characters: a sprite-like figure (or *duendecillo*) named Amor; two men (one a *limeño*, the other a recent arrival from Spain); a pair of *tapadas* (or "veiled women," whose name referred to a costume of Moorish origin that consisted of a skirt and veil known as a *saya y manto*, which covered most of the wearer's body and face with the general exception of her eyes);[46] a *negra* slave; and her mistress.[47] The *saynete* follows the two men as they first encounter the mysterious *tapadas* and attempt to court them with flirtatious remarks and promises to fill their wardrobes with more sumptuous costumes. The main action centers on the *tapadas'* testing the seriousness of the men's intentions by asking them for everything from money to sweet treats. After completing one such errand, the suitors eventually return with handkerchiefs full of candy, eager to revel in the *tapadas'* gratitude and affection. But the men soon discover that the women standing before them in *sayas y mantos* are not the *tapadas* with whom they first became enamored, but rather a mistress and her identically dressed *negra* slave out for an evening stroll.[48]

The story ends with the character Amor issuing a warning about "*los engaños de un manto*," or the deceptions of the veil.[49] The *saynete* thus functioned as a cautionary tale, along the lines of other plays and poems about *tapadas* that circulated in early modern Spain. It urged men to avoid falling victim to *tapadas'* manipulative seductions and criticized *tapadas* for the insatiable material desires that drove men to lose their wits and drain their finances.[50] But what set *El Amor Duende* apart from its Old World counterparts was its particular preoccupation with the ability of a *negra* slave to hide beneath the *manto*'s fabric. The true *engaño* of the *manto*, in Lima at least, was that it had the power to conceal not only a woman's legal status but also her racial identity.

Although fictional, the *saynete* addressed the kinds of real-life conditions and attendant preoccupations that ultimately helped guide Armendaríz to revisit the 1723 law just a few months later, in September 1725. And while the *manto*, or veil, was a particularly literal form of disguise, it also served as an apt proxy for the broader issue surrounding the way clothing was confusing and even erasing status and racial boundaries in the region (however temporarily). For Armendaríz (and the judge before him), this called for drawing a strict color line across colonial society. The goal was to put Spaniards on one side of that line, where they would enjoy unique and unfettered access to luxury, and everyone else firmly on the other.

But for so many Spaniards in Lima, the idea of having unique and unfettered access to luxury would always include the right to put themselves *and* their slaves on elegant display. This was a tradition with roots too deep and too wide to forsake, and no amount, or kind, of sumptuary legislation would prevent them from claiming what they saw as their due. Which helps explain why, upon their visit to Lima in the 1740s, Spanish travelers Jorge Juan and Antonio de Ulloa wrote what stands as one of the quintessential descriptions of the city's Spanish women in the colonial period: "[T]hey especially shine in their long dresses with trains, which they wear to chapel on Holy Thursday; on that day, they attend masses accompanied by two or four female *negra* or *mulata* slave lackeys, who arrive dressed in identical costumes."[51]

IDENTICALNESS AND ALTERITY

In an essay on clothing as a social sign, Webb Keane notes how nobles in old Sumba (in the South Pacific), rather than wearing what was known as *ikatted* cloth themselves, dressed their slaves in it instead. Even when draped over slaves' bodies, the cloth was nonetheless "indexical of being noble," since "the displacement of that clothing from master's body to slave is iconic of the nature of nobility, as a quality that expands and transcends any particular embodied form."[52] That a slave could wear clothing that projected his or her owner's status was clearly not lost on Spanish slaveholders in Lima, who found no shortage of occasions for such displays. But they did not leave themselves out of the spectacle. Indeed, above all of the previously discussed evidence of Spaniards' aesthetic of mastery in Lima, there looms a compelling question: Why were Spanish slaveholders so eager to have their slaves dress just like them? This is a separate question from why they embraced an aesthetic of mastery to begin with. We already know why slaveholders had long drawn a sense of status from their ability to acquire luxury goods for themselves and conspicuously adorn their human property with them as well. But what is less clear is why their aesthetic of mastery hinged so much on identicalness. Why did they not seem to share lawmakers' belief or worry that luxurious clothing blurred status and racial boundaries or adhere to other models (such as that of nobles in Old Sumba) that would have allowed them to dress their slaves in a specific clothing item that could communicate their owners' status?

Perhaps slaveholders in Lima simply viewed their slaves' bodies as so fundamentally different from their own that no amount of luxury could change that. For these owners, slaves were not just property but tools. In forming part of their owners' retinues, pageants, and performative traditions, slaves were to protect and to ornament. They were not, by any means, meant to express their own socioeconomic interests or aesthetic priorities or to be unyielding in any way. Even though they were in possession of their own faculties, they were by no means in full control of them. Seen from this perspective, male and female slaves could dress identically to their owners without ever taking on any aspects of their owners' identities. In fact, the act of dressing in identical livery, silks, laces, or veiled costumes was the ultimate statement and sign of alterity.

The sight of a uniformed colonial official and his liveried slave, then, signaled the former's masculine power and authority and the latter's dependence and subordination. Or, to use another example, the sight of a *tapada* and her identically dressed slave signaled the former's protected and nurtured status and the latter's lack thereof.

Perhaps these kinds of displays held additional appeal to female slaveholders because they could also showcase the women's (socially constructed) beauty in relation to their slaves. A passage from French traveler Amedée Frezier's account of his visit to Lima in the early part of the eighteenth century provides some grounding for this possibility. In describing the city's Spanish women, Frezier notes that they "are beautiful enough, with a more engaging air than women elsewhere, perhaps because their beauty owes in part to its contrast with the *Mulâtresses, Noires, Indiennes,* and other hideous faces that outnumber them in the country."[53] If women of African, indigenous, and mixed-racial ancestry were inherently "hideous," or ugly, then the similarities between the costumes worn by Spanish women and their female slaves would only put that fact in starker relief.

A return to the denouement of *El Amor Duende,* the *saynete* performed in 1725, however, helps illustrate one of the pitfalls of the previous logic. In their own discussion of the play, literary scholars Esther Castañeda Vielakamen and Elizabeth Toguchi Koyo refer to the figure of the *negra* as "*la sorpresa no deseada,*" or the unwanted surprise, the opposite in every way of "the beauty and whiteness of the *tapada limeña.*"[54] To be sure, the enslaved woman underneath the veil functions in the story as a source of disappointment to the two amorous suitors: even though her costume was apparently identical to that worn by the first two *tapadas,* and that of her owner, her racial difference made her undesirable. But still her costume managed to confuse the men long enough to lure them into nearly giving their amorous attention to an undeserving woman.

Yet, enslaved women in colonial Lima occupied a far more complicated position in relation to Spaniards. They were more than mere aesthetic inferiors to Spanish women and unwanted foils to Spanish men. Records from the period show that Spanish men pursued them as wives and concubines and engaged in other intimate (and often forcedly sexual) relationships with them.[55] And as colonial officials were all too aware, enslaved and free women of African descent had both enjoyed access to elegant clothing and other luxurious goods thanks to their ties to Spanish men. So there was hardly a uniform consensus among Spaniards in Lima regarding female beauty. But it is clear that a significant number of slaveholders in Lima adhered to the belief that slaves were not just social inferiors but aesthetic ones as well.

'TIL DEATH DO THEY PART

The ability to enlist slaves in status displays was so integral to Spanish selfhood in Lima that it even extended to end-of-life celebrations. In a city where royal *exequias*, or funerary rites in honor of deceased monarchs, had long stood out as the most sumptuous of the city's ceremonies, there was a rich tradition to draw on. Among other protocols, the royal *exequias* generally involved the participation of hundreds of mourners wearing long and rich black funeral cloaks, processions led by high-ranking officials and elegantly liveried slaves, the delivery of extensive sermons in honor of the deceased, and the burning of thousands of candles on catafalques and at masses held in cathedrals around the city.[56] And while it was financially and practically impossible for individual persons to carry out such spectacles on the same scale as those organized in honor of Spanish monarchs, *limeños* generally did their best to ensure that their own final passages were marked in ways that said something about their earthly status. Most prominent among them were the funerals of elite Spaniards who organized funerals calling for the use of numerous wax candles, the construction of large and ornate *tumulos* (burial mounds) and the hiring of *lloronas* (professional wailers), as well as the wearing of expensive *lutos* (mourning dresses) among survivors of the deceased, including family members and slaves. For the men and women who had spent their lives paying careful attention to dress and comportment and generally presenting their best selves to the public, it is hardly surprising that the same considerations would inform how they marked their final passages. They were also well aware that these choices would shape or bolster their legacies. On July 6, 1758, for example, the *Gaceta de Lima* noted the pomp that characterized the funeral of one Señora Doña Rosa de Ilardy y Sabedra, which, the paper explained, "was a tribute to her merit, *calidad*, and her sumptuous fashions."[57]

Equally unsurprisingly, lawmakers found serious fault with the splendor of funerary practices in the region, which not only were excessive in their own right but also set a bad example for the rest of colonial society. In 1740, Viceroy José Manso de Velasco cited these problems when he imposed restrictions on the color and fabric of mourning cloaks and coffin adornments, along with other funerary garb and practices. The viceroy also prohibited elite Spaniards from outfitting their slaves in mourning dress – acts he described as "exorbitant and superfluous expenses" that inspired emulation among the lower classes.[58] More than thirty years later, in 1771, Viceroy Manuel de Amat y Junient issued similar legislation, which pointed to the "lutos of particularly immoderate decoration" being worn by *mulatas, negras*, and other "*gente de color.*"[59] And once again, on August 31, 1786, Viceroy Teodoro de Croix issued a decree that sought "to correct the detestable luxury that has been so flagrantly introduced into this populous Capital." De Croix was referring to the cost and spectacle of funerals, burials, and *exequias* that, in his words, were contributing to "the detriment of the public and ruin of families" throughout the viceregal capital of Lima.[60] His multi-page proclamation devoted ample space to reiterating the efforts of his predecessors and conveyed a palpable degree of frustration over the seemingly intractable gap between law and social behavior.

CONCLUSIONS

Frustration would be one of the only enduring legacies of sumptuary legislation in the region. So, too, was eventual capitulation. By the close of the eighteenth century, it was clear that official zeal on the subject of luxurious sartorial display would never bend colonial society to its will. In fact, the former appeared to have finally and fully succumbed to the latter: in February 1798, a tailor named Antonio Beluzo recorded a wardrobe order for five male slaves belonging to

Ambrosio O'Higgins, the Marques de Osorno and Viceroy of Peru. The list of requested attire was extensive and elaborate and, among other items, included five pairs of shoes; five large straw hats; fifteen dozen metal buttons for five suits (three dozen buttons for each suit); white buttons for ten dress shirts; and five ponchos with ribbon collars.[61] Whereas his predecessors had nearly always taken the lead in seeking to restrict slaves' access to finery, the current viceroy chose to fall in line with – and implicitly endorse – a more inexorable tradition.

Lawmakers in eighteenth-century Lima ultimately failed in their efforts to regulate access to clothing as a means to assert a color-based social hierarchy because those efforts, along with the logic that propelled them, were incompatible with two fundamental truths about colonial society. The first was that too many Spaniards – including other government officials – had come to view their slaves as central to their sense of selfhood in the region. Incorporating those slaves into an aesthetic of mastery was crucial to their cultural, gender, and racial identity, as well as to their notions of beauty, attractiveness, power, and hierarchy. And it would hold steady even in the face of persistent legislation.

The second truth was that, despite the prevalence and enduring power of the idea that slaves were to labor in service to Spanish selfhood, these men and women were more than just the mobile avatars of their owners. They were mothers and fathers, brothers and sisters, daughters and sons, friends and lovers, all with their own subjectivities. Along with free people of African, Indian, and mixed-racial ancestry in Lima, they also had their own culture of elegant self-presentation that had little to do with Spaniards. As the next two chapters will show, they acquired their own finery, outfitted themselves in accordance with their own sense of selfhood, and betrayed no willingness to bend to legislation that sought to restrict their behavior. In short, just as lawmakers in eighteenth-century Lima had wrongly assumed that Spanish slaveholders had the will to put a stop to the problem of importunate sartorial display, they also believed they alone had the power to do so.

2 Legal Status, Gender, and Self-Fashioning

On a summer day in 1732, an enslaved man, Juan Ramos, and woman, Margarita Zaya, took a walk through the streets of the neighborhood in Lima that they both called home. For this particular occasion, Ramos chose to wear something special. Perhaps he wanted to impress Zaya with his look and all the attention it brought him, for he was certainly hard to ignore. Indeed, one neighbor later described the man as looking "very gallant" that day, noting that the white shirt he had on was particularly "rich." Another said of his shirt that it was the kind of thing "a gentleman would wear."[1]

The neighbors' accounts come from a criminal investigation in which workers at a local hospital alleged that Ramos had entered the premises and stolen a white shirt and several chickens. Prosecutors in the case gathered a bevy of witnesses who, in addition to providing the aforementioned statements, described Ramos as a man with a "public and notorious" reputation for stealing. At times, they claimed, he benefitted from the help of accomplices; other times he seemed to have acted alone. In every reported instance, though, clothing and material goods were involved in some way, whether it was a pair of capes (one made of a fine blue wool known as *paño azul*;[2] the other, white with gold braiding and apparently from London), a hat, a basket of laundry, a wooden box (which he was later seen giving to Margarita Zaya), or the white shirt at the center of the 1732 case. There were further reports that Ramos went by the nickname *Camparón*, which in English roughly translates to "the distinguished one." The name seemed to lend credence to the accusations against him, in that it crafted an image of a man so accustomed to receiving flattering attention that he was willing to go to great lengths – including stealing – to continue standing out.

The case offers a useful entry point for analyzing two interrelated themes. The first is how enslaved men and women in Lima acquired and used elegant clothing to lay claim to their bodies as sites of pride and pleasure. The second is how they used clothing, money, and other valuable material goods – which they kept for themselves as often as they distributed them to social intimates – to nurture relationships and fashion dynamic social identities. Whereas the previous chapter showed how slave owners incorporated their human property into public sartorial displays to communicate their wealth, power, and racial dominance, this chapter draws attention to the meanings slaves themselves assigned to dress. It does so by focusing mostly on the experiences of *jornaleros*, or hired-out slaves, whose obligations to perform work in exchange for daily wages came with a certain measure of physical distance from their owners and their watchful scrutiny. Their relative freedom of mobility as they sought out employment in building projects, food service, and artisanal labor (among other roles) exposed them to goods, money, and people, including other slaves and free *castas*. These conditions set *jornaleros* apart from their enslaved counterparts at the center of the previous chapter, whose roles in domestic service and obligations to accompany their high-status owners in public (as carriage drivers and escorts) meant that their bodies performed both physical and symbolic labor.

Of course, because of their legal status as property, even *jornaleros* faced serious and often insurmountable struggles to acquire anything beyond basic necessities. Despite the fact that owners were obligated to supply their human property with food and clothing, they tended to transfer that burden to slaves themselves, which the latter paid for out of their meager wages.[3] Consequently, not only was purchasing sumptuous finery exceedingly difficult for slaves but also, for some, it was so distant a priority (compared, e.g., to saving money for self-purchase) that, even with adequate resources, they may simply have had no interest in partaking. But there were other slaves who not only found ingenious ways of gaining access to elegant dress but also managed to extend the reach of their access to their social intimates. Their routes, resources, and relationships occupy the central focus of this chapter's analysis.

SLAVERY, LAW, AND CLAIMS-MAKING: AN EXTRALEGAL TURN

For the past two decades, scholars have paid increased attention to the various ways in which slaves in colonial Lima made use of secular and ecclesiastical tribunals to negotiate and improve their status. This rich and growing body of research has shown that slaves took to the courts to file lawsuits against a range of targets. Among other charges, they accused their owners of inflicting cruel and excessive punishment (through whippings, burns, hair pulling, and other acts that fell under the banner of *sevicia*) and sexual abuse, hirers of withholding wages, and the executors of their owners' estates of disregarding or overturning posthumous manumission provisions and bequests.[4] They also filed lawsuits against other slaves and free *castas*, such as those belonging to fellow and rival *cofradías*, or religious brotherhoods, to secure high-ranking roles within their organizational hierarchies as well as favored positions during religious processions.[5] And while enslaved litigants were not always successful in their challenges, when backed by favorable judgments, they were able to effect important changes, from securing improved treatment and recovered wages to finding new owners and even gaining their own freedom.[6]

These claims and the changes that resulted from them were particularly remarkable in light of the fact that the majority of slaves in Lima – along with most of the city's population in general – were unable to read or write on their own.[7] Yet, as José Ramón Jouve Martín has argued, slaves in the region were nonetheless exposed to various legal, religious, and literary discourses, thanks to having heard literary texts, legal decrees, biblical verses, and religious sermons read and performed aloud in the homes, city streets, and churches where they worked and worshipped.[8] Hence, they did not need to be able to read to gain knowledge of legislation or scripture, nor did they need to be able to write in order to convey or make use of such knowledge, which they shared with one another and used to enlist the help of local scribes, lawyers, church officials, and judges to obtain redress where possible.

This scholarship joins an ongoing and larger conversation about how slaves in Latin America used litigation to assert their humanity and lay claim to various rights and dispensations. This subject has provided tremendously valuable insight into the ways in which slaves mobilized their understanding of the law, not only for their own benefit but also for that of their children, family members, extended kin, and the generations who benefitted from their efforts and followed their examples.[9] But we cannot limit our examination or understanding of slaves' claims-making to the lawsuits they filed. To do so is to overlook those slaves who were unable or unwilling to take their grievances to court. This is a crucial point in light of the fact that a key barrier to litigation was access to money to pay for a lawyer, or to social networks that would provide surety on a claimant's behalf.[10] Further, there is evidence suggesting that enslaved women outnumbered enslaved men as litigants in colonial Lima, in both ecclesiastical and civil tribunals, by a ratio of more than two to one, meaning that a litigation-centered focus is often a female-centered one (at least from the perspective of the claimants).[11] The nature of the claims themselves helps explain these differentials, as women were more likely to face sexual abuse at the hands of their owners and be the primary caregivers for their children (who were fathered by other slaves, free men, or the women's own masters). Therefore, they were more likely to file claims of *sevicia* and to petition on behalf of their children's freedom. But there were also more complex factors at work, which scholars of slavery in Lima have generally attributed to enslaved women's greater exposure in the domestic sphere to their owners' conversations and informal promises – of freedom, license to marry, and preservation of family units. These promises tended to result from intimate, or affective, ties between masters, mistresses, and enslaved women, which in turn gave the latter group a greater sense of confidence and entitlement to pursue litigation.[12]

For their part, enslaved men were more likely to engage in *cimarronaje* (running away) and violence (such as attacks on their owners or acts of collective rebellion) than their female counterparts.[13] This trend also applies to the available data on other crimes such as theft. For the period between 1723 and 1795 (which roughly corresponds to the first half of this book's focus), there are 216 extant criminal investigations from Lima's *Real Audiencia*. Of those cases, twenty-seven accuse male slaves of stealing, while only three accuse female slaves – and two of those cases involve the same woman (more on this later).[14] With these gender differences in mind, an examination that gives specific attention to acts of theft committed by slaves can open up several new ways of seeing. For one, it allows for an understanding of how – through acquiring, wearing, and distributing clothing, money, and other material goods in particular – enslaved men found means other than filing lawsuits to challenge their condition and claim certain rights. At the same time, such an analysis pushes beyond framing men's challenges to slavery purely in terms of flight or violence by showing the ways in which they chose to stay put and peacefully (but not necessarily passively or legally) assert themselves. And, finally, because criminal theft investigations also include testimony from and references to the accused perpetrators' neighbors, alleged accomplices, and social intimates, an analysis of these records provides a rare opportunity to put enslaved men and women, along with the wider social worlds they inhabited, in the same analytical frame. In the process, this chapter highlights not only the role of gender in shaping access and relationships to dress but also the role of dress in shaping access to (decidedly gendered) relationships as well.

In mining criminal theft investigations not only for the accusations they contain but also for the details they provide about slaves' sartorial behavior, it is possible to read the records in ways that yield insight into a world of extralegal practices – which is to say, those taking place outside of the domain of the law – that played meaningful parts in enslaved men's and women's lives. It also allows for a consideration of enslaved men's and women's motives and subjectivities. While this way of reading requires drawing information from the same category of sources – lawsuits filed in colonial tribunals – that has animated the work of other scholars, here I do so with an eye out for those moments when slaves were the targets rather than the initiators of lawsuits, and when their bodies served as meaningful, visible, and at times even contentious sites of claims-making.

This approach draws particular theoretical insight from Stephanie M.H. Camp, who has shown how enslaved men and women in the nineteenth-century American South undertook a range of efforts to lay claim to their bodies as sites of pleasure, pride, and self-expression. They hosted secret parties (known as "frolics") in the woods, where they played music, danced, and enjoyed one another's company away from their owners' sight lines and spheres of influence.[15] In anticipation of these gatherings, enslaved women – eager to escape the forced androgyny of slavery – would stay up late into the night after a day of grueling labor and taking care of their own families, to make dresses out of fabric scraps and design hoopskirts made of tree branches and grapevines. For their part, enslaved men made their own instruments to play and helped acquire the necessary items for meals and performances – often from their owners' homes. In other words, ingenuity was at the heart of slaves' cultural practices. What they could not do openly, they shrouded in secrecy; what they could not buy, they made with their own hands; and what they could not make, they justified procuring by other means. Together, these practices – however short-lived and infrequent they may have been – functioned in opposition to slavery's economic imperatives and the attendant burdens placed on enslaved men's and women's bodies. Further, according to Camp, by conserving and diverting their energies toward preparing for and experiencing pleasurable amusements, rather than toward fulfilling their owners' labor expectations, these men and women also "insulted slaveholders' feelings of authority."[16]

To be sure, there are important distinctions to draw between the plantation South and viceregal Peru, beginning with the obvious divides between rural and urban life, between the early US republic and late-colonial Spanish America, and between the specific labor demands imposed on slaves in these two contexts. But even when accounting for those differences, Camp's notion that slaves could clothe and use their own bodies in ways that not only provided individual gratification but also undermined slaveholders' dominion finds particular resonance in Lima. Moreover, applying Camp's framework to Lima helps build on her thesis, to show how slaves' access to elegant clothing provided a highly visible means by which to communicate as well as challenge ideas about legal status, gender, family, and honor.

THE DISTINGUISHED ONE

As a *jornalero*, Juan Ramos (whose 1732 case opened this chapter) spent his days performing work for hire in exchange for wages that he was obligated by law to surrender to his owner, a woman named Doña Clara Manrique. The precise details of this arrangement are unclear, since neither Ramos nor other witnesses indicated the kind of work he performed in his capacity as a *jornalero*. In any case, his ability to move around the city was evinced by his diverse social network that included Margarita Zaya (whom witnesses later described as accompanying Ramos on a neighborhood stroll while the latter was looking particularly "gallant") as well as an assortment of neighbors, acquaintances, and friends. Several of these (enslaved and free) people were called to testify against Ramos in the case involving the theft of the white shirt, with each sharing details about the man's lifestyle, self-presentation, and reputation around the community.

By referring to Ramos as a man of distinction who took to strolling about in "the kind of shirt a gentleman would wear," the witnesses in the case managed to link the accused with a certain brand of colonial masculinity. The image of a gentleman was more closely associated with elite Spaniards in colonial Lima than it was with African slaves, given that it referenced the ability to enjoy what historian Fred Bronner called a "lordly style of life." This lifestyle was made possible thanks to pure blood, legitimate birth, and access to titles and patronage and made comfortable thanks to elegant clothing, material goods, and the ability to enlist human property to do one's drudgery.[17] For neighbors to describe the white shirt as redolent of a gentleman – or the sort of man who enjoyed comfort and leisure – suggested that Ramos himself was convincingly able to embody a similar kind of persona in spite of his own racial, legal, and socioeconomic status.

While certainly flattering to Ramos, such a characterization was also emblematic of the threats slaves could pose to Lima's social order, in that with a mere change of clothes they could be seen and treated with the kind of esteem generally reserved for elite Spaniards. This is not to overstate the depth or duration of the esteem cast in Ramos's direction, but rather to acknowledge the man's ability to push the limits of his condition. His skill at doing so was further evinced thanks to another common thread in the witness testimony against Ramos, which was that he was in regular trouble with his owner, Doña Clara Manrique. One such account came from an enslaved woman named Ignacia María, whose familiarity with Ramos owed to the fact that she belonged to one of Manrique's relatives. In her testimony, Ignacia María noted that Manrique frequently sent Ramos to a local slave prison as punishment for various misdeeds. While the witness did not elaborate on the offenses that resulted in these punishments, other sources from the era help ground her claims. Known as *panaderías*, because their primary functions were as bakeries, the prisons formed part of a punitive ecosystem within the institution of slavery in Lima. For, in addition to serving as sites of slave labor, slaves were sent to *panaderías* for all manner of alleged or convicted crimes – including stealing and running away – as well as for the duration of court investigations.[18] *Panaderías* also served as spaces where owners who had no plans to sell or imprison their slaves could make use of certain facilities and resources to punish or torture them.[19] Given the numerous shackles, whipping posts, and irons that were readily available in most *panaderías*, it is easy to imagine the kinds of terror to which enslaved men and women were subjected in these spaces, either at the hands of their owners or one of the facilities' operators (known as *panaderos*).[20] In short, Ignacia María's reference to Ramos's frequent visits to these prisons served to indicate that Ramos had a history of getting into trouble, and of facing harsh punishments as a result.

Ramos's owner was not the only person in his life who found him to be a troublemaker. Other witnesses linked Ramos to a man known simply as Thoribio, who they described as a habitual criminal and regular accomplice to Ramos's alleged acts of thievery. And in her own testimony, Margarita Zaya admitted to sharing an "illicit friendship" with Ramos, which she claimed that friends and acquaintances urged her against to avoid getting involved with a man they described as a "thief with bad habits."[21] Her remarks indicate just how complicated Ramos's standing in his community was, in that he seemed to receive praise for his self-presentation, suspicion of how he spent his time, and criticism of his character all at once. Zaya's testimony also indicated the extent to which the man seemed to wield a certain amount of charisma and charm, for even in the face of so many warnings to keep her distance and to refuse anything Ramos tried to give her, Zaya would not cut off contact with him.

By the time Ramos gave his own testimony, he had to answer to both the original charges (of stealing a white shirt and several chickens) and a litany of damning assertions from those who knew him. When called to give his own testimony and asked if he understood why he had been arrested and imprisoned, Ramos responded that it was because he and an accomplice had, in his words, "stolen some chickens" (a vaguely phrased admission that did not make clear which or how many chickens he was talking about, or from whom he had stolen them). He denied having committed any other acts of thievery and rejected the substance of the other witness claims. Ramos further insisted that the box that neighbors saw him give to Margarita Zaya (the contents of which no one knew and he did not explain) had come from his owner, not from the church; that he had purchased the "very rich shirt" he was seen wearing from a friend; and that he had no idea where Thoribio (whom witnesses described as an accomplice) had gotten the "London cape" that was allegedly stolen from the tailor. Further, Ramos seemed eager to posit Thoribio as the real criminal, adding that he had actually seen the man wearing the white cape a few nights before they stole chickens from the church. Given that Ramos admitted to one theft and denied involvement in the others (which he implicitly blamed on Thoribio), it is possible that he was telling the truth in his testimony. Another possibility is that he considered the chicken theft a lesser offense than the other crimes of which he had been accused and was thus only willing to offer a partial confession to lessen his potential punishment.

Whatever their logic, Ramos's denials, evasions, and redirections were ultimately no match for the prosecution's tactics. In the face of such a vast arsenal of incriminating witness testimony, the judge in the case ultimately declared Ramos guilty of the crime of stealing the chickens and shirt from the church. He was sentenced to 100 lashes and expulsion, which required him to move away from Lima for a period of four years.[22] Both the corporal punishment and forced removal from the city were common penalties reserved for slaves committing all manner of offenses[23] and, in this case, represented a particularly cruel and ironic turn of events for a man who used clothing to claim his own body for his own purposes. In addition to suffering the immediate pain of the whip, Ramos would have been left with deep and lingering wounds resulting from the repeated contact between lash and flesh. With this in mind, the punishment likely extended beyond the moment in which it unfolded, since he would have carried the scars with him for the rest of his life. The sentence thus served as a harsh reminder of the fact that, whatever Ramos may have thought of himself and gotten members of his community to believe about him, in the eyes of the law he was a still a slave. Not only did his own body not fully belong to him but also it was subject to the court's decisions as to where it could or could not reside. In this way, the punishment also served as a kind of warning to other slaves considering similar acts of thievery or impudence, akin to the scars worn by runaways throughout the Americas whose bodies presaged what their fellow captives might experience should they undertake similar attempts at escape.[24]

To be sure, the outcome of the case says a great deal about Lima's slave society. For one, it shows that Ramos was a man on display. As he made his way through daily life and down the streets of the city he called home, he seemed always to have eyes trained on him. Of this Ramos was surely aware, and in fact, the man was adept at courting his share of attention. But he also thought that there were times when no one was looking. His moment of reckoning likely came with a large dose of surprise over just how often he had been seen by neighbors, associates, and friends. This is not to say, of course, that observers always eyed him with negative judgments, for his neighbors' accounts of how "gallant" he looked on his stroll with Zaya, in fact, reveal just the opposite.

Nor is it clear whether neighbors willingly offered their testimony against him, or if it was taken under duress. As discussed in this book's introduction, criminal records from slaveholding societies challenge historians to not mistake detailed witness testimony for willful candor or complicity in proving guilt, since enslaved witnesses were especially vulnerable to harsh interrogation tactics and threats for noncooperation. Still, regardless of the circumstances of their collection, when marshaled in an investigation of a slave's presumed guilt, witness testimony could and did amount to bad news for the accused. The outcome of the case against Ramos also highlights how, when a man of his status and condition was found in violation of the law, no matter his offense or reasons, the punishment would be swift and brutal.

At the same time, Ramos's (alleged and admitted) actions also shed light on the cracks within the institution of slavery in eighteenth-century Lima. His behavior in the period leading up to and following the church theft reveals how slaves' physical mobility enabled them to build connections and access resources that served interests beyond their status as property.[25] Further, the frequent and brutal punishments did not seem to stifle Ramos's desire to acquire elegant clothing. Perhaps the repeated assaults on his bodily autonomy lent even more urgency to his desire to fashion himself in a way that instilled a sense of pride and pleasure. The case against Ramos, then, serves to highlight the kind of premium that enslaved men could place on elegant self-presentation, not only in terms of what it could do to shape others' conceptions of them but also for how it could nurture their own sense of self-regard. The outcome of Ramos's case does not erase the image it captured of a man in pursuit – and at times in full command – of his own mode of self-presentation.

Indeed, while certainly remarkable, Ramos was by no means unique among his contemporaries in eighteenth-century Lima, nor, for that matter, was Margarita Zaya. Enslaved men frequently found themselves under suspicion of stealing, and the ensuing investigations revealed the men's distinctive use of social ties and material goods. For their part, even though enslaved women rarely appeared on record as the specific targets of criminal investigations, they were nonetheless highly visible throughout such cases, as the girlfriends, friends, acquaintances, relatives, and wives of the accused. They appear either by way of witness testimony linking them to the men in question, or through their own explanations of their relationship to them. And often, they appear as the – alleged or actual, reluctant or willing – recipients of stolen goods, or of goods purchased with stolen money. The women's visibility in these records offers important hints and details about enslaved men's motivations for acquiring and distributing elegant clothing, as well as both groups' social lives, identities, and attendant responsibilities.

HUSBANDS AND WIVES

As was true elsewhere in Latin America, the church in Lima did not prohibit enslaved men and women from marrying.[26] In fact, it offered a modicum of support for such unions by encouraging owners to jointly purchase husbands and wives and to recognize couples' conjugal needs and personal responsibilities.[27] But slaveholders did not always yield to ecclesiastical expectations, particularly when they perceived those expectations to run counter to their own economic interests and control over their human property. Consequently, even when they were able to marry, enslaved men and women often belonged to different owners – or lived apart for other reasons, such as when one member of the couple was free while the other was enslaved[28] – which meant that they had to work to maintain their relationships from separate households or even from different cities.[29] Beyond physical separation, their status as human property dictated the contours of their daily lives and responsibilities in ways that hindered the nurturing of intimate relationships and the preservation of spousal and familial bonds. Enslaved couples thus had to struggle to spend time together, attend to one another's needs, and offer as much protection and support as they could from afar.

Some slaves turned to the courts to improve their circumstances, such as by appealing to church officials to intervene when owners sought to block marriages or conjugal access, asking for permission to find new owners closer to their spouses, or even by filing claims on behalf of spouses abused at the hands of owners and overseers.[30] In those instances, slaves' knowledge of the law enabled them to put pressure on the legal system to grant the rights and protections to which they were entitled. Yet there is ample evidence to show that slaves also used extralegal (and at times illegal) means to honor the sanctity of their unions. A case from 1740 helps put this into relief. In it, a man named Pedro de Vargas Machuca accused an enslaved *zambo*[31] named José Alvarado of colluding with María Dominga de Loayza (Vargas Machuca's slave and Alvarado's wife) to extract money and goods from his home and then absconding with her. According to the claim, Vargas Machuca had recently purchased Loayza and taken her into his home. Since then, various household items had begun to go missing. One day it was a pair of socks, and another day it was a few handkerchiefs, until suddenly, 600 pesos' worth of clothing, nearly 1,000 pesos in silver, and Loayza herself were gone. In explaining why he suspected Alvarado, Vargas Machuca recalled that when Loayza first arrived at his home, she was barefoot and had only the clothes on her back, which consisted of a short-sleeved cotton blouse and yellow patchwork skirt. Within a matter of days, however, she had begun spending time with her husband and wearing several new outfits, including a striking yellow skirt. When Vargas Machuca asked Loayza where the clothes came from, she said that her husband had bought them, having paid about 80 pesos in total. Of this, Vargas Machuca was dubious. For one, in his estimation, the new wardrobe was worth more than 300 pesos, and besides, "a poor slave could not afford such luxuries."[32] (Amid all his explications, there was no mention of why, in the face of Loayza's ex-owner's warnings and his own mounting suspicions, Vargas Machuca bought and kept her anyway.)

The prosecution called several witnesses to testify in the ensuing investigation, including neighbors and friends of Pedro de Vargas Machuca, as well as individuals who knew José Alvarado and María Dominga de Loayza. Without a doubt, the witnesses' statements paint an image of a couple guilty of the crimes for which they stood accused. But they also tell a story of a husband and wife whose determination to support one another pushed them to take bold measures. To begin, two witnesses, both residents of the neighborhood where Vargas Machuca lived with Loayza, testified to having once seen the enslaved woman pass her husband a large basket of white clothing from the upstairs balcony. One witness further noted that she remembered when Loayza first arrived in the neighborhood looking "very disheveled" and was surprised to see such a drastic change in the woman's appearance. Another witness claimed that Loayza had recently been spending money in a way that, to him, "did not correspond to her status as a slave." Based on these statements, it seems that the couple had been stealing from the claimant's home to finance new outfits and expenditures. Such a scenario gained credence thanks to other witness statements. When it was his turn to testify, Alvarado's owner, a man named Sebastian de Alvarado, noted with more than a hint of resignation that "José Alvarado's habit of stealing and selling stolen goods is notorious." Another witness, a free *parda* named Magdalena Zorilla, stated that Alvarado had enlisted her on several occasions to ferry several items – including a shirt, apron, and three bolts of cambric from the market in Callao – to Loayza when she was still living in Vargas Machuca's home in Lima.[33] Apparently, Loayza supplied her husband with goods to sell for cash that Alvarado would then use to purchase his wife fine clothing, which, with the help of a third party, he would deliver to her at Vargas Machuca's home.

José Alvarado, however, had a slightly different view. When asked about the three new outfits Vargas Machuca described in his wife's possession, Alvarado stated that there was only one and that it did not cost upwards of 300 pesos as Vargas Machuca insisted, or even 80 pesos as Loayza herself had claimed (per Vargas Machuca's testimony), but rather 59 pesos, which Alvarado paid for with his own money. And, finally, with regard to the accounts placing him outside of Vargas Machuca's home in receipt of a basket from Loayza, Alvarado acknowledged that witnesses were correct in what they saw but downplayed the significance of the incident, saying that what they described as a basket filled with laundry was in fact only a pair of white socks. In other words, Alvarado did not deny the fact that his wife was wearing new clothing items and, instead, took full responsibility for purchasing them. Through his testimony, then, Alvarado was able to at once defend his wife's innocence and honor by denying that she did anything wrong, dismiss the possibility that his wife had given him anything of value from Vargas Machuca's home to sell, and take full credit and responsibility for her new appearance. Likewise, when Loayza was finally discovered in hiding in the neighboring city of Callao and brought to give her own testimony, she supported the bulk of her husband's assertions. She said that from the moment she arrived at her owner's home she did not have any clothes of her own, and it was only thanks to Alvarado that she was able to acquire a wardrobe. But the wardrobe was more extensive than Vargas Machuca had realized and that Alvarado had indicated in his testimony. Among other items, it included a blouse, a cambric (light wool) apron, hair ribbons from Holland, a rose-colored skirt made with Castilian wool, two pairs of shoes, several pairs of silk stockings, and a "covering" cloth (a type of handkerchief, similar to a mantilla, used to cover one's hair or face).[34]

In their statements, Vargas Machuca, Alvarado, and Loayza made clear how they perceived their own, and one another's, roles and responsibilities. As a slaveholder, Vargas Machuca was obliged by law to feed and clothe his human property, yet, by his own admission, he did nothing in response to encountering Loayza in her meager condition. No one was more aware of such indifference or its consequences than Loayza, who alone had to experience the pain and frustration of performing her duties in bare feet and tattered clothes. And while the conversations that took place between Loayza and her husband during this time are impossible to recover, the sentiments they contained are somewhat easier to discern. To an enslaved woman, an owner's disregard for her safety and comfort may not have been surprising, but it was certainly upsetting. Indeed, the subtle difference between the woman's testimony and her owner's is replete with meaning: while Vargas Machuca said Loayza arrived at his home with very little, Loayza contended that she arrived with nothing. Surely she was not naked when she walked through her new owner's door, but from her perspective she may as well have been.

Looking back on some of the witness testimony in the case helps explain why Loayza would have reacted so strongly to her circumstances. As neighbor Petrona de Lazaro, a free *negra*, had recalled in her statement, Loayza arrived at her new owner's home looking "very disheveled." This information appears in the record as part of the prosecutor's effort to build a case against Alvarado. For, if she had originally arrived at her owner's home in such a tattered state, her newly acquired wardrobe certainly would have been a cause for suspicion. But the witness's observation also hints at the way in which Loayza may have been regarded or treated by her neighbors when she moved in with her owner. Perhaps they stopped and stared at her when she went outside, thereby heightening her sense of deprivation and degradation. Her feelings were apparently keen enough that Alvarado, her husband and confidant, sprang into immediate action to furnish her with new clothes in just a few days.

In a highly honorific culture such as that of eighteenth-century Lima, the married couple's actions are particularly significant. Of course, Alvarado and Loayza did not actually live together, and by law, Vargas Machuca still held ultimate control over Loayza, but the couple nonetheless undermined the basis of Vargas Machuca's patriarchal authority in meaningful ways. By informing her husband of her situation, Loayza was calling attention to Vargas Machuca's failure, not only as an owner but also as a head of household, and appealing to a relationship outside of the master-slave dynamic to meet her needs. For his part, rather than seeing his wife continue to work barefoot and in near tatters, Alvarado found a way to put shoes on her feet and new clothes on her back. And there was more: by acquiring and wearing such accessories as lace stockings and a covering cloth, which was primarily used among the city's elite Spanish women to cover their heads and faces while out in public,[35] Alvarado and Loayza were also countering Vargas Machuca's legally sanctioned claims about the kind of woman Loayza was. More than just a laboring body, she was capable of being cared for, supplied with elegant material goods, and looking beautiful. She was also deserving of both symbolic protection in the form of the covering cloth and removal from harm's way. And although Loayza did not address it during her own testimony, another witness who spoke with her while she was in hiding testified that the woman had endured "punishments and bad treatment" while at Vargas Machuca's home. Loayza's disappearance was also the culmination of the couple's efforts, which began with their working together in the extraction of goods from Vargas Machuca's home, to undercut the man's dominion over his household and property. In short, nearly every aspect of the couple's behavior served as either a challenge to or an indictment of Vargas Machuca, as both a slaveholder and head of household. Where Vargas Machuca would not provide for his slave, Loayza made room for her husband to provide for his wife. And, finally, although Vargas Machuca presumed his property rights to be inviolable, Loayza understood her needs, and Alvarado his duties as a husband, to be just as sacred if not more so.

The case adds new dimension to recent scholarship, signaling the importance of marriage to enslaved men and women. In Lima and elsewhere in colonial Latin America, marriage served as a crucial source of social standing for enslaved and free people of African descent.[36] It enabled men and women to shield themselves from insult, or to at least lay claim to recourse should they find themselves under attack. For enslaved men and women, marriage also provided a way for them to present themselves to the courts as "honorable, law-abiding" subjects when engaged in disputes with their owners, as well as to ensure that their children and descendants might see improved status.[37] Marriage, of course, also contained duties, and those who did not live up to their spousal obligations could imperil their financial circumstances and community standing. As Sandra Lauderdale Graham has shown in the case of nineteenth-century Brazil, enslaved and free blacks placed tremendous stock in their reputations, as their livelihoods depended on their ability to garner respect and confidence among peers. This fact was as true for women as it was for men. In her analysis of the divorce proceedings between former slaves Henriqueta and Rufino, Graham shows how an illiterate, African-born woman could dissolve an abusive union in which the male partner did not live up to his financial obligations.[38]

The case against José Alvarado and María Dominga de Loayza joins these larger narratives about slave marriage, showing that both husband and wife drew a sense of standing from their relationship, as well as an expectation of spousal duty. It also shows how, for enslaved couples, marriage could act as a cudgel against owners' pretensions about their own honor and status. For Loayza, access to material goods carried several meanings. For one, it meant an improvement on her earlier, shoeless condition, enabling her to perform her work with some measure of comfort. It also meant being able to indulge in the latest fashions and assert her own femininity while looking the part of an elegant, protected woman. At the same time, the clothing allowed Loayza to convey a certain kind of worldliness, given the foreign provenance of the goods (such as the Holland ribbons and the skirt made of Castilian wool). For Alvarado, it meant being able to ensure that his enslaved wife not only had what she needed but that she even enjoyed a few of the things she wanted as well. Even though there is no mention in the case of how Alvarado himself dressed, his careful attention to Loayza's wardrobe nonetheless formed part of the man's own self-presentation. In fact, by providing for his wife, Alvarado was behaving in accordance with the kinds of prescriptions familiar to a *paterfamilias*, or head of household as described in the first chapter– better, even, than Vargas Machuca himself was.

But neither husband nor wife was content to limit the benefits of these material acquisitions to themselves or the bounds of their marriage. In her testimony, witness Magdalena Zorilla (who admitted to ferrying goods between Alvarado and Loayza) stated that Loayza had once encouraged her to join Alvarado on Mercadores Street in Callao to pick out a skirt to her liking and for which Alvarado would then pay. Perhaps the gesture was intended to serve as means of ensuring complicity or silence, but Zorilla's self-description in her testimony as a "poor meat vendor" indicates that the couple was acting at least in part out of concern for the woman's own financial circumstances and material desires even though she, unlike Alvarado and Loayza, actually had her freedom. By offering Magdalena Zorilla a shopping trip in exchange for transporting clothing from Callao to Lima, the couple's actions revealed the extent to which access to clothing could serve multiple and often overlapping purposes. In addition to providing a tool for individual enjoyment, self-expression, and the nurturing of romantic relationships, it also provided a means to care for members of extended family and kinship networks.

FAMILY UNITS

In 1755, for instance, a Spaniard named Juan Bautista Angel accused Francisco Calvo, the forty-year-old slave he had contracted to help build some houses on the north side of the Rimac River near Lima's Plaza Mayor, of stealing 1,000 pesos. For the duration of Calvo's employment, Bautista Angel had permitted the man – who "seemed trustworthy" – to sleep in a small room near his own bedroom, which housed a trunk containing a large and "steadily increasing" quantity of silver coins. Bautista Angel and some of the witnesses called to testify in the ensuing criminal investigation alleged that after completing his work for Bautista Angel, Calvo began to "play and laze about" instead of looking for another job. They also claimed that despite being unemployed, Calvo made several payments and purchases in the weeks following the alleged robbery. Mateo Melís, the Spanish manager of a local tavern, testified to Calvo's many visits to his establishment, where he bought food and drinks with the same kind of two-peso coins described as missing from Bautista Angel's trunk. And a woman named Manuela Bolaños, who lived in the house where the unmarried Calvo had moved into a room (along with his sister, Margarita, and nieces, Eusebia and Dominga) after leaving Bautista Angel's construction site, claimed that Calvo came home one day with elegant new shawls and stockings for Margarita and Dominga to wear to a bullfight. Through it all, despite allegations of his numerous leisurely activities and expenditures, Calvo even continued to supply his owner (a woman named Isabel Peresbuelta, with whom – in a not unusual circumstance – he apparently did not reside) with a daily wage.[39]

For all the limitations of his legal status and racial background, Calvo had nonetheless found ways to cultivate a dynamic social identity. It contained elements that were especially familiar to elite male heads of household but also within reach of some enslaved men. According to Bautista Angel, not only did the accused use stolen money to eat and drink in taverns but Calvo – a man who "maintains a horrible family ... administering to all of their needs" – also used the occasion of the theft to begin "outfitting his family in notable decency."[40] By acquiring elegant clothing and distributing it to the female members of his household, Calvo appeared to be behaving in accordance with the prescriptions of an elite patriarch. For their part, as the alleged recipients of these material gifts, Calvo's sister and niece appeared to be adapting notions of colonial femininity to their own realities: in addition to outfitting themselves in the kind of finery worn by ladies of the upper classes, Margarita and Dominga also attended a bullfight – exactly the kind of social event frequented by their presumed social superiors.

A curious aspect of the case concerns the relationship between Francisco Calvo and his other niece Eusebia, who apparently was left out of Calvo's gift giving. There are several possible explanations for this. The young woman may already have had resources of her own, either in the form of money, or even a lover or husband, which could have obviated the need for her uncle to provide for her in the way he had done for Margarita and Dominga. Or perhaps there were tensions at play in her relationship with Calvo that clothing could not smooth over, no matter how elegant and useful it may have been. It is also possible that the niece had her suspicions of how Calvo had come into contact with the goods and refused to accept them for fear of ensnaring herself in a complicated situation. Finally, there is the chance that she simply did not care for, or want to be seen in, the clothes. In any case, she would not have been alone in refusing to take advantage of ill-gotten gains. When a *negro* named José Orrantía was accused of stealing clothing and personal effects from a *mulata* named Estefanía Guerrero, one witness in the case testified to Orrantía having propositioned her to purchase some of the goods. According to the witness, an enslaved woman named Manuela Saurez, Orrantía offered her three skirts ("one made of gauze; another of cotton") and five blouses for 16 pesos. She refused, telling the would-be salesman that the price was too high considering that two of the shirts were "in very bad condition." Orrantía then approached another enslaved woman, Brigida Tagle, who took a look at the offerings and demurred. In her testimony she claimed that it was for two reasons: the first was that she did not know "*de quien era,*" (or, "whose they were"), and the second reason was that she did not know "whether they had been stolen."[41]

Suarez's and Tagle's testimonies suggest that enslaved women could be discerning customers when it came to clothing. They cared about the quality and condition of the goods, as well as their provenance, meaning that, to at least some degree, enslaved women were concerned about the status and style of the previous wearer, or that they wanted to be sure that their clothes had been acquired through licit channels so as not to attract suspicion on the eventual purchaser and wearer. The witnesses' testimonies in the case thus provide a context for understanding the reasons why Francisco Calvo's other niece, Eusebia, may have refused to take part in his material distributions.

That being said, it is clear that enslaved women saw much to gain from accepting gifts of clothing. In so doing, female slaves – much like their free counterparts and presumed superiors – were able to make their way about town in the kind of finery that suggested a protected and privileged status. Moreover, elegant clothing could also help them recover aspects of their femininity denied to them by the strenuous nature of the work they performed, their responsibility to enable their female owners to lead leisurely lifestyles, or the kind of dress typically required for manual labor.

At the same time, the case against Calvo further underscores how, for enslaved men, gaining access to clothing was not only about outfitting their own bodies in finery (as was true for Juan Ramos, the slave in the "rich" white shirt whose case opened this chapter). It was also a way of ensuring that their companions, wives, and female kin could look and feel good as well. In the process, these acts enabled enslaved men to assume roles as heads of household, even if they did not reside in traditional households or head traditional family units. Their social behavior shows that, much like their elite counterparts, they valued such matters as acquiring and distributing material resources. But they did so in ways that not only accommodated but also legitimized their particular modes of family formation.

PATRONS

In addition to the men who acquired elegant clothing for their own use and the ones who did so for the women in their lives were those who used theft to satisfy their desire for both personal adornment and showing consideration for social intimates. In 1766, a man named Juan Antonio Suárez accused Domingo Calderón, a twenty-six-year-old *jornalero*, of stealing 60 pesos from a safe in his room. Suárez – who had employed Calderón to sweep his tavern and the bedrooms upstairs in exchange for a *jornal* (daily wage) that Calderón would supply to his owner – claimed that since the day of the alleged crime, the accused, in addition to buying himself a new shirt, began "spending money excessively and immoderately on meals and gifts for others in his sphere, [and] idling about without working." "The worst part," Suárez added, "is that [Calderón] tried to provoke his friends to join him in his indolence, by offering them money so that they could pay their respective *jornales*."[42] The disparaging and hyperbolic tone of Suárez's complaint – he used the term *porquerías* (which roughly translates as "garbage") to describe Calderón's economic and social activities – offers a revealing glimpse of slaveholders' conceptions of unacceptable uses of slaves' time and money. It also suggests that slaves' social ties could undermine those expectations by infringing on the privileges that many believed were reserved for only free people, and in particular for Spaniards.

For his part, Calderón might not have seen anything wasteful about his decision to invite friends (who apparently were also enslaved) to share food and drink or about offering them the means to fulfill their financial obligations to their owners while enjoying a bit of rest and leisure.[43] Moreover, in a city where a slave could be jailed, tortured, and sold[44] – or worse – for failing to supply an owner with a daily wage, Calderón's behavior also stands out among the possibilities for slaves to use the economic tools at their disposal to shield one another from potential physical harm or isolation from family and friends.[45] Cultural anthropologists and sociologists specializing in gift studies have long been interested in the socioeconomic importance of practices of giving, receiving, and reciprocating.[46] Scholars in this field largely examine the motives and meanings behind money and material exchanges and argue that they are the building blocks of social life and interaction.[47] These activities call for particular attention from historians of slavery, as analyses of gift giving and commodity exchanges offer insight into the social, cultural, and economic lives and influence of Africans and their descendants in the Americas. Indeed, for many enslaved men and women in Lima, extending gifts and favors was fundamental to the building and maintenance of their social ties and contributed in important ways to the stability of their communities.[48]

Their practices also complicate a prevailing narrative among scholars of colonial Peru, who have generally argued that relations between and among enslaved and free people of African descent were rarely communal, and instead largely characterized by caste- and status-based hierarchies fueled by concerns with daily survival and upward mobility.[49] These arguments are primarily rooted in analyses of caste- and status-specific *cofradías* that restricted membership to *mulatos* or *pardos* or free blacks only. According to Christine Hünefeldt, free blacks created complex structures of "internal differentiation," wherein *bozales* occupied the bottom rung and "at the apex of this pyramid were the *quarterones*, and *quinterones*, who thought of themselves as white and had the greatest chance of obtaining freedom."[50] Even in mixed-caste *cofradías*, historians have observed tendencies toward fragmentation and have cited the prevalence of *mulatos*, *pardos*, and others in positions of leadership and authority over *negros* as proof of the extent to which these organizations "accommodated the master-slave relation."[51]

Without denying the potential for formal organizations such as *cofradías* – which were heavily circumscribed by the church – to reproduce colonial hierarchies, daily life offered a wider range of interactive and relational possibilities. Slaves formed part of mixed-status marriages and romantic unions, belonged to family units in which some members were free, shared rooms and homes with free *castas*, and generally operated within diverse social circles. And slaves entered into and navigated these relationships with the help of clothing, money, and material goods. In 1792, a woman named Juana Maria Lobatón stood accused by her then owner, Doña María Dolores de Iturrigaray, of stealing money. Lobatón was just one of two enslaved women to face prosecution for theft in the period between 1723 and 1795, and the ensuing criminal investigation into her alleged crime filled two dense volumes of allegations and testimony. The first volume – which likely detailed the precise nature of Iturrigaray's complaint, such as the amount and denomination of the allegedly stolen money – is missing from the case file. Nonetheless, the remaining record contains valuable testimony from Lobatón's family, friends, and past accusers, who revealed that the woman had a reputation for "committing acts of theft against the owners she has served."[52] In one instance, she and Cayetano Dávila (a man described by witnesses as a free *cholo*, or of indigenous ancestry, with whom Lobatón also had a child) were accused of stealing and later selling a valuable horse carriage belonging to one Doña María de Alba.[53] Lobatón had also been jailed on several occasions – once for having stolen a silver carafe – and each time she was released she quickly resorted to the same acts of thievery.

Dávila was often Lobatón's primary accomplice – helping her extract and sell countless goods – but when their relationship eventually ended, Lobatón found another lover and accomplice of sorts named José Tadeo Acuña (a *sargento de pardos*).⁵⁴ While apparently not an active participant in her crimes, Tadeo Acuña certainly benefited from them: when Lobatón stole some gold coin from a neighbor named Natividad Herboso, she gave him a few pieces as a gift. Her gift, in addition to serving as a token of affection, also likely functioned as a means of ensuring his silence and complicity – until, that is, he was called to testify against her. In addition to her lovers, Lobatón also frequently enlisted the aid of neighbors, friends, and relatives (including her aunt Doña Jacoba Oyaque, a free woman, perhaps of indigenous ancestry given her surname, with whom Lobatón lived when she was not under arrest). While imprisoned for stealing from Iturrigaray, Lobatón sent a message through Antonio Europeo, a young man who lived in a room in Oyaque's home, to a *negra* named Gabriela. Hidden in a cushion in Lobatón's room were six ounces of gold and 14 pesos (totaling 418 pesos and presumably consisting – at least in part – of the money stolen from Iturrigaray), which Gabriela was to collect, package, and deliver to María Ignacia de Vargas Machuca, who belonged to the owner of the prison where Lobatón was being held. In her testimony, De Vargas Machuca admitted to passing along the parcel of money to Lobatón, which Lobatón intended to use to purchase her freedom.⁵⁵

With all the testimony and evidence against her in the 1792 case, Lobatón was eventually sentenced to exile and forced to find an owner outside of the city, a particularly tough blow given that Lima was home to her wealth of contacts (who included Indians, whites, and her mother, a free *negra*) and impressive social influence. The city was also where she had made significant strides toward being able to purchase her freedom. The sentence did nothing, however, to curb Lobatón's appetite for theft: the following year, Martin José de Asco y Arostegui (Lobatón's new owner and the governor of the highland region of Huarochirí), accused her of stealing more than 600 pesos in gold, as well as a trunk full of clothing.⁵⁶ The amount of the money stolen, along with the clothing, suggested that the woman remained devoted to her efforts to secure her freedom.

In addition to counting among the small handful of instances in which enslaved women stood directly accused of stealing, Lobatón's case stands out for the explicit links the woman made between the pursuit of theft and the pursuit of freedom. For her, access to money and material goods were not enough on their own; they were primarily valuable insofar as they allowed her to get closer to self-purchase. This is not to say that her male counterparts did not share the same desire for freedom, or that their experiences were any less compelling for having not prioritized freedom in the same way. Because they still found ways – thanks to their access to clothing and money – to enjoy a certain amount of dignity and esteem and to act in consideration of their social relationships. Whether they were stealing money to share with friends, stealing clothes to please a lover, or perhaps stealing some combination of money and goods for some combination of reasons, slaves were keenly aware of the currency and meaning that could be derived from their illicit activities. As the case against Domingo Calderón shows, sharing resources among friends could serve the interests of larger social networks, enabling slaves to fulfill immediate obligations and perhaps return the favor at a later date. At the same time, sharing resources could serve an individual's self-interests as well, in that Calderón may also have been able to secure his friends' loyalty or gratitude in a way that might benefit him down the line, whether over the course of a criminal investigation or under other circumstances. These relationships and resources – along with the myriad ways in which slaves wielded them – deepen historians' understanding of the role of honor in the lives of lower-class individuals in Latin America. Rather than viewing honor as a fixed quality belonging solely to elite Spaniards, men and women of various colors and classes found ways to lay claim to social status, at times even in the face of ridicule or dispute from presumed social superiors.[57]

In Lima, the circumstances detailed in Domingo Calderón's story suggest that urban slaves' culture of honor contained codes that were tailored to their specific realities. That is, while slaves may have at times followed models of colonial masculinity conveyed by elite whites, Calderón's financial consideration of his friends shows that slaves could imbue those models with their own meanings. Elegant self-presentation and material distributions between men and women enabled slaves to conceive of themselves as ladies and gentlemen. At the same time, defining themselves as such also seemed to encompass acts of patronage within larger social networks. Given their diverse African origins, slaves in Lima may also have drawn on gestures of patronage already familiar in other contexts or inherited social practices from the elders and neighbors among whom they lived.[58] The 1755 case against Francisco Calvo provides a useful framework for exploring these possibilities. In her testimony against him, neighbor Manuela Bolaños claimed that in the days following the alleged theft, she overheard Calvo say that he was "amazed to see that he was living like a free man, and to know that his sister and nieces enjoyed the same benefit." What did it mean, in eighteenth-century Lima, for a slave to live like a free person? Manumission letters from the period are particularly helpful here, as they contain a generic definition of freedom as it was employed by notaries and endorsed by slave owners. "From today on," reads one such letter signed by Juana Foronda for a *mulato* named Joséf Foronda, "he will enjoy his freedom without burden or obligation; be able to make and declare a last will and testament; give and donate any goods that he possesses and acquires; make deals and contracts; reside where he wishes; and undertake any operations that he can, as would any individual born into freedom."[59] While the recognition of an individual's legal and economic rights is a hallmark of freedom in its juridical sense, the investigation into Calvo's alleged theft reveals how a slave – without a manumission letter of his own – could find ways to access many of the privileges reserved for free people.

In his confession, Calvo denied stealing Juan Bautista Angel's money, but when asked how he was able to eat and drink in Mateo Melís's tavern, he claimed that he had earned extra money by building a mule corral for patrons of the bullfight he attended with his relatives. As for his sister's and niece's new clothes – allegedly purchased by Calvo to wear on their outing – Calvo asserted that any clothing in the women's possession would have been purchased with money from their own jobs. As a day laborer, Calvo contracted himself out to several employers and put his carpentry skills to use, not only to earn the daily wage he supplied to his owner but also to earn extra money he used at his discretion. The bullfight he attended with his sister and niece was at once a leisurely activity, an economic possibility, and an opportunity to live like free people.

In fact, the scope of Calvo's alleged and admitted activities matched the prevailing definition of freedom almost to the letter. Over the course of only a few weeks, Calvo apparently managed to give and donate goods, make deals and contracts, reside where he wished, and undertake any operations that he could, as would any individual born into freedom. But it was precisely this degree of temporal, economic, and social discretion, and the sense of autonomy they engendered, that was troubling, not just to slaveholders and hirers but also to men and women outside of the master-slave dynamic in eighteenth-century Lima. In this case, Calvo's accuser, Bautista Angel, appeared to be as concerned with the social and economic behavior that surrounded the original criminal act assigned to the accused as with the crime itself. A close reading of the accuser's claims – echoed by several witness statements – reveals a remarkable degree of disdain toward Calvo and his relatives, discomfort with his freedom of movement and economic practices, and distrust of the means by which he attained them. That Calvo's behavior in the weeks following the theft indicted him as the culprit sheds light on the extent to which slaves' efforts to make use of the social and economic tools at their disposal could meet with suspicion and frustration. For Bautista Angel, Calvo's "elaborate spending," coupled with his apparent "laziness," in addition to his relatives' newfound elegance, corresponded neither to Calvo's station nor to theirs and, thus, could only have been attained through illegal means.[60] Furthermore, the fact that a man legally defined as property could consume and distribute property, while also finding ways to satisfy his obligations to his owner without always appearing to perform visible work, seemed to undermine the very logic of chattel slavery in Lima.

Along with others, Juan Ramos, Francisco Calvo, and their alleged accomplices behaved in ways that complicate our understanding of the importance of freedom to slaves. In choosing to use access to clothing and money to nurture interpersonal relationships and improve their social standing, rather than to funnel toward the eventual purchase of freedom, the men raise questions about just what kind of value they placed on juridical freedom. While the men certainly prioritized a certain kind of liberty – one that enabled them to apportion their time and resources in ways they saw fit – they did not seem convinced that manumission or self-purchase was the only condition under which they could exercise those liberties. This is not to say that they held no ambitions to gain freedom or that they were content to spend the rest of their lives as slaves; rather, they looked for ways in which they could carve out as much autonomy, dignity, and self-regard as they possibly could and share it with as many of their intimates as their resources would allow.

BODIES UNDER SCRUTINY

Ultimately, however, these men were apprehended and investigated for stealing precisely because they were enslaved. For even when they moved between shadows or spoke in hushed voices, they seemed always to have eyes and ears trained on them, thanks to all the men and women who made it their business to carefully detail where they were going, who they were with, and how they looked. Indeed, for all their dramatic turns, the men's cases provide rather ordinary snapshots of a fact of life in Lima: regardless of where or with whom they lived, they were besieged by intense and unrelenting surveillance. It was a reality familiar to many *limeños* but especially to the city's slaves, who found themselves with a certain freedom of mobility that was not without its share of attention and criticism. This was especially true when spending their money and time however and with whom they wished.

Certainly, the kind of neighborly scrutiny to which these men were exposed was in large part a by-product of urban living. Because they lived in close quarters and generally shared entrances, exits, courtyards, and passageways with their neighbors, urban dwellers had many useful vantage points from which to observe and report. Moreover, their living conditions had a profound impact on their ideas about public and private space, and on the relationship between personal matters and communal concerns. For them, whatever transpired in building doorways, halls, and courtyards – interstitial zones that belonged to no one in particular and to everyone at once – merited attention and scrutiny.[61] This helps explain the frequent appearance of neighbors' witness testimony in criminal cases from the period, since they found justification for being in the right places at the right times to note each other's comings, goings, and movements. But living in close quarters does not fully explain why slaves were such frequent targets of their neighbors' scrutiny. What about them was so suspicious?

The answer was largely found in the codified assumptions of colonial officials, who used allegations of slaves' thievery to justify the imposition of legal restrictions like curfews and sumptuary laws. In this way, conjecture and colonial reality became fully intertwined: suspicions of slaves fueled investigations (and convictions) of slaves, which in turn justified owners', hirers', officials', and the larger culture's holding of slaves in suspicion. Even slaves were called on to do their part in monitoring or sharing information about their counterparts, whether they wanted to or not. When, in July 1767, an enslaved woman named Clementina del Carmen found herself entangled in a criminal theft investigation after her owner, a widow named Doña Josepha de Salaverde, accused an enslaved man named Manuel (Clementina's male companion) of stealing several household items, witnesses in the case included several other slaves who lived in the building. Two of them, Maria and Sipriano, were slaves who belonged to the claimant in the case. While their testimony was undoubtedly valuable given their daily proximity to Clementina and residence in the same household from which the goods in the case were allegedly stolen, their legal status put them in a precarious position. Their owner, after all, was counting on their testimony. Indeed, the witnesses confirmed that Clementina and Manuel shared a so-called illicit friendship, which they claimed to know because they often spotted the pair speaking to one another at night in the doorway of the ground-level room Clementina occupied with her owner.[62]

Michel Foucault's theory of the panoptic schema can be usefully brought to bear in evaluating this context. Originally conceived as a prison tower by British legal theorist Jeremy Bentham, the Panopticon was an ideal site from which to observe behavior. Because inmates can never know who sees them (either because their cells are arranged in a way that obstructs view of the tower, or because the tower is constructed in a way that conceals the supervisor[s] inside), the Panopticon induces what Foucault calls "a state of conscious and permanent visibility," which assures self-discipline.[63] For Foucault, the Panopticon was more than an architectural site; it was a way of seeing that he called "panopticism." As such, its applications extended beyond the walls of the prison to include patterns of "generalized surveillance."[64]

Yet in Lima, the power of the slave system rested on a wider web of generalized surveillance that emanated not just from owners but also from hirers, from men and women outside the master-slave dynamic, and even from enslaved men and women themselves. Indeed, the institution of slavery in Lima, despite both its benign superficial appearance relative to plantation regimes and the implied autonomy of the hiring-out system, was tightly restricted and oppressive in its own ways. From house to street, enslaved men and women had to face a reality in which all eyes and ears were steadily fixed on them. Ultimately, for slaves, what likely mattered more than the reasons for the scrutiny they faced was the near constant fact of it. Thanks to both owners and hirers, slaves were exposed to ever greater numbers of people who felt entitled to police their behavior and movements.

Even slaves who found rooms to let by themselves, or – more often – shared residences with enslaved and free relatives, extended kin, and other roommates faced intense scrutiny and surveillance. Living under these circumstances certainly provided opportunities to escape the labor demands imposed on them and the constraints of the master-slave dynamic. However, since slaves paid for their housing out of their own daily wages, it also meant splitting crowded rooms in crowded buildings to limit the weight of their financial burdens. In those spaces they found themselves subject to unremitting scrutiny. In part this owed to ideas about home and community that were formed in densely populated urban environments, but it also was due to the increasingly prevalent view that slaves had a particular propensity toward criminality.

That enslaved men and women were so concerned with self-presentation in a city like Lima, where scrutiny and surveillance were facts of life, is particularly striking. Why would they invite more attention than they were already guaranteed? Absent their own explanations, it is impossible to reconstruct the thought process guiding the actions of the enslaved. But it is worth considering what the psychology of a person in their situation may have been. The work of psychoanalyst Jacque Lacan is useful to this exercise, particularly his description of the "gaze imagined by me in the field of the Other"[65] as part of the enduring realization that we are generally "beings who are looked at."[66] For the object of the gaze (the being who is looked at) there is not simply exposure but a certain kind of dialectic power, since the gaze is not just experienced but also solicited, directed, manipulated, and even distracted. Lacan thus imagines the object of the gaze saying to its subject, "You want to see? Well take a look at this!"[67]

Might Juan Ramos and his counterparts have said the same to all those whose eyes were trained on them? Perhaps Ramos knew that regardless of his behavior and actions, he would never fully escape scrutiny and, rather than attempt to remain as inconspicuous as possible under such circumstances, he chose instead to turn the burden of his ingrained visibility into an opportunity. For Ramos, taking control of how he appeared in others' fields of vision clearly served several ends. Beyond allowing his neighbors to view and refer to him as a gentleman, his intentional self-presentation provided a kind of diversionary tactic. A common thread in the witness testimony against Ramos is one of confusion over his legal status. Even Santiago Granados, who described himself as a slave and good friend of the accused, did not know for certain whether Ramos was enslaved or free.

CONCLUSIONS

For historians, the challenge of studying enslaved men and women who had little to no access to writing is that we are often confronted with teasingly brief glimpses into the lives and experiences of the people we seek to understand the most. As a source base, criminal theft investigations, by their nature, are particularly frustrating in this regard. Because prosecutors in such cases were primarily concerned with proving guilt or innocence, the kind of testimony that appears on record is necessarily constrained. Witness statements usually do not tell us about the wants, needs, or wishes of enslaved men and women, and when we hear the voices of the enslaved more directly, their words are mediated by the nature of the questions they are answering, and by the scribes recording their answers.[68]

Nonetheless, the details of the criminal cases at the center of this chapter provide profound insights into the accused perpetrators' motivations. Whereas some enslaved men used clothing to outfit themselves in ways that conveyed a sense of personal distinction, others used it to provide for their loved ones and social intimates. As we have seen, a husband providing his wife with elegant clothing enabled him to fulfill his spousal duties, and her to embrace her sense of femininity. Enslaved men also sought to ensure that they could spread the reach of their access to elegant material goods even further to include extended kin and acquaintances. In other words, whether operating in pairs or in teams, or working alone and distributing pilfered resources around social networks, these men were unmistakably social actors. Not only did they assert their sense of individual status and advance meaningful social agendas of their own but also they helped the people around them to share in and benefit from those efforts. As a result of their access to elegant clothing, enslaved men and women were able to push the limits of their legal status in ways that had broader societal implications. As the next chapter will show, clothing also contributed to a broader – and for some, more troubling – confusion over the boundaries of racial identity and privilege in Lima.

3   Black Bodies and Boundary Trouble

On September 18, 1741, a woman named Doña María Cayetana de Escobar y Barrantes filed a petition in Lima's ecclesiastical court to annul her marriage to a man she identified as Joseph de Ypinsa. According to her claim, she had married De Ypinsa because he was "a rich and noble man" who, over the course of their courtship, had portrayed himself as the legitimate son of a judge in the *audiencia* of Chile, a student preparing to graduate from an esteemed Jesuit college, and a slaveholder. And because he always dressed with such elegance, she took him at his word that he was an ideal match for a woman "of distinction and *superior calidad* [quality]" such as herself. But soon after the union, the woman claimed, she learned that she had been *"totalmente engañada,"* or completely deceived. Instead of marrying a moneyed man of privilege, she said she had become legally bound to someone who turned out to be of unknown parents, possible illegitimate birth, and *"malas costumbres"* (or bad customs). Not only that, but the petitioner had reason to believe that her husband was also hiding his true racial identity, for there were rumors going around that he was a *chino*, which meant that he had some degree of mixed African and indigenous ancestry.[1]

When distilled to its basic facts – a woman claimed she married a man under false pretenses – the case was hardly unusual for its time. There are approximately 140 extant annulment petitions from eighteenth-century Lima housed in the archbishopric archive, each containing claims by husbands and wives who sought to dissolve unions for a variety of reasons, from parental disapproval to allegations of a spouse's dishonesty or undesired (and heretofore undiscovered) traits. But the specifics of the petition make it especially useful to a study of the relationship between race, clothing, and status in colonial Lima. Where the previous chapter illustrated slaves' ability to negotiate and challenge their legal status through dress, this chapter examines the way clothing enabled free people of African descent to challenge ideas about race in the region.

CLOTHING AND *CALIDAD*

The 1741 case reveals the extent to which a man's personal narrative and manner of dress worked together to help him carry out a stunning act of deception, at least from the perspective of his wife, her parents, and several other third parties. To begin, by claiming an affiliation with the Colegio Real de San Martin, a Jesuit college founded in the sixteenth century, Joseph de Ypinsa was able to establish firm footing in an elite and distinguished realm.[2] Matriculates of the school came from wealthy and noble families and went on to become archbishops, judges, and other high-ranking religious and government officials.[3] The mere fact of attending the school, then, stood as proof of De Ypinsa and his family's status. And by outfitting himself in the school's uniform *casaca*, or frock coat, De Ypinsa was able to telegraph his membership among the cream of colonial society to all whose paths he crossed. The man further burnished his public image by regularly perambulating around town in a "very costly wardrobe," as one observer described it, and by telling another acquaintance that his mother had a diamond-paneled chest at home that was filled with an assortment of "very rich" costumes, including velvet skirts.[4] In addition to his statements and displays were other behaviors that upheld De Ypinsa's self-presentation as a wealthy man from a privileged background, including giving his intended a gold ring and arriving at her house one day in a carriage with two female slaves inside.[5] The latter act served as a way of giving his intended a glimpse of the kind of life she would lead with De Ypinsa as her husband. The presence of the slaves suggested Joseph's ability to provide a comfortable home where she would receive personal service and domestic help; and the carriage they rode in provided her with the assurance that whenever she traveled outside of their home she would do so in style and under protected cover. With all this, De Ypinsa convincingly presented himself as a man of sufficient prestige, future promise, and financial resources as to be an ideal mate.

The record does not indicate what, exactly, led the woman to ultimately decide that De Ypinsa was not the man he said he was, or when she first began to suspect as much. But the ensuing investigation into her claims provides some insight into what might have happened. One witness in the case, a friend of the woman's family, testified to having heard an unnamed acquaintance refer to Joseph as a "*chino*," which suggests that a rumor was at least in part responsible for the shift in the young woman's perception of her husband. Added to that was the fact that De Ypinsa appeared to have a less-than-stellar reputation around town. According to several witnesses, it was "public and notorious" knowledge that De Ypinsa was a man of so-called bad customs and that, on at least one occasion, he had discussed a plan to steal money from his own mother.[6]

The above testimony appears at odds with the image of De Ypinsa that had so thoroughly convinced the woman and her family that he was an ideal marriage partner. As we have seen in the previous chapter, witnesses in court cases had several reasons to speak negatively about individuals who were under official investigation, owing to personal biases, grudges, and other circumstances. Because of the context surrounding the cases (such as the financial circumstances and interpersonal relationships of the various individuals' involved), we cannot always take witnesses' claims or insinuations about an accused person's guilt at face value. It is possible that Joseph may have had enough bad dealings with, and inspired sufficient envy or disdain among, those he encountered that they would only ever see him as a fraud. That being said, the evidence of De Ypinsa's negative reputation nonetheless raises the question of whether the woman knew more about her husband than she was letting on in her petition. Perhaps it was her parents who belatedly learned of the chatter surrounding the man's possible origins and bad reputation and were pressuring their daughter to annul the union to silence further discussion or at least prevent their family's name from being dragged into it.

For his part, despite his wife's accusations and all the testimony against him, De Ypinsa insisted that everything he had said and shown of himself was true. He held firm to the claim that he was the son of a judge from the *audiencia* of Chile, that he had purchased the clothing he wore with his own money (rather than stealing it as some witnesses implied), and that any claims of deception on his part were entirely without merit.[7] In the end, however, the judge in the case took the woman's side, assented that De Ypinsa had misled her into believing that "he was a man of distinction and *sobresaliente calidad*," and granted her an annulment.[8] This is not to say that De Ypinsa was in fact lying or guilty of deceiving anyone. Another way of interpreting the situation is to see both parties as having told their own truths. It is possible that De Ypinsa was honest all along about where he went to school, the extent of his financial resources, and who his father was. At the same time, it is possible that his wife and others were right that De Ypinsa was a *chino*. In any case, he never addressed the matter of his racial identity one way or the other, not during his courtship of his wife or in the annulment petition that followed. For him, it was all the other aspects of his biography that mattered more.

With this in mind, the annulment petition provides a window into the daily workings of, and tensions over, racial identity in colonial Lima. While records from the period are filled with terms such as *español/a*, *negro/a*, *mulato/a*, *indio/a*, and *mestizo/a*, among others, those terms were more often inscriptions rather than factually accurate descriptions of a person's ancestry.[9] The notaries, court scribes, ecclesiastic officials, and census takers who entered those terms into the colonial record were engaging in a subjective process that was largely based on a constellation of factors, including phenotype, legal status, and socioeconomic condition, as well as, to some degree, how the individuals who were being recorded characterized themselves and how third parties described them. This process was also mediated through the notaries, court scribes, ecclesiastic officials, and census takers' lived experiences and ideas about racial difference. Well before putting pen to paper, they carried internal data sets based on previous encounters, socially constructed prejudices, and generally complex understandings of the colonial society in which they lived. Thus, the practice of putting race on the record was as much about the people being recorded as it was about the people doing the recording.

Further, the recorded terms were not fixed labels. They could change over time, such that a man listed in his marriage certificate as a *negro de casta congo* would appear years later in military records without any racial classification whatsoever.[10] They could even change or be contested in the pages of a single document, as in the case of a man who described himself in a civil suit as a *pardo* (a generic descriptor referring to a person of varying degrees of African and European ancestry), but who was described by witnesses in the case as a *zambo* (a person of mixed African and indigenous ancestry).[11] And while these terms could carry certain connotations – the term *negro/a*, for example, was often synonymous with an enslaved status, and terms like *indio* and *mestizo* implied obligations to pay tribute to the Crown – they were hardly useful or universally understood indicators of an individual's lifestyle or social status. As the annulment petition against Joseph de Ypinsa so clearly illustrates, a man who some described as a *chino* could dress and comport himself in ways that were fully consistent with a person of so-called *sobresaliente calidad*. While the term *calidad* was not an explicitly racial term in the way that *chino* was, it did signify one's Spanish ancestry, *limpieza de sangre*, and freedom from racial stigma. The term also referred to a range of circumstantial and behavioral attributes, including legitimate birth, honorable status, wealth, and occupational prestige.[12] In other words, it was a socio-racial marker. Thus, for De Ypinsa's wife to use the term *calidad* instead of *español/a* or *blanco/a* (neither of which appeared in this particular record at all) was to describe herself and her family as deserving occupants of an elite status position. It was a position that, for awhile at least, she believed she shared in common with her husband.

Again, the fact that De Ypinsa was so convincing to the woman and her family did not mean that he was actively deceiving them or anyone else. As Joanne Rappaport has argued in her study of racial difference in colonial Bogotá, men and women who found themselves accused of omitting or disguising their racial origins were often, in fact, "not passing for anyone other than themselves."[13] Rather than engaging in intentional acts of deception, they were instead simply navigating their sociocultural environments to the best of their understandings and abilities. Seen in this light, Joseph de Ypinsa was less remarkable a character for his time and place. In fact, many free *castas* in Lima enjoyed similar lifestyles and status markers as the kind he conveyed during his courtship. They possessed sumptuous wardrobes, owned slaves, and were generally surrounded by privileges and material comforts that paralleled and sometimes even exceeded those of Spanish ancestry and presumably superior *calidad*.

FREEDOM AND STATUS

An example of one such free *casta* would be Ana de Ariola, an unmarried *morena libre* who recorded her will in 1710. She detailed a wardrobe that included skirts and blouses made of lace and heavy woolen fabric, as well as an assortment of gold and pearl jewelry, among other personal items.[14] Similarly, *cuarterona libre* Petrona Cortes, who was also unmarried, described her wardrobe in her 1720 will as consisting of a lace blouse, five skirts made of silk brocade, and various pieces of cotton clothing.[15] Both women's inventories highlighted the extent to which free people of African descent had contributed to both the need for and the failure of sumptuary laws in colonial Lima. As discussed in Chapter 1 of this book, since the seventeenth century, lawmakers had consistently zeroed in on enslaved and free women of African descent as populations in need of particular control and barred them at various points from wearing laces, silks, cotton, and woolen clothing. But those lawmakers placed much of the onus for adhering to the restrictions on slaveholders who were outfitting their human property in finery and on Spanish men who were providing their African-descent wives with elegant dress. Yet despite the fact that they did not have obvious ties to Spaniards (either through the bonds of enslavement or through marriage), women like De Ariola and Cortes were also contributing to lawlessness. Indeed, their wills detailed the exact kinds of clothing that ongoing sumptuary laws had expressly prohibited them from wearing.

De Ariola's will also revealed that she owned at least seven slaves. This group included five young women and girls, one adult male, and a little boy. Given the extent of her human and immovable property – which included a home, furnishings, and cash reserves – the woman was clearly a woman of means.[16] Perhaps, like her Spanish counterparts in early modern Spain as well as in colonial Lima, she sought to further signal her status by dressing her slaves in one of her five silk brocade skirts for public outings around the city (to pick from several possible examples from her wardrobe). In this way she would have doubly undermined reform-minded officials' zealous efforts to restrict African-descent women's access to elegant dress by outfitting herself and her human property in sumptuous fabrics.

While there is no concrete data to enumerate how many slaveholders of African descent resided in Lima, they were not uncommon archival presences. For example, when Gabriel de Quiroz, a self-described *negro libre*, recorded his will in 1766, he listed the following among his possessions:

> Two old blue jackets with antique design;
> Two waistcoats, one of plumed baize with gold ribbon, the other of pink wool with gold ribbon;
> Two pairs of very old velvet pants;
> A muslin cloak with red velvet stitching;
> Four old *sayas* (skirts), one of sky-blue damask, the other three of a shiny material;

A little black hat with silver ribbon;
A *negro* named Miguel, de casta Lucumí;
Four machetes;
Two lamps;
A *negra* named Maria Rita de casta Popó;
Another old *negra* named Maria de los Santos;
A slave named Maria Josefa; and
A *negrito* named Joseph, aged 8 months.[17]

De Quiroz had been widowed twice: first by a woman named Maria de Soto (who is not marked in the record with any racial classification); and the second time by a *negra libre* named Rosa Mendoza, who named her husband the beneficiary of the aforementioned Maria Josefa. The testator's references to his status as a widower suggested that the only women who resided in his home were enslaved. And yet his will detailed several items of women's clothing. Perhaps these items originally belonged to one or both of his deceased wives, and he kept them as mementos. Another possibility is he kept or obtained the clothing to outfit his slaves in finery to publicly showcase his status.

Another testator, a *parda libre* named Agustina Balcazar, listed the following items among her possessions:

Two female slaves named Thomasa and Isabel, the latter having a son named Carlos, which makes three slaves in total;
400 pesos in cash;
A pair of Pinchbeck bracelets with antique gold finishes;[18]
A large gold reliquary;
A rosary with large beads strung on handmade Jerusalem thread with a large gold cross;
A rosary with large gold beads, a little gold cross, and four charms;
A rosary with blue beads and a cross embedded with eleven fine pearls.[19]

Balcazar's will also included a statement of fealty to Christianity, which was a common (though not inherent) feature of colonial wills.

Recognizing "the Father, Son, and Holy Spirit as three distinct beings," in addition to professing "to have lived and continue to live as a faithful Catholic" were standard prefaces to last wills and testaments. No mere catalogues of possessions, wills offered individuals the opportunity to leave written records of their commitment to religiosity – even in consumption. For testators like Balcazar, these records represent a balancing act between their piety and their indulgence. The impressive amount of religious paraphernalia she described, coupled with her apparent penchant for (real and imitation) precious stones and metals, suggests that such a balancing act was resolved through an indulgence in sumptuous rosaries. This kind of indulgence might also have been a way to sidestep legal limitations on sumptuousness in dress, since a trove of religious ornamentation, no matter how costly, served to exemplify the extent of her piety rather than mere materialism.

The aforementioned testators stand out in the record for various reasons. To begin, free men and women of African descent (who appeared with racial labels like *pardo/a, negro/a, cuarterón/a,* and other similar terms) comprised a small minority of testators whose wills are housed in Lima's colonial archives.[20] The numbers are especially low when considering that for nearly the entirety of the eighteenth century, free people of African descent steadily represented around twenty percent of Lima's total population.[21] Of these testators, the majority detailed rather meager possessions, if they had any to speak of at all. For them, their wills primarily functioned as mediums through which they could profess their Christianity and guarantee proper passage into the next world. These were generally people who lived in or on the edge of poverty, were likely to have been previously enslaved themselves, and could scarcely afford the expenses of daily life. Manuela Aspertía was typical of this type of testator. A *parda libre* who recorded her will in 1761, Aspertía was relatively terse in her will, which mentioned only her marriage to Pascual de Caseres, her childless state, and that she would die "desperately poor and without any property."[22]

But for Petrona Cortes, Ana de Ariola, Gabriel de Quiroz, Agustina Balcazar, and others like them, their wills provided space in which they could list and arrange for the distribution of valuable property. These testators were joined by women like Buena Ventura Pastrana, a free *parda* who named six slaves among her worldly possessions, in addition to money and household furniture.[23] Others, like Maria Javiera Ramires, a free *quarterona* who recorded her will in 1775, listed a small collection of dresses and some gold and pearl jewelry among her goods.[24] For her part, when Maria Josefa Pintado – who described herself as a *morena libre de casta chala* – recorded her will in 1777, she claimed possession of 1,500 pesos in cash.[25] Both women also described themselves as slaveholders.

When considering the content of these wills alongside the 1741 annulment case against Joseph de Ypinsa (which opened this chapter) it becomes clear that there was nothing about the man's alleged status as a *chino* that would have foreclosed his having access to the status markers he showcased during his courtship of his wife. Just as it was possible for *cuarterones*, *morenos*, and other free people of African descent to own sumptuous wardrobes, possess significant material goods, and be slaveholders, it was likewise possible for De Ypinsa to have done the same. Moreover, it was possible for free people of African descent to own personal property that matched and, in some cases, even surpassed that of Spaniards. Compare, for instance, the details of the former group's immovable and human property to those of Doña Theresa Catalina de Espinosa, who in 1744 recorded a will and inventory that included five slaves and a set of diamond-encrusted candles,[26] and Doña Francisca Casal, whose 1741 will lists the following possessions, among others:

> First, A *negra* named Theodora, of Terranova caste;
> A *mulatilla* named Enferma;
> Another *negra* named Theresa;
> 4 silver candelabra;
> 1 large silver and glass vase;

2 drawing room rugs, one large and the other small;
1 *saya* with a train and two scapularies;
1 *saya* for horseback riding, with a silver fringe;
3 silver engravings (one of the Holy Trinity);
1 pyre with the image of *San Juan de Dios*, made of gold and diamonds;
1 blue rosary with pearl beads; and
1 gold cross.[27]

The absence of racial labels and the presence of the honorific title "Doña" generally implied Spanish ancestry or a white racial identity, which was the only thing that seemed to set De Espinosa and Casal apart – at least on paper – from Ana de Ariola and the other free people of African descent whose wills are discussed here. Of course, we cannot take these similarities to mean that there were no meaningful differences between these diverse testators in the realm of lived experience, for reasons that will be discussed later in this chapter. For now, it is important to emphasize the fact that African ancestry was not an inherent marker of an inferior socioeconomic status. Likewise, Spanish ancestry was not an inherent guarantor of a superior socioeconomic status.

CLOTHING AND COMPLICATED INTIMACIES

The relative paucity of African-descent testators, and the scant mentions of elegant clothing that were contained within their wills, should not be taken to mean that these men and women rarely had access to elegant or sumptuous clothing. As the previous chapter made clear, enslaved and free people of African descent had myriad opportunities to make use of their social networks to outfit themselves in finery, regardless of their legal status or the state of their personal finances. Moreover, if we consider the diverse ways in which racial terms could shift in and out of view in colonial documentation, it is also worth considering that many of the testators we now read as Spanish, or "white," could actually have been of African descent.

In any case, even those wills recorded by Spaniards, or by individuals unmarked by color terms, provide useful insight into the kinds of clothing and resources to which African-descent people had access. This is especially true of wills recorded by testators who bequeathed clothing and money to slaves and free people of African descent. The 1744 will of Doña Juana de Rivas, for example, stipulated that upon her death, her slave named Gregoria de Rivas be given her freedom and that the testator's clothing "be divided equally between said Gregoria de Rivas and Doña María Theresa de Solís."[28] The bequest is interesting for several reasons. First, it shows how a woman like Gregoria could make the transition from slavery to freedom armed with clothing that signaled the change in both literal and symbolic terms. Even the used – but perhaps still high-quality – castoffs of her former owner would have served an important purpose: Gregoria could literally dress like a free Spanish woman. Put another way, even though the items might have held equal appeal to all of the women involved, they certainly offered each of them different possibilities. Juana's bequest is also interesting for how it sheds light on the layered meanings female slaveholders assigned to clothing. While Chapter 1 showed how Spanish slaveholders were invested in dressing their slaves in ways that highlighted their own wealth and status, Juana's will and bequest to Gregoria suggested a different way of thinking. As Amanda Vickery has shown in her study of eighteenth-century Northern England, material goods could play important roles in mistress-servant relationships, functioning as forms of payment and currency, of course, but also carrying profound emotional weight.[29] Although Juana did not provide a reason for bequeathing freedom and clothing to Gregoria, the fact that she included the enslaved woman alongside a bequest to another (presumably) Spanish woman indicates that she shared similarly powerful bonds with them both.

Juana did not include an explanation of why she had elected to arrange freedom and an inheritance for her slave Gregoria. Nor did other owners like Doña Francisca Casal, whose 1741 will stipulated that upon her death her slave Enferma (who was possibly a young girl, as suggested by the label *mulatilla*, a diminutive of *mulata*) be given her freedom and the quantity of 100 pesos.[30] Similarly, when Don Francisco de la Sota recorded his will in 1758, he arranged for Maria Josefa de la Sota, a *samba*, to be given her freedom as well as 200 pesos, all without explaining why.[31] But the documents nonetheless offer possible clues. Recall that the *mulatilla*, or young *mulata* who Doña Francisca Casal singled out for freedom in her will, was named Enferma, which in English roughly translates to mean "sick." Given her name, it is possible that the young girl or woman was born with an illness, or contracted one at an early age. Perhaps her owner had chosen to grant Enferma her freedom because she was simply too ill to continue performing work as a slave, was near death, or had become too burdensome to retain and difficult to sell. Such actions were not uncommon in Lima or in other slaveholding societies in Latin America. As Nancy Van Deusen has shown in the case of sixteenth- and seventeenth-century Lima, owners often granted freedom to their sick slaves, or "donated" them to a hospital or convent where they could live out their remaining days while receiving some measure of care.[32] And Sandra Lauderdale Graham's analysis of a case involving a nineteenth-century slave owner in Rio de Janeiro reveals how, when faced with the possibility of paying medical expenses for her moribund slave (who had possibly been infected with a sexually transmitted disease by the owner's former husband), the owner granted the sick woman her freedom and installed her in a hospital for freed blacks.[33]

The previous cases only scratch the surface of the scenarios that lay behind a given will's provisions. Fortunately, testators did occasionally take care to explain just what compelled them to make such provisions, making it possible for us to understand at least some of the motivations behind these decisions. When Narsisa de Espinosa recorded her will on April 5, 1741, for instance, she made specific provisions for a *mulata* named Nicolasa, who, as she put it, "protects and supports me, not as a slave would but as if she were my mother." To acknowledge this relationship, the will stipulated that Nicolasa should be given her freedom upon the testator's death.[34] The statement highlighted how the degree of intimacy shared between masters and slaves could lead to mutual reliance. This was perhaps especially true for slaves who lived in close quarters with their owners or apart from members of their own families or communities, since they would have experienced a heightened need to provide and even accept some degree of care and nurturing, even if it came from the same person or persons responsible for their bondage and suffering. However, given the inherent power dynamic between them, De Espinosa's characterization of the women's relationship cannot and should not stand in for Nicolasa's. Just because De Espinosa saw Nicolasa as a mother figure does not necessarily mean that Nicolasa saw herself in such a role. This is particularly worth noting in light of the age difference between the two: Nicolasa was just twenty years old at the time of the will's creation, while De Espinosa was a much older woman. Moreover, it was, after all, Nicolasa's job to "support" her owner (to use the testator's own language), by providing direct service such as household chores, laundering clothing, preparing food, and generally fulfilling whatever duties her owner assigned her. While this could easily and understandably be confused with nurturing, it was not the same.

In her examination of probate materials from nineteenth-century Brazil, Sandra Lauderdale Graham shows how a female slave owner used the space of her will to grant bequests of freedom, money, and even human property to a family of favored domestic servants.[35] Lauderdale Graham explains the bequest as resulting from the "authentic emotional confusion" that could arise when masters and slaves formed central parts of one another's social worlds and daily lives.[36] But such a characterization suggests that the actors involved did not truly understand their own feelings, or that those feelings were somehow not entirely genuine. Perhaps a better way of characterizing these relationships is to describe them as complicated intimacies.

Acknowledging the complicated nature of the master-slave dynamic serves several ends. For one, it highlights the extent to which guilt, love, respect, appreciation, and other emotions could put slaves on the receiving end of their owners' material resources. It also reminds us that there was nothing inherent to the gift of clothing or other material goods that would have lessened the pain of the master-slave relationship from a slave's perspective or that would have suggested that the owners were somehow more kindly than those who did not bequeath freedom or goods to their slaves. As we have seen in other slaveholding societies, the same mistress who provided gifts of sweets and clothing to a favored slave, for instance, could also administer whippings to the young woman for acts of alleged "impertinence."[37] Likewise, a master who freed his newborn son and provided him with financial resources and a specialized education could leave that same child's mother in bondage.[38] An owner's special consideration could be mercurial, divisive, or otherwise dispensed in ways that made it impossible to forget the power imbalance, manipulation, and harsh reality of slavery.

These sorts of issues could also have had bearing on how slaves related to the clothes they inherited. In both a physical and abstract sense, they bore traces of their original wearers. Their threads and folds might hold lingering scents, from perfumed waters, fragrant flowers, and – less pleasantly – the wearer's own body odor. And in their cuts, colors, and textures, they could communicate everything from the original wearer's aesthetic judgments and preferences and their negotiations with tailors, as well as the limits of their purchasing power. And, for better or worse, they could hark back to all sorts of occasions, such as public ceremonies, theater performances, bullfights, and salons, or to more prosaic walks through city streets and home-based activities.

To the enslaved women tasked with laundering and pressing such items, or with helping their original owners fit into them, some of these details would be deeply familiar. Perhaps their intimate associations with these goods even created a sense of covetousness, which, if expressed clearly enough (but with enough care as to avoid suspicions of theft should those same items disappear), could result in one or several items being set aside for her to inherit. But there is also the chance that familiarity could breed contempt, such that repeated contact with another person's soiled goods might render even the finest apparel less appealing, even once cleaned and ironed.

These considerations should serve as a caution against romanticizing the relationships that formed between masters and slaves. Theresa Catalina de Espinosa's 1744 will provides a particularly sobering example of why, in that it stipulated that her niece, María Bitalina de Espinosa, be given two of her five slaves, in addition to a set of diamond-encrusted candles.[39] Theresa did not indicate what would happen to the other three slaves, but it is likely that they would have been sold to cover any potential debts she left behind. And African-descent slaveholders could be similarly selective or indifferent. For example, the *negro* testator Gabriel de Quiroz only granted one of his slaves her freedom upon his death and made provisions for the other four to be sold away.[40] Put another way, there were times when slaveholders acknowledged their slaves' humanity and right to freedom, and other times when they very easily referred to slaves as no different than inanimate household objects that were meant to be bought, sold, or bequeathed.

Despite the fraught circumstances and relationships that unfolded at the margins of colonial wills, the documents nonetheless further our understanding of why colonial officials would continue to struggle to regulate access to clothing in Lima. For, beyond the Spaniards who used their slaves as indices of their own status, and the slaves who stole clothing to outfit themselves and their social intimates in finery, were slaveholders who facilitated slaves' ability to dress in ways that reflected their own sense of self (particularly as they gained access to freedom). When considering these details alongside African-descent testators' descriptions of their own material circumstances, the picture that emerges is one in which enslaved and free people of African descent were able to take aim from multiple directions at Spaniards' sense of racial privilege and dominion in Lima.

Yet just as we acknowledge slaves' experience of surveillance in Lima, we must also recognize that for free people of African descent, including those of immense privilege, legal freedom was no guarantee of freedom from scrutiny. One of the striking features of the 1741 annulment petition against Joseph de Ypinsa (the alleged *chino*) was the kinds of scrutiny and criticism he faced. After all, his marriage crumbled under the weight of his wife and others' belief that he had stepped outside the limits of his racial identity to pursue her. Seen in this light, De Ypinsa's case was less remarkable for his actions than for the responses they provoked. For his wife and her parents, their belief in De Ypinsa's status as a *chino* made it necessary to sever any legal or personal connections to the man. The marriage was threatening the family's status, and were the couple to have children, there would have been a stain on the family's bloodline. That the judge agreed to annul the marriage was proof that they were not overreacting; their response to the situation was perfectly rational for the time and place in which they lived. The case thus exposed the fact that, even though the bounds of racial identity and privilege in Lima were remarkably fluid, there were still people who wanted them to remain fixed and unbreachable.

CONCLUSIONS

A popular late eighteenth-century ballad, written by Spanish-born poet Esteban de Terralla y Landa, signaled how widespread were Spaniards' concerns over the boundaries of both legal and racial status in Lima. Titled *Lima por dentro y fuera* ("Lima inside and out") the text was written as a satirical guidebook addressed to the author's visiting friend and pilloried Lima's inhabitants for their wasteful penchants for luxury and indulgence. Although it echoed the concerns of colonial officials by taking aim at elite Spaniards' habits of outfitting their slaves in finery, the true targets of Terralla y Landa's scorn were the city's men and women of African descent. Not only did they outnumber Spaniards (who by 1790 represented just one-third of the city's total population),[41] but they also used their seemingly unfettered access to the city's comforts and pleasures to dress and behave in importunate fashion. As Terralla y Landa wrote:

> You will see that the *negros* wear bordered capes
> With the most luxurious hats,
> And the best cuts of silk, lace, wool, and velvet.[42]

They even outfitted themselves in ways that made it easy to mistake them for Spaniards, the narrator warned his friend:

> Never should you approach a *tapada*
> To engage in a flirtation,
> Because you might find a *negra*
> Or some other horrible creation.[43]

According to Terralla y Landa, it was not worth the risk to seductively approach a tapada (typically a Spanish woman who wore a unique costume known as a *saya* and *manto*, or a skirt and shawl that covered all but the wearer's eyes), because beneath her concealing layers may have lurked a dark surprise. Again, as was the case with the amorous suitors discussed in Chapter 1, who found themselves in similar pursuit of a veiled woman only to find an enslaved *negra* concealed underneath it was the Spaniard who was at risk of manipulation.

Beyond the prospect of trickery, though, was the possibility that African-descent men's and women's dress and comportment threatened to subordinate Spaniards as well:

> You will see few *blancos*, but many *negros*,
> The *negros*, in fact, are the *blancos*
> In both estimation and appearance.
> You will see that the *negros* are the masters,
> And the *blancos* are the *negros*,

> And soon the day will come
> That the *blancos* will be their slaves.⁴⁴

Here, the satirist signaled an even deeper concern than whether a woman could trick a man into believing she was someone else. From Teralla y Landa's perspective, which was shared by other Spaniards in Lima, African-descent men and women were a danger to the entire social order. So formidable was this threat, in fact, that absent effective sumptuary legislation, Spaniards would come to seek out other mechanisms by which to assert and preserve the fiction of European racial superiority on which colonial society had been built. The nature and effect of those efforts is the subject of the next chapter.

4 *Casta* Painting and Colonial Ideation

Colonial officials in Lima faced a host of challenges when it came to enforcing sumptuary legislation that would limit the kinds of clothing worn by *negros, mulatos, indios,* and *mestizos*. As we have seen, they expected that Spaniards would do their part to help regulate access to finery as a means to assert and enforce a color-based hierarchy. But the slaveholders among them stood firmly in the way of such efforts, as the pull of outfitting their slaves to communicate their status was simply much too strong. Adding to the problem were slaves themselves, who were finding myriad ways around the limits of their condition to engage in their own forms of elegant self-presentation. And if officials were unprepared to confront these truths, they were even less equipped to address the extent to which free *castas* (a group that also included slaveholders) used clothing to shape their own sense of place within colonial society. Together, these groups and their practices not only overwhelmed legislative efforts to shore up the boundaries of racial privilege in the region but also chipped at the very notion of its existence.

Nonetheless, officials – along with other Spaniards in the region – remained committed to realizing a vision of an ordered and hierarchical colonial society. The emergence of a distinctively Peruvian genre of *casta* painting in the latter part of the eighteenth century formed part of that effort, giving particular, prescriptive attention to issues of dress and deportment. This chapter examines the context in which this pictorial genre took shape, as well as the content of several key images contained therein, to show how it functioned alongside sumptuary legislation as a discursive platform on which to advance specific ideas about the relationship between race, clothing, and status.

REIMAGINING LIFE IN LATE COLONIAL PERU

In 1770, Viceroy Manuel de Amat y Junyient arranged for a series of twenty illustrations to be sent via the frigate *Hercules* to Spain's Prince of Asturias (Charles III). To alert the prince of the shipment's impending arrival, the viceroy sent a separate letter that also explained his intentions in commissioning and sending the pieces. Desiring with "utmost vehemence" to contribute to the formation of the prince's *Real Gabinete de Historia Natural* (Royal Cabinet of Natural History), Amat wrote that the illustrations reflected the "notable mutation of appearance, shape, and color that results from the successive generations of mixing with *indios* and *negros*, which," he noted, "is usually proportionately accompanied by inclinations and qualities."[1]

Although the images do not bear an artist's signature, they have since been attributed to the workshop of Cristobal Lozano, who served as Viceroy Amat's principal painter. They comprise the only known collection of Peruvian *casta* paintings and were numbered and labeled as follows:

No. 1. *Indios infieles de montaña.*
No. 2. *Indios serranos. Tributarios Civilizados. Yden.*
No. 3. *Español. Yndia Serrana. O Cafetada. Produce Mestiso.*
No. 4. *Mestizo. Mestiza. Mestizo.*
No. 5. *Español. Mestiza. Producen Quarterona de Mestizo.*
No. 6. *Quarterona de Mestizo. Español. Produsen Quinterona de Mestizo.*
No. 7. *Español. con Quinterona de Mestizo. Producen Español o Requinteron de Mestizo.*
No. 8. *Negros bozales de Guinea. Yden.*
No. 9. *Negra de Guinea o criolla. Español. Producen Mulatos*
No. 10. *Mulata. Y Mulato producen Mulato.*
No. 11. *Mulata. con Español. Produsen. Quarteron de mulato.*
No. 12. *Español Quarterona de Mulato. Produce Quinteróna de Mulato.*

No. 13.   *Quinterona de Mulato Requinterona de Mulato. Español.*
No. 14.   *Español. Requinterona de Mulato. Produce Genteblanca.*
No. 15.   *Español. Genteblanca. Quasi limpio de su Orígen.*
No. 16.   *Mestizo. con Yndia. Producen Cholo.*
No. 17.   *India. con Mulato Producen Chinos.*
No. 18.   *Español. China. produce Quarterón de Chino.*
No. 19.   *Negro. con Yndia. Producen Sambo de Yindio.*
No. 20.   *Negro. con Mulata Produce Sambo.*[2]

Each image features a mother, father, and child and corresponds to one of three main categories. The first category includes the images numbered 1 through 7 (from *Indios infieles de montaña* to *Español. con Quinterona de Mestizo. Producen Español o Requinteron de Mestizo*) and focuses on Indians, Spaniards, and their Indo-Spanish offspring. The first image is the only one featuring an Indian father; all subsequent ones feature Spanish fathers. The second category of images, consisting of those numbered 8 through 15 (from *Negros bozales de Guinea. Yden* to *Español. Genteblanca. Quasi limpio de su Orígen*), features Africans, Spaniards, and their Afro-Spanish offspring. And with the exception of the African father in the first image, Spanish fathers are present throughout. "It should serve as a key," Amat explained of the first two image categories, "that the child that is represented in the first marriage is, regardless of sex, the mother or father in the second; and the child of that union will be the mother or father in the third; and so on."[3] For their part, the last category of images, numbered from 16 to 20 (from *Mestizo. con Yndia. Producen Cholo* to *Negro. con Mulata Producen Sambo*) follows a slightly different logic in that these images combine members of all the aforementioned groups but focus on a set of (mostly unrelated) families in which Spaniards do not play a part.

The image numbers and titles invoke the labeling system introduced by Carl Linnaeus in his seminal 1735 text, *Systema Naturae*, and popularized by artists and naturalists around the world. In it, Linnaeus made order out of nature's "chaos" by appending Latin names and corresponding letters to identify and classify plants. By using a plant-based scientific method to number, label, and categorize Peru's human inhabitants, the images make a striking conflation between human and natural history.[4] This link is further underscored by the fact that the canvases were joined on their journey to Spain by a parcel of fifty coconuts, four dyed pelts, several bolts of white wool, and a wooden weapon known as a *macana* – all of which Amat intended to be housed in the same museum. The items aboard the ship were indigenous to Peru: the coconuts grew from Andean palms, the pelts were skinned from native animals and later hand-worked and dyed by Indians, the wool came from highland alpacas, and the *macana* had Incan origins.[5] Together, the collection of items represented an attempt to showcase Peru in the best possible light. The weaponry sample provided evidence that the once powerful Inca were fully subdued, the textiles served as proof of indigenous productivity under Spanish rule, and the fruits represented the region's diverse natural bounties.

For their part, the paintings held several layers of importance, all in keeping with the celebratory aims of the larger shipment of which they formed part. Produced by local artists, they served as an additional instantiation of the range of human talent in Peru. Beyond their provenance, the paintings also showcased local flora, along with clothing items and material goods from around the world. The latter reflected the viceroyalty's position as a busy trade hub and depot of luxurious imports. As one late eighteenth-century observer put it,

> Peru does not have to envy the glories of other lands, since whatever it lacks in natural resources it finds at its ports: China sends its silks and marble; India its drugs and spices; Spain its textiles and velvets; Milan and Naples its brocades; Rome its steel; Venice its glasses; and Turkey its rugs. ... For all the silver and gold Peru produces for Spain, and for all the liberal and prodigious distributions it makes throughout the world, it remains as rich as ever.[6]

Moreover, whereas the other items en route to Spain on the *Hercules* were tangible artifacts of conquest, colonial rule, and nature's cornucopia, the paintings were intended to convey an idealized image of the colonial world from which they originated.

CASTA PAINTING AS A PICTORIAL GENRE: ORIGINS AND COMPARISONS

Analyzing the content of the images first requires an understanding of the larger visual tradition to which they belonged. The paintings' most obvious analogues are the *casta* paintings of New Spain, which were originally produced around the early part of the eighteenth century. Scholars such as Magali Carrera, Ilona Katzew, Susan Deans-Smith, and others have given significant attention to the genesis, development, and meanings of these images, drawing on rich and varied visual and documentary sources to shape compelling analyses.[7] Given the vast array and diversity of *casta* paintings from eighteenth-century New Spain – as well as the strength of subsequent analytical interpretations thereof – a comprehensive discussion of the original genre is neither integral to nor within the scope and goals of this project. Nonetheless, a brief sketch of the genre's broad features, and scholars' interpretations of such, will provide a useful framework on which to rest a discussion of the Peruvian images.

Manuel Arellano is largely credited as a pioneer of *casta* painting, thanks to his 1711 *Diceño de Mulata yja de negra y español en la Ciudad de Mexico* ("Drawing of a *mulata* daughter of a *negra* and Spaniard in Mexico City," not pictured). It features a sumptuously dressed young woman adorned in pearl jewelry and wearing a silk dress over a partially exposed, lace-trimmed corset. The ornamentation of her costume, with its blue ribbons tied at the sleeves and decorative skirt fringe, was typical of rococo style and conveyed both an ability – and reason – on the part of the wearer to keep up with the fashions of the time. A companion image also dates from 1711 and showcases the woman's male counterpart, a *mulato*, in buttoned finery. In addition to this pair were Arellano's two depictions of so-called *Chichimec* Indians – one male, one female (with child) – who appear in their respective renderings with facial markings, feather headdresses, and little else. The contrasts between the *mulatos* and Indians in the set are clear: the former subjects represent urban types whose costumes connote access to sartorial splendor, whereas the latter subjects – unmistakably indigenous and distinctly rural – stand bereft of such options.

A few years later, in 1715, Juan Rodríguez Juárez drew on Arellano's work to produce another early set of *casta* paintings that introduced a compositional innovation: where Arellano's images generally focus on one central figure at a time, the Rodríguez Juárez images include mother, father, and child in the same frame. The latter group of paintings is also larger in number (there are about twenty-one extant images, including one series of seven and another of fourteen) and depict a wider range of racial combinations and gender pairings, including African men with Indian women, Indian men with mixed-race women, Spanish women with mixed-race men, and so on. Their differences aside, the Arellano and Rodríguez Juárez images share striking visual similarities. The poses, markings, and nearly naked forms of Rodríguez Juárez's *Indios Bárbaros* are nearly identical to the Indians depicted in Arellano's work. Likewise, the urban subjects – regardless of their parentage – are all outfitted in finery similar to that of the *mulatos* of 1711, echoing Arellano's suggestion that life in Mexico City and other urban centers offered obvious material comforts.Together, the 1711 and 1715 images established the defining features of a new pictorial genre: the depiction of families of three, including mother, father, and child; the inclusion of labels assigning color categories to each family member; and the careful detailing of rich costumes.

Over the course of the eighteenth century, *casta* paintings maintained these core characteristics but evolved in numerous ways. In contrast to the early examples featuring subjects posed against plain backdrops, the work of later artists situated families in a variety of indoor and outdoor settings. Further, as Ilona Katzew has shown, while the images of the early eighteenth century – such as Arellano's depiction of a *mulata* draped in sumptuous lace and shimmering pearls – tended to celebrate the wealth of the colony and showcase its extension onto the bodies of *castas*, those produced from mid-century onward focused more on social stratification. The paintings of Miguel Cabrera in the 1760s, as well as those signed and dated by Andrés de Islas in 1774, to cite two major examples of the genre, show two different worlds of familial life and interaction. They present Spanish men in dominant positions as household authorities and exclusive possessors of culture and outfitted along with their families in rich costumes; in contrast, they show *castas* engaged in trades and in scenes of domestic conflict and wearing humble garb.[8]

When considered alongside the images from New Spain, Peruvian *casta* paintings share both subject matter and labeling techniques but also bear several distinguishing traits. First is their intended audience. As Susan Deans-Smith and others have shown, a diverse network of patrons – including viceroys, archbishops, middling bureaucrats, and merchants – financed the *casta* painting industry in New Spain.[9] These patrons commissioned images that would help advance their specific interests or agendas, such as a desire to critique indigenous popular customs or to showcase the same groups engaged in productive activities and gainful employment.[10] And, once complete, the images circulated widely. They adorned the walls of private homes, public offices, and viceregal palaces in New Spain, and some even made their way across the Atlantic to Spain, where they were hung in private residences and – by the nineteenth century – in Madrid's *Gabinete de Historia Natural*.[11] For their part, the Peruvian images had a single patron – Viceroy Amat – and, once complete, were immediately dispatched for display in the *Gabinete de Historia Natural*. In other words, rather than forming part of the colony's own visual landscape, where they could shape local attitudes and debates, the Peruvian *casta* paintings were intended for a distant, scientifically minded audience.

A second element that set Peruvian *casta* paintings apart was their nomenclature. Scholars have frequently noted the mix of curious terminology appended to the subjects of Mexican *casta* paintings. They include such zoology-inspired terms as *lobo* and *coyote*, Old World descriptors like *morisco* (meaning "moorish"), pejorative labels including *zambaigo* (literally, "knock-kneed"), and even directives like *salta atrás* (jump backward), all of which had been in use in colonial documentation prior to being employed in the language of the paintings.[12] In contrast, many of the Peruvian images introduced an entirely new language of description that had no precedent in the region's colonial documentation. In keeping with the desire to appeal to a taxonomically inclined audience, the images contained confounding pseudoscientific labels like *quinterón de mulato* and *quarterón de mestizo* (one-fifth *mulato* and one-fourth *mestizo*, respectively). Meanwhile, census records from early- to mid-eighteenth-century Lima divided the city's population into five groups: *españoles* (Spaniards, including Iberian-born *peninsulares* and American-born *criollos*), *mestizos* (of mixed Spanish and Indian ancestry), *indios* (Indians), *pardos* (brown), and *negros* (black). From parish to parish, when it was time to be counted, there were thus only five possible categories to choose from. *Limeños* certainly used other terms in other circumstances to describe themselves and the people around them, like *morena* or *zambo* or even less specific regionalisms like *sacalagua* (which refereed to a person of African and Spanish ancestry), but not the terms coined in the image titles. The cumbersome racial categories spelled out in the paintings carried an implication of a precise, known genealogy, an uneasily probed subject during what Ann Twinam has described as "the century of illegitimacy" in Spanish America.[13] This created challenges for both "those doing the classifying and those being classified," to borrow Joanne Rappaport's phrasing.[14] To record a woman as being, say, a *requinterona de mulato*, would require knowledge of the racial origins of five generations of her ancestors for the label to carry any literal meaning. Likewise, the *requinterona de mulato* would have to have known the same.

Another difference between the two genres of *casta* painting rests on the roles they each assign to Spanish women and to men of African, Indian, and mixed-racial ancestry. Mexican *casta* paintings generally show both groups as active participants in the race-mixing process, appearing as parents of *mulato, mestizo,* and *morisco* children. Although such images are relatively few in number compared to those featuring Spanish men paired with women of African, Indian, and mixed-racial ancestry, they generally tell similar kinds of stories. In a Mexican image painted by an unknown artist in 1780 and titled *De mulato y española, sale morisco* (not pictured), for instance, a *mulato* father and Spanish mother sit at the table playing cards while being served coffee by their young *morisco* son. Standing to the right of the family is a dark-hued woman, whose outstretched hands suggest that she is prepared to serve the family at a moment's notice. That the family is engaged in a leisurely activity while apparently being attended to by a servant suggests that Spanish women could perform the same status-enhancing and redemptive role in mixed families as could Spanish men. This is not the case in the Peruvian genre, which is conspicuously and completely absent of Spanish women. And, with the exception of a handful of images, African, Indian, and racially mixed men are missing as well. Instead, Spanish men predominate in the series, and their presence largely conveys genealogical and socioeconomic progress.

Finally, and perhaps most importantly, Peruvian *casta* paintings lacked the kinds of contextual details that were so common in *casta* paintings from New Spain. With the exception of the Arellano and Rodríguez Juárez images, the majority of *casta* paintings from New Spain show families at work, at home, or in a variety of other situations. The depiction of mothers, fathers, and children in front of fruit stands, serving *raspado* (flavored ice) in ice cream parlors, enjoying leisurely afternoons, and preparing meals in household kitchens serves several purposes. In addition to showcasing New Spain's agricultural products, material bounties, and cultural pastimes, these settings are filled with details that help convey the families' socioeconomic status. The nature of their labor – or the conspicuous lack thereof – and the condition of their homes are key to understanding the impact of race mixing on the subjects of the paintings.[15] In contrast, the Peruvian images dispense with situational framing of any kind. The families in this collection are positioned before plain, dark backdrops, as though sitting in an artist's studio.

As a consequence of this artistic choice, the viewer's focus draws immediately to the subjects' hues, facial features, and, especially, their dress. In fact, dress constitutes the primary language of racial, generational, and socioeconomic difference in the images and the site of the most significant difference between *casta* painting in New Spain and Peru. Certainly, both genres pay detailed attention to costume, and the Peruvian images, like their counterparts from New Spain in the late eighteenth century, show Spaniards and their families in greater elegance than their African and Indian counterparts. But where the Peruvian images go further is by affixing to their African-descent subjects a specific and consistent set of material markers of difference.

FROM *NEGROS BOZALES DE GUINEA* TO "ALMOST PURE OF ORIGIN"

The first marker of racial difference – a white headscarf – appears in the beginning of the series of Peruvian images originally numbered from 1 to 8, and only gradually disappears over genealogical time. The first image in this series, *Negros bozales de Guinea. Yden* (Fig. 4.1), depicts an African-born family in which parents and child appear in humble attire.

While mother and father wear similar ponchos and shirts that hint at the forced androgyny of slavery, the mother also wears a white headscarf. The child, in turn, wears a threadbare white shirtdress with a tear in the left arm and a piece of red cloth tied with a sash around her waist. The simplicity of the family's dress is brought into relief by the second-generation image, *Negra de Guinea o criolla. Español. Producen Mulatos* (Fig. 4.2), which shows a family comprised of a

figure 4.1 *Negros bozales de Guinea.Yden*, Museo Nacional de Antropologia (Madrid, Spain). Printed with permission.

negra (the now-grown child from the previous image) and a Spanish man with their *mulata* child.

The Spanish man appears in a red jacket worn over a white blouse with lace-trimmed sleeves. He wears a brown cape draped over his shoulders and carries a hat in one hand, while gesturing toward the *negra* with the other. No longer the child in tattered clothes that was featured in the previous image, the *negra* has made a compelling sartorial transformation. Unlike her own African-born mother, she wears pearl-and-diamond earrings, a blue-and-white paisley blouse with gold lace trim worn over a long-sleeved shirt, a skirt with ruffled lace trim, and a flower in her hair. And the *mulata* child in her lap appears in a cleaner and more elegant version of the white shirtdress the *negra* wore as a baby in the previous image. Accentuated by a piece of red cloth and belted with a sash matching the paisley pattern

figure 4.2 *Negra de Guinea o criolla. Español. Producen Mulatos*, Museo Nacional de Antropologia (Madrid, Spain). Printed with permission.

of the mother's blouse, the *mulata*'s costume further illustrates the image's message of generational progress. Another detail that signals this progress is the cross drawn above the child's head, which, as Fermín del Pino Díaz has noted, serves as an index of the child's legitimate birth, formal baptism, and Christianization.[16] But one generation of race mixing can only offer so much distance from the past. For, despite all the improvements to the *negra's* condition, one marker of her origins nonetheless remained visible: wrapped high across the woman's forehead is a rolled white headscarf.

The white headscarf makes frequent appearances in other images throughout the series, but only on certain individuals. The next sequential image, *Mulata. Y Mulato producen Mulato* (not pictured), is faded beyond recognition, but the child from that image is

figure 4.3 *Mulata. con Español. Produsen. Quarteron de mulato*, Museo Nacional de Antropologia (Madrid, Spain). Printed with permission.

represented as the *mulata* mother in the fourth-generation image, *Mulata. con Español. Produsen. Quarteron de mulato* (Fig. 4.3).

Dressed in the same billowy laces and silks as the Spanish father of her child, the mother also wears a white headscarf, the presence of which suggests that her mother in the previous, unreadable image, likely wore something similar (but more humble). The child in the image is dressed in a plain white shirt, with a pink blanket tied at the waist with a blue-and-gold sash. And, like her *mulata* ancestor, she appears with the subtle mark of a cross above her head.

The white headscarf does not make another appearance in this narrative until two generations later, but the family members represented in the next sequential image still bear other markers of racial difference. In the image originally numbered 12, *Español Quarterona de Mulato. Produce Quinterona de Mulato* (Fig. 4.4), the now-grown *quarterona de*

figure 4.4 *Español Quarterona de Mulato. Produce Quinteróna de Mulato*, Museo Nacional de Antropologia (Madrid, Spain). Printed with permission.

mulato is sumptuously attired, wearing a dress made of silk and lace, a blue-and-gold sash, elegant jewelry, and a floral crown on her head.

For her part, the child is dressed in ornate detail, wearing a floral patterned coat over a lavish silk-and-lace dress tied at the waist with a blue-and-gold sash. The same pattern of the sash is repeated in the trim of the red skirt. The child is accessorized from head to toe, with a cross above her head, colorful flowers and ribbons in her hair, earrings, a gold necklace, and gold shoes with blue detail and a diamond buckle. The shoes, in particular, stand out since the feet of previous generations of children are either bare or covered by blankets. And both the mother and the child bear white marks on their temples.

The mark also appears on the mother (but not the child) in the next sequential image, *Quinterona de Mulato Requinterona de Mulato. Español* (Fig. 4.5).

figure 4.5 *Quinterona de Mulato Requinterona de Mulato. Español*, Museo Nacional de Antropologia (Madrid, Spain). Printed with permission.

In addition to being dressed in a billowy silk-and-lace dress (with a red-and-gold sash tied at her waist), she also wears a white headscarf, which makes her the only woman in the entire series to appear with both the facial mark and the headscarf. What do the two markers mean, both individually and when taken together? Part of the answer can be found in their generational timing. For example, the facial mark also appears on women (and their children) in the series' Indo-Spanish narrative, though it emerges only in the last three generations (as it does in later generations of Afro-Spanish women). The timing suggests that the facial mark is a symbol of racial improvement – perhaps even a beauty mark, since it resonates with similar (though differently colored) facial marks on women in contemporaneous portraiture from Spain and Mexico, who wore them as symbols of fashionable prestige.[17]

figure 4.6 *Español. Requinterona de Mulato. Produce Genteblanca*, Museo Nacional de Antropologia (Madrid, Spain). Printed with permission.

In contrast, the headscarf appears to be a marker of African ancestry and racial inferiority. It appears on the first five generations of African and Afro-Spanish women in the series, alongside the beauty mark on the sixth-generation *quinterona de mulato* (making her own body the link between her family's past and future), and then it disappears in the seventh and final generations – at least from the heads of the mothers. Instead, the headscarf adorns two new subjects in the series. In *Español. Requinterona de Mulato. Produce Genteblanca* (the image originally numbered 14 in the series and reproduced here as Fig. 4.6), the headscarf appears on a dark-hued man or woman who stands in the background of the portrait and appears to be the family's servant or slave.

The mother in the image wears a now familiar silk-and-lace dress, with earrings, a pearl necklace, and a floral headpiece. Her

figure 4.7 *Español. Genteblanca. Quasi limpio de su Orígen*, Museo Nacional de Antropologia (Madrid, Spain). Printed with permission.

child, the *genteblanca*, wears a costume similar to her that of her mother, with an ornately patterned skirt. Her accessories are impressive as well: a floral crown, colorful hair ribbons, a pearl necklace, and gold shoes with red detail. The mother and child each bear beauty marks on their temples, which, in addition to elegant dress, serve as a sign of racial progress.

The final image, *Español. Genteblanca. Quasi limpio de su Orígen* (originally labeled number 15 in the series and reproduced here as Fig. 4.7), which depicts the family's eighth generation, is quite different from the others.

It is the only image among the collection of Peruvian *casta* paintings in which no child appears to mark the family's genealogical progress. Instead, a dark-hued figure appears where the child would have been. Fermín del Pino Díaz has argued that the image is further distinguished from the others in the series in that it is the only one to take place outside, perhaps along one of Lima's popular public boulevards (where elite *limeños*, especially, enjoyed taking afternoon strolls in fashionable attire). Del Pino Díaz further asserts that the third figure in the image is a "*demandero* negro," or an itinerant beggar of African descent.[18] Although the backdrop of the image does not suggest an outdoor setting any more than the other backdrops in the series, the *español* does appear to be handing a coin to the dark-hued figure (whose short hair and shapeless clothing make it difficult to assign a male or female identity). In any case, the presence of this third figure serves to affirm the couple's racial identity, hierarchical status, and leisurely lifestyle. But since reproduction could not necessarily promise a child "almost pure of origin," the absence of the child not only speaks to colonial expectations of the possibility of whitening over generations of race mixing but also hints at certain colonial anxieties about the failure or dangers of race mixing as well. Could this nearly white mother possibly produce a child who would carry the same dark color as her ancestors? While Spanish women do not form the trunk of any of the family trees in the image collection, the *requinterona de mulata* and the *genteblanca* appear to stand in for Spanish women by representing the genealogical possibility of whitening. The women's status is made most visible through the combined visual effect of their pale hue, their sumptuous attire, and – perhaps most importantly – their total contrast to the dark hue of the slaves who are wearing headscarves in the images. Thus, from *Negros bozales de Guinea. Yden.* to "almost pure of origin," the original family transforms over the course of eight generations from dark-hued and humbly outfitted to lighter in color, richer in costume, and higher in status. While the subjects gradually move further and further away from their African origins, the women remain marked most of all by their headscarves until, finally, they bear no physical or material traces of their dark family origins, becoming almost pure at last.

Where did the white headscarf originate as a marker of racial difference? Concomitant with the rise of *casta* painting in New Spain

figure 4.8 Jorge Juan and Antonio de Ulloa, *Relación histórica del viaje à la América Meridional*, 82. "A. Limeña en el trage de Saya de montar; B. [Limeña] En el trage Casero; C. Español en trage del Peru; D. Mulata; E. Negro criado; F. Mulata a l modo que andan a Caballo; G. Calesa al modo de Lima; H. Vicuña; I. Huanaco ó taruga; J. Llama ó carnero de la tiera." (Courtesy of the John Carter Brown Library at Brown University). Printed with permission.

was the emergence of another pictorial tradition of human classification. When Spaniards Jorge Juan and Antonio de Ulloa published their account of their journey to South America that began in 1735, a curious engraving accompanied their description of Lima. It bore the signature of an artist named Diego de Villanueva (1715–74), who taught drawing in Madrid at the *Escuela de Bellas Artes de San Fernando*. There is no evidence to suggest that Villanueva traveled to Peru himself. Instead, the artist likely consulted with Juan and Ulloa or read drafts of their account for guidance. The resulting image (Fig. 4.8) – a collage of Peruvian flora, fauna, and human types – thus represents a combination of the authors' first-person views and the artist's distant perspective.

In it, we see the kinds of coastal city-dwellers described in Juan and Ulloa's narrative of Lima, including Spanish women, a *mulata*, a *negro,* and others. But rather than placing them against an urban backdrop, the artist has transplanted them – along with the kind of horse-drawn carriage Juan and Ulloa described seeing on Lima's streets – to a mountainous landscape. There, they appear alongside such highland creatures as the vicuña and the llama – though not, notably, alongside highland Indians. The caption in the top-right corner of the image provides a key:

A. *Limeña* wearing a *saya*
B. [*Limeña*] in homemade dress
C. Spaniard in typical Peruvian costume
D. *Mulata*
E. *Negro criado*
F. *Mulata* on horseback in riding wear
G. Lima-style horse and carriage
H. Vicuña
I. *Huanaco* or *taruga*
J. Llama[19]

As for the human types in the image, the *limeñas* (designated by the letters A and B) and the Spanish man (C) are dressed in the elegant fashion conveyed by Juan and Ulloa's descriptions.[20] Similarly, the two *mulatas* (D and F) are wearing the same kinds of shoes, jewelry, capes, and sumptuous dress as their *limeña* counterparts. But here the artist adds new details: each of the *mulatas* appears in the image wearing headgear. Their triangular scarves (or hats) serve as dual markers of difference, not only between the *mulatas* and *limeñas* but also between the authors' and the artist's perspectives. At no point in Juan and Ulloa's account of Lima do they identify *mulatas* or any other person wearing headscarves or hats. Why did Villanueva put them there?

Perhaps the artist found some of Juan and Ulloa's descriptions – and Lima itself – lacking. As Chapter 1 has shown, while Juan and Ulloa acknowledge the existence of distinct racial groups in Lima, the overall impression in their narrative is of a city in which everyone could wear what he or she could purchase. But if *negras* and *mulatos* were able to dress in a similar fashion to Spaniards, what difference, then, did race make? Villanueva's inclusion of headscarves suggests a desire to inscribe obvious material markers of racial difference on his subjects, even if it they did not exist in reality (or even in Juan and Ulloa's narrative).

RACIAL REGENERATION AND THE CHALLENGE OF "*SAMBAJE*"

A similar effort to inscribe material markers of difference is visible throughout the third and final series of Peruvian *casta* paintings. While the first two narratives in the collection (which is to say, those originally numbered from 1 to 7 and from 8 to 15) chart the process of so-called blood mending, or whitening, the third and final narrative is the most distinct and least straightforward. Unlike its predecessors, it does not depict different generations of the same family throughout:

No. 16.	*Mestizo. con Yndia. Producen Cholo.*
No. 17.	*India. con Mulato Producen Chinos.*
No. 18.	*Español. China. produce Quarterón de Chino.*
No. 19.	*Negro. con Yndia. Producen Sambo de Yindio.*
No. 20.	*Negro. con Mulata Produce Sambo.*

In fact, with the exception of images 17 and 18, the families in the series do not appear to be related. Moreover, of the five images, just one features a Spanish man, and with his darkened hue and facial expression he bears little resemblance to his Spanish counterparts elsewhere in the collection. And the series ends not with a Spaniard or even an "almost pure" product of race mixing but instead with a *sambo*, or an Afro-Indian.

The image titled *Mestizo. con Yndia. Producen Cholo* (Fig. 4.9), features a family that includes a *mestizo* father, an Indian mother, and their *cholo* child: The father in the image looks similar in dress and features to the *mestizo* father in image 4 in the collection. He wears a heavy wool cape over his shoulders, a blue jacket, and a white shirt

FIGURE 4.9 *Mestizo con Yndia. Producen Cholo,* Museo Nacional de Antropologia (Madrid, Spain). Printed with permission.

unbuttoned to his navel. The shirt, coupled with the headscarf tying back his shoulder-length hair, suggests a life of manual labor. Similarly, the mother in the image wears a slightly more feminized version of the costume, along with a rosary around her neck. Their child is outfitted in a similar fashion to his parents, with an unbuttoned white shirt that heralds the labors of his future. It is also in this section that we see that while the headscarf is the most obvious material marker of difference in the images, it is certainly not the only one. For the *mestizo* and *negro* men in this narrative, difference is marked by how they wear a particular item of clothing. For instance, the *mestizo* man in the image *Mestizo. con Yndia. Producen cholo* wears a red cape over a blue frock coat and white blouse that is unbuttoned nearly to his navel. It contrasts sharply with the images of the Spanish men, who appear in every image wearing neckties

figure 4.10 *Negro. con Mulata Produce Sambo*, Museo Nacional de Antropologia (Madrid, Spain). Printed with permission.

under their buttoned-up shirts and coats. Like their *mestizo* counterparts, the *negros bozales* in the image *Negros bozales de Guinea. Yden.* and the *negro* in the image *Negro. con Mulata Produce Sambo.* (Fig. 4.10) both bear markers of difference.

While the former wears a heavy cape over a plain dark-blue cotton shirt, the latter is dressed very much like the Spanish men pictured in the images – in a blue cape over a red embellished jacket and ivory damask vest – but both men are set apart not only by their skin color but also by their unbuttoned shirts, which may imply physical labor as well. And while the white headscarf marked only African-descent women, the unbuttoned shirt marks both *mestizo* and African-descent men, suggesting that the artists viewed the differences among the two groups to be less meaningful than their

120　EXQUISITE SLAVES

figure 4.11 *Español. China. produce Quarterón de Chino*, Museo Nacional de Antropologia (Madrid, Spain). Printed with permission.

distinction from Spanish men. The difference is particularly pronounced when comparing the aforementioned images to *Español. China. produce Quarterón de Chino.* (Fig. 4.11), which happens to be the only one in this particular series to include a Spanish male.

Despite the Spanish man's curiously ruddy hue, he is dressed in the same elegance as the other Spanish men in the collection. Likewise, the mother in the image appears in the kind of finery typical of the other mixed-race women paired with Spanish men in the images, serving as a reminder of Spanish men's valuable role in granting access to sartorial splendor.

That the depictions of African and Indian family formation appear last, as a series of comparatively few examples, suggests that Viceroy Amat and his artists sought to subordinate the images' importance relative to the first two sets. While the very inclusion of the images acknowledges the fact that men and women of African and Indian ancestry managed to come into social and sexual contact with one another (despite official efforts to keep them apart),[21] the images actually uphold the overarching narrative of the entire series of Peruvian *casta* paintings: without Spanish men, African, Indians, and their mixed race families would remain inferior, toil in manual labor, and enjoy access to neither luxury nor leisure.

Because of the letter he sent with the collection of *casta* paintings he had commissioned for the Prince of Asturias, we know that, in addition to hoping that the images would be housed in a European museum alongside other New World artifacts, Viceroy Amat wanted the paintings to tell a particular story about race and status in eighteenth-century Peru. For Amat, it was a story that acknowledged the region's human diversity while conveying the presence of a fixed racial hierarchy in which Spaniards occupied the top, in which Spanish women were shielded from race mixing, and in which Spanish men would lead Indians, Africans, and their descendants into genealogical purity. Along the way, Spaniards alone would control access to elegant material goods, while Indians and – especially – Africans would carry material markers of racial inferiority.

Most of the images in the series depict race mixing as a tightly controlled process in which Spanish men formed marriages with women of African, Indian, and mixed-racial ancestry over the course of successive generations. The children born to those unions carried such labels as *quarterona de mulato* (one-fourth *mulato*) and *quinterona de mestizo* (one-fifth *mestizo*), terms that reflected an attempt to apply Enlightenment-era scientific classification to the realm of human reproduction.

Amat's *casta* paintings made very narrow room for depicting African and Indian family formation in Peru and plainly disregarded families that were headed by single mothers, those composed entirely of extended kin, and other nontraditional units. As we have already seen in previous chapters, Lima's colonial and ecclesiastical archives are filled with details about these kinds of families, for whom social ties cemented access to valuable resources and material goods as much as – if not more than – biology. For example, on October 7, 1766, Joseph Nazaro's owner signed a letter acknowledging receipt of 50 pesos from a free woman named Antonia Vásquez, a *negra de casta congo* who was also Joseph's godmother.[22] The manumission letter entitled the *negrito* (as he was described in the record) to "go, stay, and reside wherever he wishes, make deals and contracts, give and donate whichever of his goods, sign a will, and undertake any other act performed by a free person."[23] Even though he was just three months old, Joseph now had more legal rights than his own mother, Juliana, who apparently used her ties to a free woman of African descent to secure her son's freedom before she obtained her own. Whether Juliana had done so because her son's purchase price was lower due to his tender age, because she wanted his earliest memories to be of a life lived in freedom, or for some combination of reasons, her choice created a new kind of family. Part free, part enslaved, it was the kind of family common to many inhabitants of eighteenth-century Lima, where – as we saw in previous chapters – blood relatives, extended kin, husbands, wives, lovers, and friends often lived on different sides of the law.

Had painter Cristobal Lozano or one of his assistants captured Joseph's transition to freedom on canvas, the scene might have featured Juliana holding baby Joseph in her arms, with godmother Antonia by her side, all standing before Joseph's owner as he signed the manumission letter in the presence of a notary. The group would even have conveyed the same spirit of generational progress that was so embedded in the language of the *casta* paintings. But in every other way, the image would have been far from the images's idealized world. Here, Spanish men played only peripheral roles (as slave owner and notary), and two women were jointly responsible for a young boy's change in status. Thus, even without a painting to commemorate it, Juliana, Joseph, and Antonia's encounter with the law showed that the prevailing images of Peruvian *casta* paintings were at best incomplete.

More than that, the encounter hinted at the possibility that, even without the controlling measures of colonial officials and the guiding influence of Spanish men, these families would enjoy their own generational progress. In fact, this was far more than a possibility – it was a reality on full display in a record compiled in 1771, when Lima officials – undertaking the first in-depth population survey in city history – traveled from door to door, block to block, and parish to parish, gathering information on the age, sex, occupation, marital status, *casta*, and legal status of every man, woman, and child in every type of household. The exhaustive exercise formed part of a broader effort led by Spain's Bourbon monarchy to exert influence in and extract revenue from its American empire; as such, its primary purpose was to help officials identify which colonial subjects would pay tribute, fulfill labor quotas, and support militia operations. But the resulting document also revealed, in rich and varied detail, that a significant portion of the city's inhabitants lived in households headed by men of African descent, as well as those in which men, no matter their color or *casta*, played relatively minor roles, if they were present at all. Moreover, because it contains the names, ages, civil status and occupations of the men, women, and children who fill its pages, the 1771 census also adds necessary human dimension to the classificatory systems that took hold during the eighteenth century. Despite the circumstances of its creation, the census challenges the tendency of those systems to flatten human beings into categories or types, assigning labels without regard for the wide array of socioeconomic realities beneath the surface. For the same reasons, it is worth lingering on those names and biographical details.

In the parish of Santa Ana, a neighborhood east of the Plaza Mayor, officials found the home of twenty-nine-year-old *quarterón libre* and carpenter Joseph Romano. Romano headed a large household that included his wife, a *blanca* named Feliciana Martínez; their infant daughter, Martina (who is not identified by color terms, suggesting that census-takers viewed her as white); his mother, a widow and *parda libre* named María del Carmen Lugones; his brothers, Juan

Evangelista Mariluz, Joachin Pérez de Mendoza, and Manuel Pérez (none of whom is identified by color terms); his sister-in-law, María Ana, a *quarterona* who was married to his brother Manuel; and three teenaged apprentices named Agustín Negrón, Rudecindo Viera (both *mulatos libres*), and Marcelino Mendoza, a *zambo libre*.

Beginning with his white wife and daughter, Joseph Romano's household challenged the images set forth in Amat's *casta* paintings that Spanish men were the catalysts for the whitening process. Further, Romano's skills as a carpenter had apparently enabled him to provide support and training for three young apprentices, thereby underscoring his abilities to provide for his own family and prepare other generations to do the same.

Joseph Romano also owned the two stores that flanked his house. A cigarette vendor named Francisco Nieto lived and worked in one, and a *mestizo* cobbler named Joseph Aguirre lived and worked in the other.[24] Francisca Xavier Daza lived in one such household. Like Romano's, hers was large and diverse. A sixty-year-old widow identified as a *quinterona de mestizo*, Daza lived with her three daughters named Josefa, Eustaquia, and Rosa (none of whom was identified by color terms), and six slaves, including María Mercedes, Luis, Francisco, Julián, José Manuel, and María Santos, who were all identified as *morenos*. Daza also owned the two buildings on either side of her house. One operated as a *pulpería*, or tavern, and the other as a store, where a free *zamba* named Maria Antonia Aspeytia worked as a cook and lived with her daughter, María Antonía (also a free *zamba*), who worked as a seamstress, and her son, Pablo Rojas, a free *zambo* and carpenter.[25]

Joseph Romano and Francisca Xavier Daza were hardly unique among free *castas* for heading their own households and sharing those spaces with their own (immediate and extended) families and dependents. They were joined in Santa Ana and in other neighborhoods by men like Joachin Canal, a free *mulato* who lived in a small house in the parish of San Bartolomé with his *zamba* wife, Manuela (who was also free), along with their six children; and by a notary named Don

Orencio de Ascarrunz, who lived with his wife, two children, and their slave.[26] (While de Ascarrunz goes unmarked in this record by color terms, the census noted that his neighborhood of San Bartolomé was nearly exclusively home to "morenos libres y esclavos," which suggests that he was also of African descent.) But most free *castas* were generally concentrated, along with most Spaniards and slaves for that matter, in multifamily or multiunit residences, where they commingled with intimates and strangers alike. Spaniards Don Pedro Taller and his wife, Doña Maria Antonia Salazar y Beitía, owned one such home, where they shared quarters with their two teenaged sons as well as the family's four servants (a *morena* named Maria Rosa and her three children, who were all under five years old) and also let out three rooms. One went to an eighty-year-old *quarterona* named Nicolasa Ortega; another to Victoria Mendoza y Madero, also an elderly *quarterona*; and a third was shared by a thirty-nine-year-old free *zamba* named María Asempción and her five children, who ranged in age from three to twenty-four.[27] Neighbor Josepha Daza owned another such home, where she shared space with her fifty-year-old aunt named Doña Isabel de Mena and their five servants. Daza also rented out seven rooms. Their inhabitants included a thirty-year-old *blanca* named Josepha de Reina, who worked as a seamstress and lived with her two-year-old son; a thirty-five-year-old *mestiza* who lived alone and worked as a laundress; and an eighty-six-year-old *morena* named Marcela Farfán, who lived alone and worked as a cook.[28]

In addition to signaling the prevalence of traditional households in which people of African, Indian, and mixed-racial ancestry served as heads, the 1771 census also gives us a sense of the degree to which enslaved and free *castas* often joined households with other families, cohabited with extended clans, and fostered other kinds of connections that facilitated access to valuable social and material resources. The census also provides insight into a group that is completely absent from Amat's *casta* paintings: Spanish women. The women's presence in the census records reveals that, contrary to the narrative of the *casta* paintings, in which they were shielded from social and sexual interactions with *castas*, they were in fact active agents of race-mixing.

CONCLUSIONS

Given this tension between the world of *casta* painting and the extant documentation, it is worth thinking of the *casta* paintings as more than just idyllic renderings of colonial society as artists wanted it to be seen – with a fixed racial hierarchy in which there was an easily identifiable place for every race. Instead, they were indictments of contemporary colonial society and imaginings of its alternate future possibilities. In fact there is reason to believe that the images informed certain aspects of Spanish imperial legislation. Two subsequent legislative measures help bring this possibility into view. The first is the Crown's passage of the 1776–8 Pragmatic Sanctions on Marriages, which enabled parents throughout Spanish America to contest their children's marriages to undesirable partners, or to disinherit those children should they refuse to follow through with arranged marriages.[29] In this way, Spanish men in particular gained the kind of control over family formation and material distributions that were so richly illustrated by the artist(s) who produced the 1770 paintings. The paintings, therefore, could have provided Crown officials with a clear model of the Pragmatic's potential outcomes. The second transformation concerns a more minor element of the paintings but one that was nonetheless a significant feature across the series: the headscarves. For, in addition to their rhetorical function in eighteenth-century visual culture, the headscarves came to play a significant role in Spanish American legal culture. Specifically, in 1786 New Orleans, the Spanish-born Governor Esteban Miró (who arrived in Louisiana in 1778) passed legislation requiring women of color – who for so long had managed to match and often exceed the elegance of white women in the region – to wear a white headscarf known as a *tignon*.[30] Could the governor have viewed the collection of Peruvian *casta* paintings during a visit to Madrid's *Real Gabinete* and used them to help inform his sense of colonial order and hierarchy?

Regardless of whether we can draw specific lines from the 1770 images to the royal and colonial edicts that followed, the *casta* paintings nonetheless formed part of a broader discourse that sought to preserve a sense of racial difference and hierarchy in colonial Spanish America. It provided a kind of visual companion to the sumptuary legislation of the eighteenth century, which in Peru had sought to draw ever-clearer lines between Spaniards and the rest of colonial society. And while there were obvious, meaningful differences between sumptuary laws and *casta* paintings – with the latter reflecting a somewhat more realistic view of society in that they acknowledged the extent to which Africans, Indians, and mixed-race *castas* were gaining access to the luxury that abounded in the region (even when those individuals did not have ties to Spaniards) – both insisted on the idea that Spaniards wielded ultimate control over luxury and that Spanish men were the primary channels through which it was distributed.

By the end of the eighteenth century, however, it was clear that just as sumptuary laws could not guarantee social and racial hierarchy, neither could *casta* paintings impose a specific vision of colonial reality. They could not limit African-descent people's access to elegant material goods, saddle them with material markers of racial inferiority, or ensure that Spanish men were the sole guarantors and guardians of material comforts and social status. Importunate sartorial display had become too enduring a component – and symptom – of the mismatch between legally defined castes and estates, on the one hand, and the wide-open possibilities for luxurious consumption in a rich colonial city, on the other. How this mismatch would shape other discursive realms is a subject of the next chapter.

5 Print Culture and the Problem of Slavery

On October 1, 1790, the *Diario Curioso, Erudito, Económico y Comercial de Lima* became the first major daily newspaper in Spanish America. At its helm was the Spanish-born journalist Jayme Bausate y Mesa,[1] who sought to create an American companion to the kinds of gazettes that circulated in Europe at the time. Chief among them was the *Diario de Madrid*, which Bausate y Mesa had founded in 1758 and published until 1780.[2] Like its predecessor, the *Diario de Lima* (as the paper was better known) was intended to serve as font of information for a literate public in the era of the Enlightenment, and as such it covered topics in the fields of science, philosophy, and medicine.

The paper frequently looked to Spain and its Crown for models and inspiration, a fact that set it apart from the better-known *Mercurio Peruano*, which published its first issue on January 2, 1791. Helmed by the creole members of the Lima-based *Sociedad Académica de Amantes del País*, the *Mercurio Peruano* served as a platform for the expression of an elite-male creole consciousness that emerged in response to late-eighteenth-century Bourbon reforms that granted preference to *peninsulares* in nearly every aspect of colonial administration.[3] The inaugural issue of the *Mercurio Peruano* outlined the paper's goals and ambitions. Written by Jacinto Calero y Moreira, the prospectus noted that the *Mercurio Peruano* was interested in publishing articles pertaining to Peru's commerce, culture, literature, arts, astronomy, and other topics. It gave no particular place of prominence to Spain or to Europe as a source of inspiration or information (although it, like the *Diario de Lima*, was published with explicit permission from Viceroy Gil de Taboada), and instead noted that, "we are as interested in what is happening in our Nation as we are with what concerns *el Canadense, el Lapon, y el Musulmano*."

Calero promised that the paper would touch on issues "that particularly interest *las Señoras Mujeres.*" Though he did not elaborate on what those issues were, exactly, it was clear that, like Jaime Bausate y Mesa's *Diario de Lima*, the *Mercurio Peruano* was meant to be a widely relevant enterprise that counted men and women of all colors and classes among its readers. As for his paper's competitor, Calero dismissively noted that while "Lima does have a *Diario Economico*, according to its current prudent direction it deals mostly with *la vida sociable.*"[4]

Although short-lived (the *Diario de Lima* published its final issue on September 26, 1793, and the *Mercurio Peruano* lasted slightly longer, until 1795) and often at odds thanks to their founders' respective birthplaces and competing aims, the papers had two features in common. Both positioned Lima as a cosmopolitan center of ideas and nurtured in their readers – who included Viceroy Vicente Gil de Taboada along with subscribers throughout the viceroyalty of Peru and as far away as Havana – a profound sense of intellectual curiosity. And they shared a profound preoccupation with the subject of slavery in the region. By giving attention to both papers' coverage of slavery – particularly those areas relating to issues of dress and deportment – this chapter focuses on two primary subjects. The first is the way in which clothing facilitated the blurring of boundaries, particularly between slavery and freedom. And the second is the way in which newspapers contributed – alongside sumptuary laws and *casta* painting – to the discourse about racial difference and hierarchy in the eighteenth century.

REGARDING THE RUNAWAYS

Like their counterparts in other slaveholding societies around the world – from Boston to Buenos Aires and everywhere in between – slave owners in and around Lima frequently turned to newspapers for help when their human property ran away. Hopeful that a fellow reader might recognize their errant slaves and return them, local owners as well as those from neighboring haciendas and provinces filled these notices with the kinds of descriptions they thought would be of use. On October 11, 1790, for instance, the *Diario de Lima* published the following runaway notice (its first):

> A *quarterón* named Vicente disappeared in April of 1786: he is tall, with a severe nose, is missing one or two upper teeth, has a scar on one calf, and knows how to cook, shave, and sew.[5]

In many ways, the notice was a typical example of the genre. It included aspects of the man's appearance that were unlikely to change over time, such as his facial features, missing teeth, and the scar on his leg. It also listed the skills the man may have deployed during his absence, just in case a fellow reader might have noticed or encountered the man working somewhere as a cook or *criado* (or personal valet). Yet the four years that stood between Vicente's disappearance and the publication of the notice were unusual (most notices ran a couple of weeks to a few months after a given escape) and made clear the uncomfortable fact that, to this point, Vicente had successfully managed to get and stay lost.

Despite its specificity in certain areas, however, the notice was still short on useful details. Because Vicente's owner failed to provide his age or some approximation thereof, even the most attentive reader would have found it exceedingly difficult – if not impossible – to step out onto Lima's streets and distinguish the runaway from the other tall men of mixed racial ancestry who crossed his path. In fact, in a city where approximately one in every four residents was enslaved by the latter part of the eighteenth century, and nearly half the total population was of African descent, Vicente would hardly have stood out at all.[6]

A few days after Vicente's notice appeared in the paper, the *Diario de Lima* published another, similar notice:

> Hilario, a *"mulato asambado"* from Trujillo who works as a wheat cutter and goes by the name *El Pobre*, has a receding hairline, broad forehead, brown eyes, a scar above his right eyebrow, another on the right side of his beard (immediately below the mouth), and is 35 years old and 4 feet 6 inches tall. Ran away on Monday the 11th from the Panaderia de la Recoleta.[7]

As with the earlier notice, the reference to Hilario's physical features were vague. Despite being described as a *mulato*, or of mixed African and Spanish ancestry, the man apparently looked more like someone of mixed African and indigenous ancestry (hence the label *"asambado"*), although the notice did not provide sufficient detail to clarify the difference. And even though it provided the man's age and height, the details were insufficient to single the man out. Not even the scars on his face would have been unusual. As we have seen in Vicente's case, he had a scarred body as well (his mark ran across his calf). Neither of the men would have been unusual in their scarring. For one, the nature of the kinds of labor slaves performed – especially men who worked in construction and handled dangerous tools – meant that injuries were a regular part of life. In addition, slaves in Lima faced regular physical punishment for all manner of (alleged and actual) transgressions, at the hands of owners, hirers, and jailers alike, and as a result, they bore countless scars from lashings and other forms of abuse.

This is not to minimize the importance of scars and their frequent appearance in runaway notices. To be sure, they provide key insights into the brutality of slavery in the region, and parallel details contained within archival sources from the era. On June 9, 1781, for example, a free *mulato* named Pedro Nolasco Boller filed a civil suit against a man named Don Fernando Jose Salvatierra, alleging that Boller's daughter Maria Hipolita Lozano (a *mulata* slave belonging to Savatierra) was being unfairly imprisoned in a local panadería and put up for sale for spurious reasons. In the suit, Boller alleged that Salvatierra and his wife had regularly brutalized Lozano. One day, after burning a shirt she was ironing, Lozano was beaten so badly that she saw no choice but to run away. The action landed Lozano in a panadería, where she awaited sale as a runaway who failed to pay her jornales.[8] A bodily scar, then, was less a marker of an individual slave's identity than it was a general indicator of an enslaved status.

With this in mind, it is perhaps doubly surprising that so many runaway notices contained descriptions of even more ephemeral characteristics, as was the case with another notice published in the *Diario de Lima*:

> Whoever knows the whereabouts of a *mulato* named Juan Manuel, approximately 18 to 20 years old, who went missing on December 7th wearing a yellow jacket, a bordered poncho and stockings, all made of wool, with a straw hat, is asked to notify Don Andrés Salazar on Concepción street.[9]

In addition to the runaway's name and age, the notice detailed the kind of clothing the man had last been seen wearing. In fact, the owner opted to specify the colors and fabric composition of Juan Manuel's clothing at the expense of any other physical description. How tall was the man? What color were his eyes? Despite the fact that Juan Manuel had been missing for more than two weeks, during which time he could have easily disposed of some portion of his outfit or changed clothes altogether, his owner nevertheless thought that describing his clothing mattered more to ensuring his capture than did his facial features or body type.

Whatever his logic, Juan Manuel's owner was hardly alone in treating a slave's dress as a crucial identifying characteristic. Similar notices regularly appeared in the pages of the *Diario de Lima*, with varying degrees of descriptive detail about the slaves and the clothes on their backs. One described a "runaway *criada* named Librata, a *negra* who is fat, gray-haired, 40 years-old, wearing mourning dress."[10] Another described an "un-baptized *negro bozal*" who "responds to the name Francisco, has an ugly face, protruding eyes, scars on both cheeks, dark skin, his hand is almost crippled and he cannot properly bend his fingers, and he is dressed in coarse wool clothing." [11] In both cases, the runaways' owners saw fit to include even the vaguest details about what they were last seen wearing, as though their clothes were immutable physical traits like eyes and hands.

However, as other scholars have noted, runaways regularly found ways to alter their appearance to evade detection. In their work on North American runaway notices, for example, Shane White and Graham White argue that the slaves who appear in printed notices as having worn simple outfits made of broadcloth at the time of their disappearance disguised themselves by wearing colorful waistcoats, dresses, and hats.[12] With these and other scenarios in mind, David Waldstreicher has argued that runaway notices from eighteenth-century North America reflect a pattern of "slaves pretending to be something else, and, in doing so, becoming something else." Waldstreicher shows that slaves not only used clothing and material markers to conceal their identities but also used language skills, trades, and cultural knowledge to assume new personas.[13]

This would have been particularly easy for runaways like Hilario. Recall that his runaway notice mentioned his having escaped from the northern region of Trujillo. With nearly 500 miles separating the city from Lima, getting as far away as Lima was the hard part. Once he arrived there, he would have no trouble staying lost. Of course, we cannot know with any degree of certainty whether these runaways successfully avoided detection, or if the notices printed in the *Diario de Lima* resulted in their eventual return to their owners. Most notices appeared only once in the publication, which on its own is only evidence that owners in these cases either could not or saw no need to re-issue their calls for help. This did not necessarily mean that such owners were successful in their recovery efforts – some might simply have decided to spend their time and resources on they slaves they already had, or on the purchase of new ones. Certainly, some notices did provide sufficient detail as to increase the likelihood of tracking the runaway or his associates. For example, when a Quito-born man named Bernardino ran away from his owner Doña Maria Antonia de Salazar in December 1790, she published a notice (in March of 1791) describing him as "more than fifty years old, a mason and a whitewasher, with an ugly, scarred face, sparse eyebrows, and a hoarse voice." The notice also included the following information:

> This *negro* has ties to [several neighborhoods in Lima], as well as to the home of a *Serrano* (also from Quito) named Don Ramon Salazar, who lives across from the Colegio de San Carlos. He also has access to the home of Mariano Fritas on Recoleta street ...[14]

It was clear from the sheer volume of details that Bernardino's owner had put considerable thought into where the the runaway might have gone and why, and what information could be useful for his recovery. Still, Lima was an ideal place in which to hide in plain sight.[15] For his part, Bernardino managed to stay missing for at least four months. In addition to his background as a brickworker, Bernardino had ties to a social network that included free people living in various parts of the city. Together, these skills and connections amounted to an ability to find work, housing, and perhaps even protection. Further, the city's demographics and conditions of slave life made it possible for runaways – even those with conspicuous scars – to blend with others of their condition.

As previous chapters have shown, slaves in Lima had expansive social ties that facilitated their access not just to elegant clothing and other material goods but also to ways of seeing and behaving themselves that had little to do with their legal status. For runaways, then, the city held significant promise. For local fugitives it was a place to tap into social networks, which could provide a place to live or evade detection, job leads, and financial assistance, among other things. And for those who had come from outside the city, it could be a place to reconnect with social intimates (especially in cases where families or kin networks had been torn apart by sale or forced exile), or simply to start anew. In short, the city was a place for reinvention.

In addition to passing among the other slaves who traversed this urban landscape, some runaways might even have been able to pass as free. This owed in part to the fact that roughly equal numbers of enslaved and free people of African descent called Lima home, and many of the latter group lived and worked in equally humble circumstances to those of slaves. So African ancestry was not an inherent marker of slavery, nor was an impoverished condition. Further, because Lima offered an array of opportunities to gain (legal or illicit) access to clothing, a mere change of clothes would have allowed runaways to put significant distance between their fugitive selves and the versions that appeared in the pages of the *Diario de Lima*. In fact, the wearing of certain clothing items could and did make it difficult for observers to discern a person's legal status. For instance, when an enslaved man named Juan Ramos (who was first introduced in a criminal theft investigation analyzed in Chapter 2) made his way around town in a crisp white shirt that neighbors described as the kind of thing "a gentleman would wear," several of those who crossed his path later testified to having mistaken him for a free man.[16]

"SUCH RUINOUS LABORERS"

That clothing could help blur the boundary between slavery and freedom, in fleeting moments as well as for more enduring periods, was just one of many problems reflected in the pages of eighteenth-century newspapers. Both the *Diario de Lima* and *Mercurio Peruano* featured long-form complaints about household slaves and disquisitions on the dangers of race mixing. Together, these writings blended into an increasingly alarmist and decidedly anti-African ethos. Before getting into the specifics of those writings, it bears noting that, with rare exceptions, the papers' authors and subscribers were elite Spanish men. This is not to say, of course, that the papers' only readers were elite Spanish men; in fact, the editors of both publications took such pride in the idea of their broad appeal and wide readership that one boasted of how his paper "circulates among the Cabinet of the wise man as well as the ranch of the savage. Even miserable slaves use the *Diario* to teach themselves how to read."[17] Yet despite taking liberties in speaking for others, it is clear that the elite, lettered, and urban perspective embodied by the *Diario de Lima* and *Mercurio Peruano* did not stand in for the other groups on whose behalf they so assuredly pontificated. In reality, the men were only speaking for themselves.

As Bianca Premo has shown, late eighteenth-century Bourbon policies that sought to emphasize the central authority of the Spanish Crown created a "patriarchal crisis for the city's creole elite," who took to the pages of the *Mercurio Peruano* to depict themselves as "trapped patriarchal protagonists, facing the unraveling of the colonial order from inside and out."[18] Similarly, Mariselle Meléndez has drawn attention to how the *Mercurio Peruano* placed particular "emphasis on the black as an epitome of disorder and deficiency" in its various writings on the public behavior and religious traditions of enslaved and free people of African descent.[19] Together, this work shows how enslaved and free people of African descent were at the heart of the paper's writings on household and social disorder. Specifically, in publishing these essays and letters, the *Mercurio Peruano* was giving voice to men who felt as though slaves were increasingly putting their domestic dominion – and by extension, their control over colonial society – under siege.

This was true of the *Diario de Lima* as well. On April 13, 1790, for instance, the paper featured an article detailing the consequences of what it termed the "pernicious introduction of *negros*" into the Viceroyalty of Peru. Expansive in content, the piece focused on the institution of slavery in Lima, Cuzco, Potosí, and other cities in the region, beginning with an oblique reference to King Charles IV's "*Real Cédula sobre educación, trato, y ocupaciones de los esclavos*" and its attendant expectations of slaveholders. The 1789 code (which is generally referred to in shorthand as the *Instrucción de 1789*) outlined fourteen major provisions to which slave owners, "no matter their class or condition," were obliged to adhere.[20] Among other rules, the code limited the kinds of punishment owners could mete out to slaves (by restricting, for example, the maximum number of punitive lashes to 25), and required owners to instruct their slaves in the Catholic faith, provide a minimum amount of food and clothing, and to "employ them in useful work that is in proportion to their strengths."[21]

Unsurprisingly, the code prompted widespread outrage among slave owners throughout the Spanish empire (which led to its eventual suspension in 1794), who viewed it as a subversion of owners' authority and unreasonable in its expectations of their obligations to slaves. With this context in mind, it is clear that the *Diario de Lima*'s complaints about slaves also served as an indirect critique of the Crown's expectations of slave owners. Given the royalist leanings of the *Diario de Lima*, in fact, complaining about recalcitrant household servants provided a way to avoid criticizing the Crown itself, and instead gave voice to the many burdens of slave ownership. "A poor owner spends 500 or more pesos on a slave (depending on quality)," the paper complained, "and has to dress him, feed him, and teach him what he needs to know in order to be useful," only to have the slave eventually run away.[22]

The logic of the complaint was clear: for an owner, a runaway represented more than simply a loss of property – he or she also represented the potential waste of an investment (in clothing, food, and instruction). And, the concern over runaways was well founded, given that the "noticias particulares" section of the paper regularly featured requests from owners for information and assistance that could lead to the return of slaves who had taken flight. In other words, slaveholders in the late eighteenth century were using newspapers to show that instead of needing to curb any of their abusive treatment of slaves, slaves needed to correct their own behavior. In addition to runaways, owners claimed that they also had to deal with other problems as well, including the loss of household property at the hands of thieving slaves. "It is common knowledge," the *Diario de Lima* asserted, "that at the end of the year things start to disappear from these homes, including silver, jewels and clothing, among other items."[23] Here, the paper was reproducing the notion that – as was discussed in Chapter 2 – slaves had a particular propensity toward theft. But even worse than the financial costs related to stealing issues was the impact of slaves on the dynamics of the families they served. To address these issues, both papers the *Diario de Lima and Mercurio Peruano* expertly framed slaveholders' anxiety over the loss of masculine, patriarchal authority in terms of fatherly concern.

In the January 23, 1791, issue of the *Mercurio Peruano*, for example, a father wrote a letter to the editor detailing his regret over having purchased a wet nurse named Maria for his daughter, Clarisa. While he was originally supportive of Maria's presence in his home when Clarisa was just a baby, as the young girl grew older and developed a closer bond with the enslaved woman, the father began to question the wisdom of their arrangement. "Not only does [Maria] protect and guard Clarisa (who refers to Maria as '*mi mami*')," complained Clarisa's father, "but she sleeps, eats, and plays with her." Now that his daughter was getting older, he thought that she "should no longer be under [Maria's] tutelage." It seemed that the problem rested as much on the pair's closeness as on where the two spent time together: "[Maria] dresses her, takes her into the kitchen and washroom, into the streets, and anywhere else she goes."[24] The author, in other words, feared intimacy and unfamiliarity in equal measure. He worried that the bond between his slave and his child would grow to supplant his own role as father and head of household, and he harbored additional concerns that the world to which his slave exposed his child was one he did not know or control.

The father was hardly alone in expressing anxiety about slaves' unknown worlds. In June 1791, another article in the *Mercurio Peruano* noted the following practices during the feast of the Corpus Christi:

> Some [*negros bozales*, or African-born blacks] disguise themselves as devils or with feathers; others imitate bears while wearing their skins; while still others dress as monsters, wearing horns, lions' heads, and serpent tails. They all arm themselves with bows and arrows, garrotes, and shields; and paint their faces blue according to their country of origin, as if that somehow increased the effectiveness of their attacks on their enemies.[25]

The article conveyed a tone of profound derision, even going so far as to argue that such displays distracted from the seriousness of the Corpus Christi, a supposedly solemn commemoration of the institution of the Holy Eucharist:

> This type of decoration, which would be acceptable for a carnival, seems indecent at an ecclesiastic function, especially one in which the slightest impertinence mars the dignity of the Sacred act, and dissipates the devotion of the attendees.... Our children might see these and other similar abuses, the extirpation of which we demand henceforth.[26]

Not only were the revelers' costumes inappropriate for the occasion but also they suggested a failure to understand the very meaning of the day itself. The article echoed the sentiments of colonial officials who had passed repeated legislation in the 1780s that sought to prohibit members of African-descent confraternities from wearing these exact costumes on religious holidays.[27] And, in a turn that was typical of officials and the paper itself, the article gave voice to a paternalistic concern over the potential for such practices to set a bad example for the rest of colonial society.

For its part, the *Diario de Lima* shared similar concerns. In April 1792, the paper devoted a multi-part series whose central premise was that owners, by relying so heavily on specialized slaves, were courting disaster for their homes and families. The first problem was that, instead of bringing just a few multitasking servants into their homes, owners surrounded themselves with "lazy" men and women who were skilled only at singular tasks:

> If we were to go inside these houses and into their servant quarters, we would find lazy *mulatas* without much to do beyond that for which they have been hired. She who attends [to her owner] does nothing else, she who washes knows no other work, she who irons understands no other tasks, and she who cooks looks upon no other obligation.[28]

The author continued by detailing an additional litany of complaints about male household slaves, claiming that, among other things, "the black coachman knows only how to drive a carriage but not how to clean or cook." [29] However, the same paper that gave voice to such disparaging remarks also devoted space to advertisements and runaway notices that said the exact opposite. Just the day before this article was published, in fact, the "noticias particulares" section of the *Diario de Lima* featured a notice advising "anyone who wants to buy a negro, aged fourteen, capable of all tasks and valued at 400 pesos" to stop by the home of one Señor Marques de Villa-Fuerte, who lived near the Plaza of the Inquisition.[30] The owner's honorific title indicated the kind of elite household that was indulging in the single-use hiring that the paper's editorial side was so critical of, yet his description of the slaves' broad capabilities conveys a different reality. Other notices detailed the exact skills at which the slaves in question were expert: one, from 1790, described a *negro bozal* who was not only a cook but also a carriage driver and a mason;[31] and another, from 1791, noted that a *negro* runaway had worked as a mason, plasterer, and whitewasher before he ran away from his owner.[32] Additionally, that so many slaves had run away from their owners (a fact about which the *Diario de Lima* was all too aware) seemed also to give lie to the notion that owners were simply too permissive and indulgent with their slaves. Why would a slave run away from an owner whose worst attribute was his or her boundless sense of permissiveness? Obviously, there was a great deal of tension between the world described by the editorial side of the *Diario de Lima* and the world depicted in its "noticias particulares."

Nevertheless, the paper's characterization of how heavily elite households relied on multiple task-specific slaves was also rather popular in its own period. One particularly vivid and lively rendering of this type of characterization can be found in an image produced by an unknown Lima artist sometime between 1785 and 1800, titled "A Merry Company on the Banks of the Rimac River" (Fig. 5.1).

The image depicts a large gathering on a waterfront, where a panorama of merriment unfolds in the foreground: from left to right, the scene includes a man presenting a woman with a fresh flower, a couple enjoying a harpsichord serenade, a pair of ladies dancing, and another woman reclining on pillows. Each vignette also includes

figure 5.1 Lima School. *A Merry Company on the Banks of the Rímac River*, 19th century. Oil on canvas, 26 x 35.5 in. (66 x 90.2 cm). Brooklyn Museum, Gift of Lilla Brown in memory of her husband, John W. Brown, by exchange, 2012.41. Printed with permission.

(mostly dark-hued) men and women providing the services to the assembled revelers.

The vignette in the right corner of the image is particularly salient to this chapter's discussion. The small grouping depicted here includes a Spanish woman, a little girl (possibly her child), and three women of apparent African descent. The Spanish woman sits surrounded by the other three women, each of whom attends to her in different ways from head to toe: one styles her hair, another fastens a bracelet on her wrist, while a third puts shoes on her feet. Meanwhile, the child idly drinks from a silver teapot while taking in the scene. The attendants are each outfitted in the same kind of full skirts, lace blouses, shawls, and jewelry as the woman they serve. From their activities to their costumes, the figures appear in every way to embody the indulgences of which the *Diario de Lima* had been so critical in 1792.

In light of the parallels between the image and the paper's language, and how rancorously the paper described this very type of scene, it is worth examining just what message the artist sought to convey. To begin, the composition bears similarities – both in name and in content – to the "merry company" genre paintings of seventeenth-century Dutch artists like Jan Steen. These images typically showcase groups of individuals engaged in diverse forms of merriment as they reclined on furniture, outfitted themselves in clothing, and were surrounded by decorations typical of the era in which the images took place. Art historians have long noted the tendency of these genre paintings to mock their subjects and serve as a form of social criticism, given their emphasis on such vices as smoking, drinking, gambling, fighting, and prostitution. While the Lima painting does not showcase the exact same kinds of deleterious habits as its Dutch counterparts, it conveys a similar – yet regionally specific – preoccupation with its subjects' past-times. Indeed, when read alongside the *Diario de Lima*, the image appears to echo the paper's critique.

Just as the paper described households in which enslaved men and women specialized in specific activities to the exclusion of their broader utility, the image shows three enslaved women employed in distinct yet somewhat overlapping tasks. Were the acts of styling hair, affixing jewelry, and putting on shoes so different that they required three different sets of hands? Further, much like the *Diario de Lima* article argued that Lima's heads of household were indulging their wives who, in turn, were setting bad examples for their daughters by modeling laziness, the image shows a young child looking on while her mother barely lifts a finger.

Seen from this angle, the image has tremendous rhetorical power alongside the piece from the *Diario de Lima*. By describing homes bursting with "lazy" and "useless" slaves, the author of the newspaper article was able to cast domestic slavery as a threat to colonial masculinity, femininity, family structures, and, by extension, society as a whole. The presence of so many domestic slaves meant that Spanish men were essentially presiding over households in which laziness was not only permitted but also indulged. Worse yet, male heads of household were denying their wives and children the opportunity to learn how to properly take care of themselves as well as their current and future families. Such an environment could only lead to vice. "What kind of lessons will your daughters and wives learn," the author asked his readers, "if you have corrupted them so? What kind of moderation and composure will they be able to practice if they are surrounded and served by libertine and scandalous *criadas*?"[33]

According to the logic of the *Diario de Lima*, the problems created by slavery also raised a more profound, existential question: "What would Peru be like had it not introduced such ruinous laborers?" For one, the paper argued, "the population that today consists of so many *castas* and mixes would be reduced to Spaniards, Mestizos, and Indians only, and all would belong to *familias limpias* [or pureblood families]." Each family would thus be spared the taint of impure African blood, and furthermore, each family member would find his or her proper place. "The honorable father," the piece continued, "would live to his dying day knowing that his children were well educated, without having been indulged." Their daughters would "serve their households with pleasure," while their wives (and eventual widows) would "take care of their children by washing, ironing, and sewing ... just like the most honorable women in Spain do."[34]

CONCLUSIONS

Because they positioned African descent men and women as socioeconomic threats, the *Mercurio Peruano* and *Diario de Lima* were also performing a remarkable sleight of hand. They disingenuously cast Spaniards as passive victims of slaves' sexual and social predations by disregarding the power structures and abusive conditions under which slaves lived, and which they sought to escape. The papers also glided past the instances that often resulted in enslaved women enduring sexual assaults at the hands of their masters and bearing the mixed-race children that resulted from those violations.[35] And they treated the introduction of Africans into Peru – and by extension the institution of slavery – not as a great ill visited on slaves, but as the cause of irreparable damage to Spanish (and, to a lesser degree, indigenous) families in the region. The presence of domestic slaves meant that Spanish men had no lessons in self-reliance to pass onto their families and were thus bereft of any confidence in their wives and children's abilities to master the kinds of skills in self-sufficiency that were apparently central to their peninsular counterparts' sense of self.

This argument stood in stark contrast to the narrative set forth in Viceroy Amat's *casta* paintings, which – as Chapter 4 has shown – conveyed confidence in the ability of Spanish men, through generations of mixing with Africans and their Afro-Spanish offspring, to create a race that was ultimately "almost pure of [African] origin." In contrast, the papers blamed Africans for the generations of mixing with and service to Spaniards that made the latter not only susceptible to bad customs but also, when compared to their peninsular counterparts, inherently impure. In other words, where Viceroy Amat's paintings epitomized the ideal of racial regeneration, Lima's two major newspapers were sounding the alarm of degeneration. In the face of this fact, there emerged within the medium of print culture a sense of increased frustration and vitriol whose primary targets were slaves in particular and people of African descent more generally. What began as platforms for the expression of patriarchal concern soon became media for the expression of racial animus. As the next chapters will show, this would become a defining feature of nineteenth century discourse, persisting throughout the independence era and well beyond the abolition of slavery. Even as enslaved and free people of African descent contributed to the revolutionary efforts, improved their status, and gained their freedom, their self-presentation, sense of self-regard, and claims to citizenship would remain under relentless assault.

6 Ladies, Gentlemen, Slaves, and Citizens

The July 28, 1821, declaration of Peruvian independence took place in Lima's Plaza Mayor. Both the city and its plaza served as fittingly symbolic locations for such an occasion, given that the former had been a royalist stronghold committed to the preservation of Spanish rule, and the latter a centuries-long site of colonial administration and ritual. Delivering the proclamation was General José de San Martín, the Argentine liberator who invaded Lima in December 1820 with the goal of advancing a campaign that had already resulted in independence for his homeland in 1816 and for Chile in 1817.[1] Six months after his arrival, with royalist leadership and forces having withdrawn from the city, the General addressed a large assembly with his troops positioned nearby. According to one observer of the proceedings, San Martín held the flag of the new republic, stood on a large stage in the center of the plaza, and stated: "From this moment Peru is free and independent, by the general wish of her people, and by the justice of her cause, which God defends." He then raised his flag and shouted, "Viva la *Patria*! Viva la *Libertad*! Viva la *Independencia*!" The words marked a moment of triumph for San Martín and were greeted with chants and cheers from the gathered masses.[2] Together, the speaker and his audience created a scene that has come to stand as the signal moment in the establishment of republican Peru.

Most of what we know about this moment and the events surrounding it centers primarily on writings by and about elite Spanish men.[3] And while we have a growing understanding of how elite Spanish women in Lima participated in the discourse and action of the independence era,[4] there is still much to learn about slaves and free *castas* during this era. Did those men and women share in the enthusiasm that accompanied the independence proclamation?

How did they negotiate and help shape the meanings of freedom, independence, and citizenship that circulated during the period? The task of filling in this knowledge gap is complicated by the fact that – as previous chapters have shown – slaves and free *castas* were more often the subjects rather than the authors of the extant sources from the period. But even if their words are difficult to access, their actions are not.

This chapter brings together an analysis of archival materials, newspapers, visitor accounts, and visual sources from 1821 through the 1854 abolition of slavery, to give attention to how legal status, race, and gender shaped the independence period and early republican era. In so doing, it argues that even though slaves and free *castas* were excluded in different ways from participating in the political debates of the era, they nonetheless found ways to assert their ideas about and claim their place within a changing world. For them, dress and self-presentation formed a crucial – and often contentious – part of this process.

1821 AND ITS AFTERMATH

Despite the centrality of the July 1821 declaration of independence to Peru's historiography and collective memory, the proclamation itself did not end the war. Much of Peru's central highlands remained staunchly supportive of Spanish rule, and armed struggles in that region were still underway. It would not be until the 1824 Battle of Ayacucho, when General Antonio José de Sucre's forces defeated the last of the royalist troops, that the struggle for independence would reach its full and final conclusion.[5]

Slaves played a key role in this process. When a royalist surge closed in on Lima just a few months after the independence declaration, José de San Martín reached out to slaves to shore up his patriot forces. Now acting as provisional governor, San Martín issued a decree that called for volunteer conscripts and promised freedom to any slaves who joined the fight.[6] The strategy had already worked for him in both Argentina and Chile and made an undeniable difference when he first arrived in Lima in 1820. By then, of the four- to five-thousand members of the liberating army, nearly half were manumitted slaves.[7] Many among them were Peru-born blacks who, having gotten word of San Martín's promises a few years before, ran away to join the independence struggle in Chile and other parts of South America. And, now, they were returning home as freemen to liberate the land of their birth. Also counting among the returnees were individuals such as *mulato* society painter Gil de Castro, who years earlier had left Peru to join the liberating army in Santiago. After independence, he received the title Primer Pintor del Gobierno del Perú and was given the role of designing the army's uniforms.[8] Thus, from the moment of San Martín's arrival in Lima, his troops and retinue embodied several promises: freedom from Spanish rule, freedom from slavery, and socioeconomic mobility.

Consequently, San Martín's forces continued adding to their numbers even more enlistees. By 1822, former slaves comprised such a large component of the patriot forces that royalist recruiters – who had long overlooked slaves in favor of existing military forces – were forced to increase their ranks of enlisted personnel with slaves. The slaves who joined did so in exchange for similar promises of freedom made to those in the patriot armies – although in this case, the Crown promised freedom in exchange for six years of service – or through the will of their owners, who were promised compensation for enlisting their human property.[9] However, many of those enlistees soon deserted the royalist army to join the patriots, thanks to the efforts of San Martín, who in August 1821 had introduced "free-womb" legislation freeing the newborn children of slaves born after July 28, thereby increasing his appeal to conscripts who wanted more than just individual and conditional freedom.[10] Thus, for slaves in Peru and elsewhere in the Americas, the struggle for independence was a period during which the political had become personal in a most fundamental way.[11] As army conscripts, they found a path to juridical freedom. For them, putting their bodies on the line for military service was an opportunity that, on balance, had the potential to outweigh the risk of exposure to the hardships and dangers of war.

The chance to bear arms and wear uniforms must have registered as an additional bonus. While the archival record does not provide a sense of slaves' subjective experience of taking up weapons and wearing uniforms during this period, the symbolism of these actions cannot be overstated. As Chapter 1 has shown, the practice of legally barring enslaved and free people of African descent from carrying swords and other weapons dated back to the early modern Iberian world and took root in colonial Lima. Thus, the ability to legally carry weapons marked a significant break from the past. Further, as Peter Blanchard has noted, the uniforms given to slave recruits "provided slaves with a sense of pride and, like bearing arms, indicated that they had moved from property to royal or citizen soldier."[12] Though they ranged in quality and quantity, these uniform rations – which could include military coats and jackets, ponchos, canvas pants, linen vests, short breeches, ties, shirts, caps, shoes, socks, and badges for their respective corps[13] – conferred a sense of dignity and unity with their fellow soldiers and the causes for which they fought that were foundational to laying claim to a new kind of selfhood.

For their part, while enslaved women only rarely fought as soldiers, they were nonetheless highly visible as camp followers, nurses, and messengers during the war. These roles, too, came with their share of physical danger, but for wives, mothers, sisters, and members of extended kinship networks, the roles provided opportunities to serve alongside and on behalf of the men in their lives. They did so without knowing the dangers that lay ahead, but proceeded in the hope that these sacrifices would result in expanding the revolution's promises of freedom in ways that made room for them and their families. Even those women who stayed home supported their soldiers in meaningful ways by filing wage petitions on behalf of their husbands and sons.[14]

There was also the possibility of getting involved in homefront campaigns that supported the ongoing independence struggle. The pages of *La Abeja Republicana*, a patriotic daily that was published in Lima from 1822 to 1823, regularly featured entreaties to its readers to get involved any way they could. The paper extended special invitations to its female readership to "provide an example of virtue" during this time of crisis.[15] Virtue, in this context, meant understanding "that riches and rewards shall only go to those who know how to use them for the benefit of their fellow citizens."[16] One way they could do so was by donating valuable personal effects to help "defeat enemies of the Patria." The paper used by way of example the case of one young woman, who, "with the heroism of the Greek virgins consecrated at Diana's altar," made a very public scene of removing her gold earrings and pearl rosary and placing them on a table at the paper's office entrance.[17] The significance of the anonymous woman's sacrifice was clear: even the willingness to part with valuable possessions, either as a show of restraint during times of crisis or as way a of helping finance military operations, was a tremendous act of valor and nationalism. And for those women who were either unwilling or unable to offer their valuables to the national cause, the paper asked that they put their needlework talents to patriotic use by sewing shirts and other uniform components.[18]

In supplying these possibilities, the paper wanted its readers to understand that, no matter who they were, no matter how little or how much they had, everyone could play a part. And while the readership of *La Abeja Republicana* likely consisted of lettered Spaniards, there is no reason to assume that they were the only ones to hear and heed its calls, or that *La Abeja Republicana* was the only medium for disseminating such messages. Indeed, historians have given careful attention to the ways in which the public sphere and more private spaces such as salons provided opportunities for men and women throughout Latin America to discuss the written discourses of the independence era.[19]

Moreover, as we have seen throughout this book, access to the written word was hardly confined to those with formal access to literacy. Slaves and free *castas* were regularly exposed to legal, religious, and political discourses as they served in their owners' homes, moved through city streets, and communicated with one another. With these considerations in mind, it is possible that slaves and free *castas* understood that, in providing their own examples of virtue, they could reap the riches rewards promised by *La Abeja Republicana*. In other words, just as we have begun to make room for acknowledging the myriad ways in which Spanish women shaped their beliefs and forms of political participation during the independence era, so too must we give attention to how slaves and free *castas* sought to do so as well.

A NEW CLASSIFICATORY LANDSCAPE

Beyond freedom and social mobility, the independence era made room for a larger, more far-reaching transformation. When a man named Pedro Rosas volunteered for the royalist army in 1811, he had been married for more than ten years to a woman named Doña Maria del Carmen Gómez. After enlisting in the *Primera Companía de Morenos*, a unit comprised of African-descent men, Rosas died in the army's first campaign against insurgent forces from Buenos Aires in June 1814. In 1818, his widow filed a successful petition to receive payment of Rosas's wages and pension. The couple's August 28, 1798, *partida de casamiento* (marriage certificate) was a key piece of evidence for Gómez, who presented it to the court to prove that the couple had been legally married and that she was entitled to the fruits of her deceased husband's military service. The marriage certificate also revealed something else: Rosas, who appears in the 1818 pension claim unmarked by color terms (except for the reference to the army unit in which he had served), was identified in 1798 as a *negro de casta congo* and a slave belonging to María Antonia Rosas. For her part, Gómez was identified as an enslaved *negra* belonging to a man named Don Ilario Risco. Together, the two documents tell a compelling story: in just over ten years, Rosas went from slave to soldier, having earned his freedom for joining the fight against patriot forces. While his sacrifice ultimately resulted in his demise on the battlefield, it also placed his wife on her own road to freedom. Twenty years after her wedding day, Gómez had gone from an enslaved *negra* to a free widow who was labeled not by her color, but by the title Doña.[20]

By making it possible for individuals like Rosas and Gómez to gain freedom and elevate their status, the war also contributed to two significant shifts. First was the shift in the way that many free people of African descent appeared (or did not appear) in the records they produced. Were it not for her marriage certificate, we might know nothing of Gómez's former legal status and the color classification she once carried. This raises an interesting question: How willing was Gómez – a woman who now carried an honorific title generally reserved in the colonial period for elite Spanish women – to produce this indirect evidence of her origins? While she would not have been able to claim her husband's pension had she not done so, she would have been able to keep her recorded status at the time of her 1818 petition separate from her status at the time of her 1798 wedding.[21]

That an individual's color category could shift in and out of view underscores the degree to which race, as Ann Twinam has observed of colonial Spanish America, rather than being a fixed quality permanently assigned at birth, "could be changed, or even achieved."[22] This possibility was particularly significant in nineteenth-century Lima, where the war, in addition to signaling new opportunities, was helping erase old distinctions. It was also creating new categories of difference. On April 20, 1822, José Bernardo de Tagle (Peru's second president), citing the "ferocious and indomitable character of the Spaniards," signed an order containing the following provisions (among others):

> No Spaniard, with the exception of members of the clergy, can wear any kind of cape or cloak in public, under penalty of exile;

> Any gathering of two or more Spaniards, anywhere, is absolutely prohibited, under penalty of exile and the confiscation of their belongings; and
>
> Any Spaniard found carrying any weapons, outside of those allowed for clergy members, will have them immediately confiscated and face a penalty of death. The only exceptions are for those who carry proof of citizenship, or a letter of exception signed by myself.

The order, with its restrictions on clothing, public assemblies, and weaponry, was designed so that "the malicious shall tremble in fear, while the few who are not shall find solace in the knowledge that the government is just, and will never confuse the innocent with the guilty."[23] The language of the law hinted at how the upheaval of the era made it difficult to spot the enemy: either royalist insurgents (Spaniards) were using capes and cloaks to disguise themselves as clerics to avoid detection, members of the clergy were being mistaken for insurgents, or some combination of both scenarios was unfolding. But one thing was clear: in the eyes of republican officials, the word "Spaniard" was now unequivocally pejorative. As recently as 1813, the term had still referred to both peninsular- and American-born persons of Spanish ancestry – in other words, it was a de-facto racial category. But by 1822, a Spaniard was considered a supporter of monarchical rule and, perhaps most importantly, a threat to public safety. As such, it was a category that now encompassed whites, slave conscripts, free blacks, and other members of the royalist armies. By displacing racial labels in favor of political ones, the order thus marked an effort to enunciate a new categorical distinction and ensure its use and stability.

In a sense, of course, this was hardly a new practice. As discussed in Chapter 1, colonial officials had undertaken similar efforts to confine access to clothing and arms to select groups. But where colonial officials had sought to draw color lines, republican officials were now drawing lines between Spaniards (or royalists), on one hand,

and Peruvians (patriots) on the other. The 1822 order stands out for how much it mirrored colonial legislation regarding dress and adornment – only this time, royalists were being cast in the roles previously assigned to enslaved and free people of African, indigenous, and mixed-racial ancestry.

The law also provided a model for how terms like "Spaniard" and "Spaniards" would be invoked in early republican discourse. Following its lead was *La Abeja Republicana*, which took to referring to Spaniards as *"una casta maldita,* or "a damned caste."[24] Invoking the term *casta* in this way served to discursively assign royalists an ethno-racial label that had previously been used to characterize people of African, Indian, and mixed-racial ancestry. In contrast, the term "Peruvian" offered more expansive possibilities in that it included those who joined the patriot forces, regardless of their color or status. In addition to the promise of freedom, the potential of socioeconomic mobility, and the chance to wear uniforms that affirmed their sense of selfhood, fighting for independence provided a chance to escape – or at least reconfigure one's place within – the classificatory system that had been so deeply ingrained in so many ways into colonial life.

This is not to suggest that old categories of difference and hierarchical systems had fully gone away. Despite the egalitarian spirit of republicanism and its principled opposition to slavery, there was frequently a tension between ideals and reality.[25] In Peru, as one historian put it, slavery "was too well entrenched an institution for it to die with colonial rule,"[26] and it would not be abolished until 1854. While Lima's enslaved population was certainly dwindling (by 1845, there were only about 4,500 slaves left in the city, a figured that comprised just 6.9 percent of a population of more than 65,000), there remained a strong attachment to slaves' dual functionality as both manual and symbolic laborers.

Visual sources and travel accounts from the era help bring this fact into focus, while also sidestepping some of the challenges inherent to documentation from the era that makes analyses of race more difficult. In a nineteenth-century image titled *Tapada limeña* and painted by E.E. Vidal (not pictured), an enslaved female escort is dressed in a strikingly similar fashion to the *tapada* she accompanies, complete with the *saya and manto* combination that was typical of the costume. The image reflected both changing styles as well as enduring customs. When she made her 1834 visit to Lima, French traveler Flora Tristan described the newer *saya* as "a three-quarter-length skirt, which hangs from just above the hips down to the ankles. It is so clinging at the bottom it is only just wide enough for the wearer to put one foot in front of the other and walk around with small steps." For its part the *manto* continued to envelop "the whole of the upper part of the body, leaving only one eye uncovered."[27] Where earlier, eighteenth-century versions of the costume enabled *tapadas* to express their piety and modesty, the new ensemble conveyed a new set of meanings.

Conforming as closely as it did to the contours of the *tapada*'s body, the fitted *saya* drew attention to the wearer's curves. Observers of the period were particularly attuned to this aspect of the costume. European artists such as Leonce Angrand and A.A. Bonnaffé frequently depicted *tapadas* in profile or from behind, at times even enhancing the women's dimensions so their hips and buttocks appeared larger in proportion to their upper bodies. These artists likely took their representational cues from the *tapadas* themselves. In another painting from the period, by an unknown artist, a *tapada* appears in the midst of slipping her *saya* over a stuffed petticoat (not pictured). Whether the image was painted in earnest or as a form of satire, it nonetheless highlights *tapadas*' desire to highlight and even exaggerate their curves.

Perhaps their desire for bodily display was so strong because of the constraints of the *manto*, which kept *tapadas* from showing too much of their upper bodies or faces. In this way, the *saya* can thus be viewed as an effort on part of elite white women to assert their own individuality, at least sartorially speaking. But in their most fundamental sense, the costumes retained the air of mystery and mischief they carried in years past. As Flora Tristan noted, the costume "so alters a woman's appearance, and even her voice, which becomes muffled because the mouth is covered, that unless there is something obvious about her, like being very tall or very short, with a limp or a hump, it is impossible to recognize her."[28] For her part, Tristan saw the costume as akin to a man's hat; in the same way that a man would put on his cap before leaving home to make his way about town, a woman wearing the *saya y manto* "has the same freedom as he."[29]

Whatever traits observers noted among or projected onto *tapadas* and their costumes, the women themselves were certainly aware of the social mores that governed their dress and deportment. As the wives, sisters, mothers, and daughters of the city's elite white men, they were responsible for representing their families in the best possible light. They knew to dress in accordance with their high station, to comport themselves with dignity and grace, and to express their innocent and delicate natures relative to the rest of the city's population. At this they had long been expert and found in their costumes the perfect tools for their self-expression. *Tapadas* could wear fitted *sayas* in part thanks to their slave escorts, whose very presence alongside their owners signaled *tapadas'* exemption from manual labor that would have required more convenient attire. With minimal physical duties beyond walking from home to church, the theater, bullfights, and to other social activities, it mattered little to *tapadas* that they could take only small steps.

Their slaves, on the other hand, were obliged to perform labor that required more unencumbered mobility than their owners' fashionable and figure-conscious designs allowed. And yet their outfits consisted of the same kinds of fitted *sayas* worn by *tapadas*. The outfits were not quite identical: while the *tapada* in Vidal's image wears a *manto* that extends down the front of her torso and to her knees, concealing all but her right eye, her escort's upper body, in contrast, is only partially covered by her *manto*, which frames rather than covers her face (this may also have helped assuage the kind of concerns discussed in Chapter 1 over the manto's ability to conceal racial difference). And finally, unlike the *tapada*, who appears empty-handed in the image, the escort carries a prayer rug. The rug is not for the escort's personal use but for the *tapada*'s, who would kneel on it throughout the day at appointed prayer times, when bells rang from the city's main cathedral. The rug thus serves as a material reminder of both women's status and responsibilities. For the *tapada*, it serves as a reminder of her responsibility to make time for prayer; for her slave, it serves as a reminder of her responsibility to facilitate her owner's obligations.

"Garments," according to Helene E. Roberts, "signal to the world the role the wearer may be expected to play, and to remind the wearer of the responsibilities of that role, its constraints and limitations."[30] In the Victorian England at the focus of Roberts' study, elite women were "exquisite slaves" who, in adherence to prevailing dress norms, were literally confined by their clothes (such as tightly laced corsets and structured skirts) to limited physical mobility. But in the case of Peru, where slaves were themselves exquisite, garments held more layered meanings. The parallels between the *tapada*'s costume and her slave's work together to showcase the former's femininity and the latter's subordination. The image of a black slave who is dressed to fulfill her mistress's purposes also helps the Vidal image speak a specific artistic language. Like much of eighteenth- and nineteenth-century iconography, in Peru and elsewhere, the presence of a dark-hued body alongside a white one provided a means of commenting on the socioeconomic behavior of the white male or female in the image.[31] In the process, however, the slave stands bereft of her own socioeconomic personality.

This representational technique was not limited to masters and slaves. In detailing the city's sartorial bloom of the early republican era, many observers cast white men and women in starring roles and relegated everyone else to positions as supporting players. While nineteenth-century artists, rather than labeling their subjects by color or legal status, used the visual vernacular of dress to mark them, that vernacular did not always keep pace with or acknowledge the many ways in which slaves and free *castas* in Lima could gain access to elegant clothing for their own purposes. This is in part because many such artists depicted the city through the lens of their own ideas about the relationship between color and status (which may have been shaped in different regional contexts), and also because many Peruvians shared similar views.

Nineteenth-century artists often took turns representing Lima's free women of African and indigenous descent as laboring bodies who were less attractive and feminine than their white counterparts. Where they depicted *tapadas* as sensual, flirtatious, and even mischievous, they generally collapsed the city's darker-hued women into types – street vendors, seamstresses, cooks, and other laborers who were defined by their work above all else. This is not to say that the artists' descriptions were wholly inaccurate, for men and women of African descent certainly comprised the backbone of the city's laboring classes. To be sure, even with slavery on the decline, freedom did not always mark an immediate change to one's socioeconomic status, and many freedmen and women spent years – if not lifetimes – toiling in the same harsh conditions they had endured under slavery. But Lima was also home to a successful and prosperous community of free *castas*.

This group included individuals such Mercedes Medrano, a free woman of mixed African and Indian parentage who, when she recorded her will in 1847, claimed ownership of a remarkable collection of possessions, including "a fourteen-year old *sambo* named Lorenzo, who was born in my home to Natividad, who was my slave;" 200 pesos in cash; several silver plates and saucers; home furnishings including two small chairs; and an un-inventoried collection of personal clothing items, all of which she bequeathed to a woman named Doña Maria Sanchez. Though she never married, Medrano had a thirty-year-old son, Manuel Presa, with a man named Remigio Presa, and both father and son were labeled in the record as free *sambos*.[32] As a slave owner with cash reserves and personal property, Medrano had her own social reasons and economic resources to dress in ways that had nothing to do with her subservient status to a white woman.

PANCHO FIERRO AND THE COLOR OF ELEGANCE

No observer of the period captured this reality more astutely than Francisco "Pancho" Fierro. Born in Lima on October 5, 1807, to an enslaved *negra* named María del Carmen, Francisco Rodríguez del

Fierro was baptized on February 5, 1809. On the same day, his owner, a woman named Doña Mariana Rodríguez del Fierro (who also held his mother as a slave), granted the sixteen-month-old his freedom.[33] One historian suggests that Francisco Fierro's father, who is listed as "unknown" in Fierro's baptism record, was probably Mariana Fierro's brother, a white priest and vicar named Nicolás Mariano Rodríguez del Fierro y Robina. In fact, that same man bequeathed nearly one-third of his possessions to Francisco in his will, and Francisco's own death certificate referred to a man named Nicolás Fierro as his father.[34]

While the story of Pancho Fierro's upbringing and education has yet to be told, a number of scholars have noted that Fierro developed his craft in a city lacking a museum or school of fine arts, and during a period when, as one scholar put it, "the public had little interaction with centers of advanced study and the diffusion of books and magazines was severely limited."[35] Despite the dearth of formal opportunities to nurture his talent, the young man taught himself to paint and found employ producing advertisements for bullfights around the city beginning when he was just a teenager. Fierro's watercolors, which depicted various urban types in their daily costumes and habits, helped him become a fixture in the closely connected – if loosely defined – arts' scene in Lima, as well as a pioneer in the nineteenth-century artistic tradition of *costumbrismo*.

The influence of Fierro's images is visible in the work of such contemporaries as A.A. Bonnaffé, a Frenchman who produced a collection of lithographs upon his 1855 to 1857 visit to Lima, including an image titled *El Capeador* ("The Bullfighter," not pictured).[36] Some scholars describe this image as a more skillful execution of Fierro's undated *Esteban Arredondo* (Fig. 6.1), which features the same sharply dressed, dark-hued bullfighter on horseback, with a red cape draped over his right arm, a cap on his head, and a cigar hanging from his mouth.[37]

"Without a doubt," Raul Porras Barrenechea and Jaime Bayly argue, "Fierro's watercolor is technically inferior," but because it very

figure 6.1 Francisco "Pancho" Fierro, *Esteban Arredondo*. Pinacoteca "Ignacio Merino" de la Municipalidad Metropolitana de Lima. Printed with permission.

likely provided the model for Bonnaffé's lithograph, they assert that it is therefore "superior in its artistic merit."[38]

The question of Fierro's technical and artistic merits aside, the hundreds of watercolors that constitute his body of work weave observant detail and subtle storytelling into rich visual narratives of daily life in early republican Lima. They center on the city's diverse inhabitants, including *tapadas*, water carriers, carriage drivers, and street vendors, who appear in the images at a remove from the well-known backdrops (such as the Plaza Mayor and Plaza de Toros) that figure in many other paintings from the era. Posed individually and as parts of urban market scenes, religious processions, and dances, the city dwellers in Fierro's watercolors showcase the city's vibrant sartorial landscape.

In one image, titled *En Amancaes*, ("At Amancaes," Fig. 6.2), three dark-hued limeños surround a beverage stand. At the center of the image is a woman serving a glass of what looks to be *chicha* (a beverage derived from fermented corn) to a woman on horseback.

figure 6.2 Francisco "Pancho" Fierro, *En Amancaes*. Pinacoteca "Ignacio Merino" de la Municipalidad Metropolitana de Lima. Printed with permission.

With everything from the flower in her hair to the shoes on her feet, the *chicha* vendor cuts an elegant figure. The flower mirrors the kind of hair adornments worn by women like Flora Tristan's wealthy aunt and other "women of good taste" in nineteenth-century Lima, who relished them as much for their beauty as for their fragrance.[39] Beside her stands a dark-hued soldier wearing a blue and red uniform adorned with a white belt, a cap, and a sword looped through his pant leg. The uniform is interesting given both his surroundings and his pose. Standing at a beverage stand, he bows somewhat flirtatiously before the female vendor, who is serving a drink to a woman on horseback. His costume and body language stand as examples of how men of African descent could use the fact of their military service as part of their self-presentation as both gentlemen and citizens of the new republic.

Fierro's watercolors present fashionable dark-hued men and women as a common sight on the streets of early republican Lima.

To some observers, those fashions were both excessive and impudent. Upon her 1853 visit to Lima, for example, British traveler Ida Pfeiffer remarked that she was startled to witness how "richly and extravagantly" the women of Lima dressed, including those of the lower classes. "You meet milk and fruit women," she writes, "in silk dresses, Chinese shawls, silk stockings, and embroidered shoes, all of staring colors, but most of the finery more or less ragged, and hanging half off." Pfeiffer found the women's elegant costumes at once impressive and unbecoming, and the women's "yellow [and] dark brown faces" reminded her of "Sancho Panza's remark concerning his lady, who, as queen of the 'undiscovered islands,' he says, will look like 'a pig with a gold necklace.'" Pfeiffer's invocation of Sancho Panza most likely refers to Part II, Chapter 63 of Miguel de Cervantes Saavedra's *Don Quixote de la Mancha* in which Sancho Panza confides in Don Quixote to express his discomfort with the idea of governing the Island of Barataria with his wife, Teresa Panza, given their humble origins. However, in my reading of this novel, I did not encounter Sancho Panza's use of the phrase "a pig with a gold necklace" in reference to his wife. Pfeiffer seems to offer a very loose interpretation of Panza's commentary, adding her own spin to illustrate what she considered the unnatural elegance of Lima's "lower class" women.[40]

Cutting through the noise of these pejorative descriptions, Fierro offered a different perspective. According to Juan Manuel Ugarte Elespuru, writing in 1975, Pancho Fierro was considered by his contemporaries to be "an elegant dresser," in his own right, "who styled himself in colorful and eye-catching *lujo mulato* [mulato luxury]."[41] Similarly, Manuel Cisneros Sanchez has noted that Fierro was known to make his way around town "in showy, buttoned frockcoats and jackets that were sometimes even gilded, with a top hat and silver-handled cane."[42] While neither Ugarte nor Cisneros attributes these claims to particular sources, their accounts nonetheless raise some compelling questions: Did Fierro's contemporaries use the phrase "lujo mulato" to describe (or to possibly deride) his style of dress? What did they mean by it? Would Fierro have characterized

FIGURE 6.3 Francisco "Pancho" Fierro, *Convite al coliseo de gallos*. Pinacoteca "Ignacio Merino" de la Municipalidad Metropolitana de Lima. Printed with permission.

that style in the same way, and if so, did he necessarily mean the same thing? Although it is hard to know with any certainty whether, how, or by whom the term was used, to whom it was directed, or the meanings it contained, many of Fierro's images do suggest that Lima's slaves and free castas embraced and showcased unique fashions and sartorial aesthetics.

In part this owed to the degree to which they inhabited overlapping worlds of labor and leisure, which forms a dominant theme in Fierro's paintings. They show how, as slaves and free *castas* made their way through city streets in fulfillment of their labor obligations, they also found opportunities to engage in leisurely activities. In the image titled *Convite al coliseo de gallos* ("The Cockfight," Fig. 6.3), for example, Fierro depicts a procession of three dark-hued men leading a crowd to a cockfight.

At the front of the group is a man in a white shirt and pants, a long frock coat, and top hat playing a trumpet; behind him is another man who is playing a drum and wearing a short-sleeved white shirt,

FIGURE 6.4 Francisco "Pancho" Fierro, En día de fiesta. Pinacoteca "Ignacio Merino" de la Municipalidad Metropolitana de Lima. Printed with permission.

matching short pants, and a straw hat; and the third man, dressed in a poncho and slacks, carries a bird in a cage atop his head. The men's clothing suggests that, outside of this procession, they all engage in diverse sorts of labor. The trumpet player's frock coat suggests access to less physically demanding work, perhaps as a merchant or artisan. Meanwhile, the other two men seem dressed for work that requires physical mobility and time spent outdoors. As they made time for food, drink, and music, or for encounters with their social intimates and rivals, they could also find ways to tailor their clothing to suit their sartorial preferences and social personalities.[43]

This point finds further illustration in the previously-discussed image titled *En Amancaes*, ("At Amancaes," Fig. 6.2). In it, the *chicha* vendor can be seen wearing delicate, pointy-toed black slippers that were suited to a job that did not require much walking. The shoes work together with the woman's green dress, red shawl, and hat to make her outfit nearly identical to the blue dress, red shawl, and hat worn by the woman in the image *En día de fiesta* ("The Day of the Party," (Fig. 6.4).

In fact, the *chicha* vendor appears to be dressed for a party herself. Whether that constituted unnatural elegance or *lujo mulato* is open to question, but it does provide a subtle yet striking indicator that garments served as more than mere reminders of a wearer's responsibilities; they could also showcase her ability to pull from various sources of inspiration to suit her clothing to her own purposes and personality.

On their own, Fierro's watercolors stand in compelling contrast to the characterizations of *limeños* set forth by European travelers and artists. By focusing on the kinds of men and women other observers either confined to the margins or lent disparaging attention, Fierro conveys a more complex image of their humanity and aesthetic practices. Rather than simply imitating the examples of Spaniards, Fierro's subjects endowed the city's sartorial landscape with a unique flavor all their own. Moreover, when analyzed with a clear sense of the time period in which they were set, his images also help tell a compelling story about the early years of independence and the final decades of the institution of slavery, which would be officially abolished in December 1854. For men and women of African descent, it was a story about stepping outside of the roles cast for them in the past and endorsed by slave owners and observers and into the shoes of the ladies, gentlemen, and citizens they knew themselves to be.

Epilogue

On May 15, 1858, approximately four years after the abolition of slavery in Peru, Lima saw the publication of a new weekly paper. Titled *El Negro*, the first page of its inaugural issue featured a manifesto of sorts, written from the satirical perspective of the eponymous black man:

> Uju! aqui toy pue – yo tambien quere jabra yo tamie quere cribi, ahora que toro amima cribe; yo se bie que so un pobre negro criado ene galpo, ma borrico que una pura chucaro, pero maquenunca ... yo se tamie que mucha mura chicaro ta criviendo ahora [sic].[1]

Filled as it is with intentional misspellings, consonant deletions, and substitutions (e.g., the use of *pue* instead of *pues*, in the case of the former; and *toro* instead of *todo*, in the latter), mis-conjugations (*quere* instead of *quiero*), malapropisms, slang terms, and other non-standard constructions, the passage is difficult to translate into English. Moreover, any attempt at translation must also consider the danger of re-inscribing the paper's denigrating characterization of Afro-Peruvian speech patterns. That being said, it is possible to approximate and clarify the passage's meaning without advancing its intentions:

> Uju! Here I am – I too want to learn, I too want to write, now that everyone is eager to learn how to write. I know that I'm just a poor *negro* servant from the slave quarters, more dimwitted than an ass ... but I also know that never before have more dimwitted asses been writing than now.

In short, the paper characterized its namesake as a poor, ignorant servant who, despite his former enslaved status, wanted nothing more than to read, write, and participate in the discourses of the era. With that apparent display of irony, the paper announced its arrival as a platform dedicated to the relentless denigration of Afro-Peruvians' intellects, ambitions, and self-regard.

Over the course of its short life (the paper published its final issue on July 31, 1858, just a couple months after its inauguration), *El Negro* introduced a larger cast of Afro-Peruvian characters who spoke and behaved in ways the paper considered deserving of mockery and scorn. One issue featured an anecdote about a group of young white women out for a stroll along the bridge over the Rimac River, which ran along the northern border of Lima's city center. The "señoritas" were all fashionably attired, each wearing skirts over crinolines (which were structured petticoats that curved out at the rear, giving the women a distinctive, shapely appearance). Their pleasant gathering was interrupted by the arrival of a black woman who appeared to be "muy avanzada en su estado interesante" ("very far along in her interesting state"). Only, instead of expecting a baby, as the phrase implied, the woman had simply worn her crinoline in such a way that its form protruded over her stomach rather than her rear, making her look pregnant.[2] In other words, although the black woman was capable of acquiring the same costume as the *señoritas*, the paper characterized her as not knowing how to properly wear it.

The scornful tone of the anecdote was also visible in other sections of the paper, particularly in a series titled "Bufonadas," or "Buffooneries." Each installment in the series centered on slice-of-life episodes featuring Afro-Peruvians in embarrassing situations. In one such episode, a black character named Dominga arrived at the home of her friend Doña Catita, whereupon she encountered Catita's black *portero*, or watchman, at the gate. When the *portero* announced that Doña Catita was away at mass and therefore unable to receive visitors, Dominga offered to wait inside the gate until her friend's return. To her surprise and chagrin, the *portero* denied her request on the grounds that he did not have permission to grant entry to strangers.

To Dominga, the man's behavior was doubly insulting, for in addition to challenging her claims to familiarity with the lady of the house, the *portero* expected Dominga, as she put it, to wait outside "like a dog."[3]

Stunned by his impudence, Dominga insisted to the *portero* that she was no stranger and that, in fact, she had even met him on several previous visits. But the man responded that he was simply doing his job and refused to relent. By this time, the interaction had escalated to a shouting match and physical altercation (with Dominga grabbing the *portero* by his shirt collar) that was only interrupted by the arrival of Doña Catita. Scandalized by the commotion unfolding outside her home for all the neighbors to see, Doña Catita defused the situation and invited Dominga in for lunch, during which time Dominga was too busy expressing her outrage over the incident to bother eating her meal.[4]

From every angle, the scene depicted Dominga as presumptuous, aggressive, and insistent upon the *portero's* deference. But as the *portero* seemed to take pleasure in reminding her, Dominga was not special. Rather, she was no different from the *portero* himself. The paper signaled this through the characters' nearly identical manners of speech, as both Dominga and the *portero* used similar malapropisms, exclamatory phrases, and contractions. Their turns of phrase especially stood out once Doña Catita joined the scene, speaking as she did in more formal, grammatically conventional ways. In fact, in terms of speech patterns, Dominga and the *portero* were just like the paper's eponymous *negro*. Speech, then, not only bound all three characters to one another, suggesting their fundamental sameness, but also marked them as fundamentally and incontrovertibly different from white Peruvians.

With its content rooted in references to local settings and costumes, *El Negro* was very much a product of its time and place. With this in mind, it is useful to consider the ways in which *El Negro* further contributed to the denigration and discrimination that Afro-Peruvians encountered in the post-abolition era. While it is not clear whether this particular paper enjoyed wide circulation (especially when compared to the eighteenth-century *Diario de Lima*, which had subscribers as far away as Havana), Lima had always been a city in which printed materials made their way into the public discourse through various channels. People read newspapers aloud in cafes, discussed their contents in private homes, salons, and *tertulías*, and generally found creative ways to gain and share access to information. Further, colonial officials made certain that laws targeting enslaved and free people of African, indigenous, and mixed-racial ancestry were regularly read aloud by *pregoneros* (or town criers) in highly trafficked public areas to ensure that no one had any reason to claim ignorance. The contents of *El Negro* could thus have easily circulated well beyond its base of subscribers.

In fact, there is a meaningful connection between the sumptuary laws of the eighteenth century that opened this book, and the discourse within this particular artifact of the print culture of the nineteenth century that helps steer *Exquisite Slaves* toward its conclusion. Although sumptuary laws in colonial Lima ultimately failed in their efforts to restrict access to dress along racial lines, *El Negro* managed to uphold the notion that black bodies were inherently undeserving of finery. Yet it did so in a way that marked a significant departure from the discourse of the eighteenth century. When looking back to *El Amor Duende*, the eighteenth-century play discussed in Chapter 1, the veiled *negra* represented the potential for clothing to blur distinctions across legal and racial lines. Her *saya y manto* briefly deceived the white male protagonists in the play into believing the woman was white herself (and thus deserving of flirtatious attention), thereby underscoring the need to prevent her and others' access to certain tools of self-presentation. But by the nineteenth century, the lesson of *El Negro* was that no item of clothing could ever enable such a deception. Even if they did manage to gain unrestricted access to the fabrics and designs of their choosing, the paper insisted, Afro-Peruvians were fundamentally incapable of looking anything other than foolish.

For Afro-Peruvians, then, the paper provided one of many cruel reminders that no matter how much they accomplished or acquired they would continue to encounter denigration and contempt. This worked alongside the generalized climate of discrimination that Peter Blanchard has described Afro-Peruvians having to face, as they toiled in many of the same labor conditions that defined their previous lot as slaves and continued to encounter the same patterns of abuse from their employers and discrimination within the larger culture.[5]

A close reading of *El Negro* also draws attention to the specific ways in which Peruvians were working out the meaning of "blackness" in the post-abolition era. According to the paper, buffoonish speech, dress, and behavior served as unambiguous racial signifiers. Throughout the pages of the paper, Afro-Peruvians expressed themselves in ways that clearly conveyed their ancestry, laid bare their limited intellectual capacities, and undercut their claims to respectability. And, just as it was careful to define "blackness," *El Negro* implicitly defined "whiteness" as the ability to avoid, recognize, and mock the problems inherent to certain ways of speaking, dressing, and behaving.

At the same time that *El Negro* examined these differences in a specific local context, the paper also shared features in common with a more widespread tradition, in which newspapers, magazines, broadsides, plays, and other forms of print culture throughout the Americas took special aim at people of African descent, mocking their speech patterns, self-presentation, and desire for social equality and political participation in the post-abolition era. In fact, the opening lines of the first issue of *El Negro* bear a striking resemblance to the various forms of "discursive blackface" that Jill Lane has identified in her analysis of Cuban poetry and plays from the 1840s to 1860s. According to Lane, this type of "written representation of racially marked expression," which was popularized by white authors, treated black speech as an error-filled source of comedy and entertainment.[6] The paper's substance and stylistic conventions also paralleled the "Bobalition" broadsides that circulated throughout the United States in the early nineteenth century. The posters began to appear in July 1819, following celebrations put on by free African-Americans in Boston to commemorate the 1808 abolition of the slave trade. One early example of the genre featured an image of a procession of uniformed black soldiers wearing caps adorned with large, cartoonish feathers. The feathers served as a visual mockery of the dignity of the proceedings and participants, while the headline did its part: "Grand Bobalition of Slavery: Grand and most helligunt Selebrashum of de Bobalition of Slabery in de Nited Tate ob Neu Englunt, and commonwet of Bosson in the country of Massa-chuse-it."[7] From their use of the word "bobalition" as a mispronunciation of "abolition," to their misspellings and mischaracterizations of key locations, the broadsides caricatured African-Americans as inept parrots of political discourse who were undeserving of freedom and citizenship.

The "Bobalition" broadsides enjoyed wide circulation and prompted frequent emulation, with papers in New York, Philadelphia, and even London publishing reprints as well as their own takes on the "Bobalition" genre.[8] The original sources and those they inspired likely traveled to more distant corners of the globe as well, possibly even making their way to Lima. To be sure, other sections of *El Negro* conveyed an air of familiarity with the conventions and contents of print culture from other parts of the Americas. Another of the paper's recurring features was a fictional series titled *La Esclava Americana*, which followed the travails of "Jenny," an enslaved woman living in the US South. The series was evocative of Harriet Jacobs' *Incidents in the Life of a Slave Girl*, which was originally published in serial form in the *New York Tribune* at various points between 1853 and 1857.[9]

Likewise, the paper's "Bufonadas" series was reminiscent of Edward W. Clay's depictions of African-Americans in his *Life in*

Philadelphia series, which was published by *Harper's Weekly* in the 1830s. Throughout the series, Clay's drawings cruelly characterized African-Americans in the city as undeserving of freedom, citizenship, and their assorted trappings. In one such image, a dark-hued woman stands before a mirror in a hat store. Wearing a brightly printed dress with a dramatic petticoat underneath and an oversized bonnet on her head, she asks her male companion, "Whut you tink of my new poke bonnet Frederick Augustus?" The man, equally outlandish in his costume of striped pajama pants pared with a waistcoat, responds, "I don't like him no how, 'case dey hide you lubly face, so you cant tell one she nigger from another."[10]

The obvious parallels between *El Negro* and other print cultural forms of the nineteenth century push us to consider the connections between the experiences of Afro-Latin Americans, African-Americans, and other African-descent populations around the Americas in the post-abolition era. Emphasizing the connections rather than the divisions among these groups has never been an easy proposition, given the extent to which their respective histories are rooted in disparate colonial contexts and labor systems. As historian Frank Tannenbaum argued in *Slave and Citizen*, which was originally published in 1946, a key difference between Latin American and North American slavery lay in the legal frameworks upholding the institutions. Because Latin America's framework recognized the legal personality of the slave and provided routes to manumission that North American slavery generally did not recognize, Tannenbaum claimed, it enabled a more humane treatment of slaves than did North American chattel bondage, and ultimately facilitated the emergence of more democratic racial regimes.[11]

In the decades following the publication of his study, scholars rigorously challenged the merits of Tannenbaum's claims about the institution of Latin American slavery, arguing that Tannenbaum failed to acknowledge the individual cruelty of slaveholders and the role of *los codigos negros* (or "black codes," which imposed strict guidelines on slaves' behavior) in fostering the system's brutality in the region.[12] However, in recent years scholars have begun to reexamine the merits of the Tannenbaum thesis. Without diminishing the myriad hardships that slaves in Latin America had to endure, scholars have acknowledged the extent to which the law provided slaves in the region with the possibility of negotiating their status, improving their condition, and securing their freedom in civil and ecclesiastical tribunals.[13]

Further, as Herman Bennett rightly reminds us, the political and social climate of the United States during the period when Tannenbaum was writing *Slave and Citizen* gave a certain moral weight to the book's arguments.[14] The prevalence of Jim Crow laws and institutionalized segregation in the United States – which traced their roots to the post-abolition era – made Latin America seem like a bastion of equality by comparison, even though the reality was that African-descent populations in the region endured their share of racism in the post-abolition era. In addition to limited employment opportunities and social mobility, they faced exclusion from political participation.[15]

Beyond adding to our growing understanding of the challenges Afro-Peruvians faced in their pursuit of citizenship and belonging, *El Negro* provides a source base for understanding the ways in which whiteness was constructed in nineteenth-century Lima. During a period when European immigrants were arriving in the region and cleaving into disparate socioeconomic groupings (which were likewise separate from those of white creoles), the question of how limenos constructed a white identity in opposition to that of the city's African-descent population merits further inquiry.[16] The paper also signals the potential for print cultural forms to enable meaningful comparative studies of post-abolition societies throughout the Americas. From Lima to Havana to Boston and other locales in between, newspapers, plays, and broadsides provided whites with powerful tools to mock African-descent men's and women's sense of self, community, and national belonging. Future research ought to further probe the discursive and representational threads connecting these and other print culture forms, as well as what those threads can tell us about the emergence and evolution of transnational discourses about race and racial difference.

Endnotes

NOTES FOR INTRODUCTION

1 Amedée Frezier, *Relation du voyage de la mer du sud aux côtes du Chili, du Pérou, et du Brésil, fait pendant les années 1712, 1713, & 1714* (Amsterdam: Chez Pierre Hubert, 1717), 380. All translations are mine unless otherwise noted.
2 Amedée Frezier, *Relation du voyage de la mer du sud aux côtes du Chili, du Pérou, et du Brésil*, 381.
3 William Betagh, 260–1. "Maclin lace" actually refers to the style of lace produced in Mechelen, a city in Flanders.
4 Jorge Juan and Antonio de Ulloa, *Relación histórica del viage à la América Meridiona*, 72: "El vestuario, que acostumbran allí los hombres no tiene diferencia de los que se estilan en España, ni la hay grande entre las varias jerarquías, que lo componen; porque todas las telas son comunes, y las usa el que las puede comprar: y así no es reparable el ver un *mulato*, u otro hombre de oficio, con un rico tisú, cuando el sujeto de la mayor calidad no halla otro mas sobresaliente, con que puede distinguir." Also cited in Jorge Juan and Antonio de Ulloa, *A Voyage to South America*, 55–6. For more on *"calidad,"* see Chapter 3.
5 Pedro de Peralta Barnuevo y Rocha, *Jubilos de Lima*.
6 "Reflexiones históricas y políticas sobre estado de la población de esta Capital," *Mercurio Peruano*, February 3, 1791.
7 Frederick Bowser, *The African Slave in Colonial Peru*; Carlos Aguirre, *Agentes de su propia libertad*; Peter Blanchard, *Slavery & Abolition in Early Republican Peru*; Christine Hünefeldt, *Paying the Price of Freedom*; Rachel O'Toole, *Bound Lives*; Jean-Pierre Tardieu, *Los negros y la Iglesia en el Perú*.
8 Herman L. Bennett, *Africans in Colonial Mexico*, 31.
9 Ira Berlin, *Generations of Captivity*, 79.
10 Stephanie Camp, *Closer to Freedom*, 60–92.

11 Shane White and Graham White, "Slave Clothing and African-American Culture in the Eighteenth and Nineteenth Centuries," 149–86.
12 Sidney Mintz and Richard Price, *The Birth of African-American Culture*, 51.
13 Ira Berlin, *Many Thousands Gone*, illuminates the difficulty of thinking about North and Latin American slavery as all-inclusive, binary categories, by illustrating the intense degree of internal diversity within the institution of North American slavery. Berlin focuses on two centuries of North American slavery in four regions (Chesapeake, Low Country, North, and Lower Mississippi Valley), and asserts that the difference in geography, demography, economy, society, and history created profound differences in the experience of slavery in those areas. Berlin also divides this study into three parts, which correspond to what he describes as three distinct periods in North American slavery. Part I covers the period of the Charter Generation, Part II examines the period of the Plantation Generation, and Part III explores the period of the Revolutionary Generation. According to Berlin, each generation confronted distinct relationships between slave and free populations, which reflected the difference between and evolution of societies with slaves (in which slaves were marginal to central productive processes) and slave societies (in which slavery was at the center of economic production). By tracing the processes by which the two kinds of societies developed their unique characteristics, Berlin presents an interesting framework not only for students of North American slavery but those of Latin American slavery as well.
14 Frederick Bowser, *The African Slave in Colonial Peru*, viii.
15 Sandra Lauderdale Graham, *House and Street*; Lauderdale Graham, *Caetana Says No*, xxii.
16 Joanne Rappaport, *The Disappearing Mestizo: Configuring Differnce in the Colonial New Kingdom of Granada* (Durham: Duke University Press, 2014), 2.
17 Natalie Zemon Davis, *Fiction in the Archives*, 112.
18 João Jose Reis, *Slave Rebellion in Brazil*.
19 Kathryn Burns, *Into the Archive*.
20 There is an extensive body of literature that engages these questions. One of the earliest scholarly critiques of slave narratives was leveled by Ulrich Bonnell Phillips, *Life and Labor in the Old South*, 216, who argued that slave narratives "were issued with so much abolitionist editing that as a

class their authenticity is doubtful." Given the attention, however, that has been directed toward Phillips's own biases, documented most notably in Kenneth Stampp, "The Historian and Southern Negro Slavery," Phillips's critique requires its own critique. Moreover, according to John Blassingame, "Using the Testimony of Ex-Slaves: Approaches and Problems," many slave narratives were related to or edited by whites who had "no connection to abolitionists," while others were produced with such exacting verification standards that "few of them were challenged by antebellum southerners." For her part, Frances Smith Foster, *Witnessing Slavery*, has traced how early styles of narratives written by African-born blacks in simple, utilitarian prose gave way to literary narratives featuring a criminalized black protagonist, to eighteenth-century narratives with religious or philosophical themes.

21 Arlette Farge, *Fragile Lives*, 6.
22 AGN, PN, Notario Orencio de Ascarrunz, Protocolo 83, October 7, 1766, "Libertad de Joseph Nazaro"; AGN, PN, Notario Orencio de Ascarrunz, Protocolo 74, November 3, 1744, "Testamento de Doña Juana de Rivas."
23 Magnus Mörner, *European Travelogues as Sources to Latin American History from the Late Eighteenth Century until 1870*.
24 Ada Ferrer, *Insurgent Cuba*, 10.
25 See, for example, Emily Clark, *The Strange History of the American Quadroon*.
26 For a discussion of the legal and conceptual distinctions Spaniards assigned to individuals of Indo-African and Euro-African ancestry in the early colonial period, see Berta Ares Quejia, "Mestizos, mulatos y zambaigos" (Virrenato del Perú, siglo XVI).
27 Joseph Boskin, *Sambo*.
28 Fernando Romero, *Quimba, Fa, Malambo, Ñeque*, 107.

NOTES FOR CHAPTER I

1 "R.C. Aprobando un Bando del Virrey del Peru para Moderar el Exceso en los Trajes que Vestían los Negros, Mulatos, Indios y Mestizos," in *Colección de Documentos para la Historia de la Formación Social de Hispanoamerica, 1493–1810, v. 3 pt. 1*, ed. Richard Konetzke (Madrid: Colección Superior de Investigaciones Científicas, 1962), 187. The full text of the document reads: "El. Rey Marqués de Castelfuerte, Virrey,

Gobernador y Capitán General de las provincias del Perú y Presidente de mi Real Audiencia de ellas. En carta de 2 de abril del año próximo pasado da cuenta con diferentes testimonios D. Pedro Antonio de Echave y Roxas, oidor de esa Real Audiencia, que hacía oficio de fiscal en ella, de que habiéndose publicado a su instancia un bando para moderar el escandaloso exceso de los trajes que vestían los negros, mulatos, indios y mestizos de ambos sexos, de que resultaban los frecuentes hurtos que se cometían para mantener tan costosas galas, fue muy escaso el efecto que produjo esta providencia, porque dentro de pocos días se volvió a introducir el mismo abuso con mayor desorden por el amparo y abrigo que los transgresores tenían en los ministros, constando por uno de dichos testimonios que veinte y cuatro horas después de la publicación del bando le quebrantaron dos negras esclavas del Conde de las Torres, oidor de esa misma Audiencia, con cuyo ejemplar se continuaban os excesos por quedar disimulados y sin castigo. Visto en mi Consejo de las Indias, con lo que dijo el fiscal de él, se ha considerado fue justo el referido bando y que se debe practicar su contenido; respecto de lo cual os encargo y mando que le hagáis renovar y publicar segunda vez con el término de quince días, con las penas establecidas por derecho, y con la advertencia y apercibimiento de que se procederá contra los sastres que a él contravinieren. Y así lo tendréis entendido para su más puntual observancia y para castigar, sin distinción de personas, a todos los que faltaren al cumplimiento de lo expresado, que tal es mi voluntad." All translations mine unless otherwise noted.

2 Konetzke, *Colección de Documentos para la Historia de la Formación Social de Hispanoamerica, 1493–1810*, 187 (all translations mine unless otherwise noted).

3 José Zevallos Guerra appeared on record again in 1734, after having sold four of his (unnamed) slaves to a man named Antonio de Salazar for a total of 2,000 pesos. AAL, Causas de Negros, E 2, L 28, 1734.

4 Betagh, *A Voyage Round the World*, 262.

5 For an account of the 1723 celebration in honor of the marriage of Spain's Prince of Asturias, see Peralta Barnuevo y Rocha, *Jubilos de Lima*.

6 Valerie Fraser, *The Architecture of Conquest: Building in the Viceroyalty of Peru, 1535–1635* (Cambridge: Cambridge University Press, 1990).

7 Jorge Bernales Ballesteros, *Lima: la ciudad y sus monumentos* (Seville: Escuela de Estudios Hispano-americanos de Sevilla, 1972).

8 James Lockhart, *Spanish Peru: 1532–1560* (Madison: University of Wisconsin Press, 1994), offers a richly detailed reconstruction of the key years in Peru's development as a Spanish society in the New World.

9 For an understanding of the effects of silver mining on Spain and Spanish America's economies, see David A. Brading and Harry Cross, "Colonial Silver Mining: Mexico and Peru," *Hispanic American Historical Review* 52, no. 3 (November 1972): 545–79; Carlos Assadourian, *El sistema de la economia colonial: Mercado interno, regions y espacio económico* (Lima: Instituto de Estudios Peruanos, 1982); and Richard L. Garner, "Long-term Silver Mining Trends in Spanish America: A Comparative Analysis of Peru and Mexico," *American Historical Review* 93, no. 4 (1988): 898–935.

10 Gwendolin B. Cobb, "Supply and Transportation for the Potosí Mines, 1545–1640," *Hispanic American Historical Review* 29, no. 1 (February 1949): 25–45.

11 William Lytle Schurz, "Mexico, Peru, and the Manila Galleon," *Hispanic American Historical Review* 1, no. 4 (November 1918): 389–402. For a more comprehensive analysis of the early American trade with the Far East, see William Lytle Schurz, *The Manila Galleon* (New York: E.P. Dutton & Co., 1939).

12 Peter T. Bradley, *Society, Economy and Defence in Seventeenth-Century Peru: The Administration of the Count of Alba de Liste, 1655–61* (Liverpool: Institute of Latin American Studies, University of Liverpool, 1992).

13 That being said, Africans nonetheless constituted a strong presence in the highlands, including in textile mills, churches, and households in Cuzco. See, for example, Jean-Pierre Tardieu, *El Negro en Cusco: los caminos de la alienación en la segunda mitad del siglo XVII* (Lima: Pontificia Universidad Católica del Perú: Banco Central de Reserva del Perú, 1998).

14 For an analysis of the debates over the use of African or Indian labor in the silver mines during the early years of Spanish colonial rule, see Bowser, *The African Slave in Colonial Peru*, 1–25. A more comprehensive treatment of the relative status of Africans and Indians in Peru can be found in Jean-Pierre Tardieu, *Noirs et Indiens au Pérou: Histoire d'une politique ségrégationniste, XVI–XVII siècles* (Paris: Éditions L'Harattan, 1990).

15 Bowser, *The African Slave in Colonial Peru*, 96.
16 Carlos Aguirre, *Breve historia de la esclavitud en el Perú: Una herida que no deja de sangrar* (Lima: Fondo Editorial del Congreso del Perú, 2005), offers a survey covering more than 300 years of slavery in Peru, as well as an overview of the major scholarship and the questions that guide it.
17 Bowser, *The African Slave in Colonial Peru*, 52–88. We should not assume, however, that notarial classifications were neatly mapped onto precise geographic locations in Africa, or that they referenced specific ethno-linguistic heritages, since they appeared in the archive following complex trade processes that made it difficult to trace individual arrivals' exact points of origin. Terms like "Congo" and "Guinea" (the latter of which referenced arrivals from the region between the Senegal and Niger rivers in West Africa), in fact, were *inscriptions* rather than descriptions. For a particularly insightful discussion of the myriad processes by which Spaniards marked Africans as inferior subjects, see Sherwin Bryant, *Rivers of Gold, Lives of Bondage: Governing through Slavery in Colonial Quito* (Chapel Hill: University of North Carolina Press, 2014), 46–83; and for a discussion of the vocabulary Spaniards produced to constitute indigenous alterity and inferiority, see Nancy E. van Deusen, "Seeing Indios in Sixteenth-Century Castile," *William and Mary Quarterly* 69, no. 2 (April 2012): 205–34.
18 Bowser, *The African Slave in Colonial Peru*, 104.
19 Bowser, *The African Slave in Colonial Peru*, 101.
20 For descriptions of Lima's public culture in the seventeenth century, see Josephe de Mugaburu, *Diario de Lima (1640–1694) crónica de la época colonial, por Josephe de Mugaburu y Francisco de Mugaburu (hijo). Publícanlo por primera vez, tomándolo del manuscrito original.* Horacio H. Urteaga y Carlos A. Romero (Lima: 1918); Juan Bromley, "Recibimiento de los virreyes en Lima," *Revista Histórica* 20 (1953): 1–108; Bowser, *The African Slave in Colonial Peru*, 100–1; Osorio, *Inventing Lima: Baroque Modernity in Peru's South Sea Metropolis*; and José Ramon Jouve Martín, "Public Ceremonies and Mulatto Identity in Viceregal Lima: A Colonial Reenactment of the Fall of Troy (1631)," *Colonial Latin American Review* 16, no. 2 (2007): 179–201. For similar events elsewhere in Spanish America, see Cañeque, *The King's Living Image: The Culture and Politics of Viceregal Power in Colonial Mexico*; D.A. Brading, "Civic Ceremonies in Colonial Spanish America," in *Europa Triumphans: Court and Civic Festivals in Early Modern Europe*,

Vol. II, ed. J.R. Mulryne (Hampshire: Ashgate Publishing, 2004), 350–7; Stephanie Merrim, *The Spectacular City, Mexico, and Colonial Hispanic Literary Culture* (Austin: University of Texas Press, 2010); and Frances Ramos, *Identity, Ritual, and Power in Colonial Puebla* (Tuscon: University of Arizona Press, 2012).

21 Defourneax, *Daily Life in Spain in the Golden Age*, provides a useful overview of the origins and features of slavery in early modern Spain, as does Tamar Herzog, "How Did Early-Modern Slaves in Spain Disappear? The Antecedents," *Republics of Letters: A Journal for the Study of Knowledge, Politics, and the Arts* 3, no. 1 (September 15, 2012). For surveys of slavery in early-modern Portugal, see A.C. De C.M. Saunders in *A Social History of Black Slaves and Freedmen in Portugal: 1441–1555* (Cambridge: Cambridge University Press, 1982); and Jorge Fonseca, "Black Africans in Portugal during Claynaerts's Visit (1533–1538)," in *Black Africans in Renaissance Europe*, eds. T.F. Earle and K.J.P. Lowe (Cambridge: Cambridge University Press, 2005), 113–24.

22 Debra Blumenthal, "Defending Their Masters' Honour: Slaves as Violent Offenders in Fifteenth-Century Valencia," in A Great Effusion of Blood?: Interpreting Medieval Violence, eds. Mark Meyerson, Oren Falk, and Daniel Thierry (Toronto: University of Toronto, 2004) 38.

23 Debra Blumenthal, "Defending Their Masters' Honour 41. For a description of concurrent practices in Lisbon, see A.C. De C.M. Saunders, in *A Social History of Black Slaves and Freedmen in Portugal: 1441–1555* (Cambridge: Cambridge University Press, 1982), 120.

24 Defourneax, *Daily Life in Spain in the Golden Age*, 57.

25 Ibid., 150.

26 See, for example, Susan Migden Socolow, "Iberian Women in Old World and New," in *Women of Colonial Latin America* (Cambridge: Cambridge University Press, 2000), 5–15.

27 Quotation: Blumenthal, "Defending Their Masters' Honour," 38.

28 Hall, *Things of Darkness*, 211

29 Ibid., 211–2.

30 Bowser, *The African Slave in Colonial Peru*, 154–5.

31 Ibid.

32 Ibid. In addition to these measures were those intended to curtail the popularity of carriages by requiring all but the highest officials to record theirs in a citywide registry. See Bronner, "Elite Formation," 24.

33 See, for example, Mugaburu, *Diario de Lima*, 221, who describes an incident from November 1674, when a Spaniard named Laureano Gelder ordered his male slave to accompany him on an outing while outfitted with a blunderbuss. Apparently, Gelder owed a debt to an unnamed person in the amount of 400 pesos and had received a written threat indicating that he would be killed if he did not deliver the sum at an appointed time. Gelder claimed that he gave his slave the blunderbuss and instructions to use it if necessary because he feared for his own safety. But in addition to serving a protective purpose, the enslaved man's presence also conveyed Gelder's ability – even in his indebted position – to arm a slave in his defense.

34 Bowser, *The African Slave in Colonial Peru*, 155, describes additional legislation targeting armed slaves in the 1620s and 1630s.

35 See, for example, Bronner, "Elite formation in seventeenth-century Peru," *Boletín de Estudios Latinoamericanos y del Caribe* 24 (Junio de 1978): 25–6.

36 Ibid., 24.

37 Alejandra B. Osorio, "The King in Lima: Simulacra, Ritual, and Rule in Seventeenth-Century Peru," *Hispanic American Historical Review* 84, no. 3 (August 2004): (quotation, 469). For more descriptions of Lima's early-colonial ceremonial culture, see Mugaburu, *Diario de Lima (1640–1694)*; Juan Bromley, "Recibimiento de los virreyes en Lima," 1–108; Bowser, *The African Slave in Colonial Peru*, 100–101; Osorio, *Inventing Lima*; and Jouve Martín, "Public Ceremonies and Mulatto Identity in Viceregal Lima," 179–201. For similar events elsewhere in Spanish America, see Cañeque, *The King's Living Image*; Brading, "Civic Ceremonies in Colonial Spanish America," 50–357; Merrim, *The Spectacular City*; and Frances Ramos, *Identity, Ritual, and Power in Colonial Puebla*.

38 Thomas Gage, *Travels in the New World* (Norman: University of Oklahoma Press, 1958), 65.

39 Herman Bennett, "Soiled Gods and the Creation of a Slave Society," in *Africans in Colonial Mexico: Absolutism, Christianity, and Afro-Creole Consciousness, 1570–1640* (Bloomington: Indiana University Press, 2003), 14–32 (confirm quotation page). There is evidence to suggest that similar notions held sway elsewhere in Latin America as well. In colonial Brazil, for example, French painter Jean-Baptiste Debret recorded the image of a nineteenth-century official leading a procession of the members of his

household. The image, titled "Une employe du government sortant de chez lui avec sa famille" (or "A government official leaving his house with his family"), included the man, his wife, the couple's children, and five household servants of different ages and sexes (possibly a family unit of their own), all of whom are depicted wearing varying degrees of finery.

40 This data comes from Bowser, *The African Slave in Colonial Peru*, 340–1, who calculated that in 1636, Lima's population totaled 27,064, which included 14,481 enslaved and free people of African descent; 10,780 Spaniards; and 1,803 Indians and mestizos.

41 Bernabe Cobo, Historia de la fundacion de Lima: https://archive.org/stream/historiadelafun00cobogoog#page/n126/mode/2up. Also cited in Stephanie Merrim, *The Spectacular City, Mexico, and Colonial Hispanic Literary Culture* (Austin: University of Texas Press, 2010), 20.

42 Bowser, *The African Slave in Colonial Peru*, 311.

43 Mugaburu, *Diario de Lima*, 91 and 124.

44 It is possible that even African-descent women who were not married to Spanish men, but nonetheless had conjugal ties to them, could have been included among the offenders. For more on these relationships, see Michelle A. McKinley, "Illicit Intimacies: Virtuous Concubinage in Colonial Lima," *Journal of Family History* 39, no. 3 (2014): 204–21.

45 For a full accounting of the events, see Don Geronimo Fernández de Castro, *Elisio Peruano: Solemnidades heroicas, y festivas demonstraciones de jubilos, que se han logrado en la muy noble, y muy leal Ciudad de los Reyes Lima, cabeza de la América austral, y corte del Perú, en la aclamación del Excelso Nombre de muy alto, muy poderoso, siempre augusto, Cathólico Monarcha de las Españas, y Emperador de la América Don Luis Primero N.S (que Dios guarde). Inspiradas, y dirigidas por el Excelentíssimo Señor Marqués de Castelfuerte, Cavallero del Orden de Santiago, Comendador de Montizon, y Chiclana, Theniente Coronel del Regimiento de Guardias de Españoles, del Consejo de S.M Virrey, lugar teniente, Governador, y Capitan General de el Perú, Tierrafirme, y Chile &c.* (Lima: Por Francisco Sobrino, Impresor del Santo Oficio en el Portal de los Escribanos, Año de, 1725).

46 References to *tapadas* are visible in travel literature and visual iconography from the sixteenth through the nineteenth century and receive careful attention in Laura R. Bass and Amanda Wunder, "The Veiled Ladies of the Early Modern Spanish World: Seduction and Scandal

in Seville, Madrid, and Lima," *Hispanic Review* 77, no. 1 (Winter 2009): 97–144.

47 Jerónimo Monforte y Vera, "Saynete Intermedio para la comedia que se represento en Palacio en la feliz aclamación del Rey N.S. Intitulado: El Amor Duende," in *Elisio Peruano*, 133.

48 Ibid.

49 Ibid., 134.

50 Poets and playwrights in early-modern Madrid and Seville frequently wrote of *tapadas* as deceitful figures whose veils concealed ugly faces and even frightful cadavers. See, for example, Bass and Wunder, "The Veiled Ladies of the Early Modern Spanish World," 122–131.

51 Jorge Juan and Antonio de Ulloa, *Relación histórica del viage à la América Meridional*, 78. The original Spanish reads: "Con el vestido de cola lucen mas particularmente el Jueves Santo; porque para visitar los Sagrarios salen acompañadas de dos, o quatro Negras, o Mulatas, esclavas vestidas de uniforme a manera de lacayos."

52 Webb Keane, "The Hazards of New Clothes: What Signs Make Possible," in *The Art of Clothing: A Pacific Experience*, eds. Susanne Küchler and Graeme Were, (London: UCL Press, 2005), 1–16.

53 Frezier, *Relation du voyage*, 381. "Generalement parlant elles sont assez belles, d'un air vis, & engageant plus qu'ailleurs, peut-être aussi doivent-elles une partie de leur beauté à l'opposition des Mulâtresses noires Indiennes, & autres visages hideux qui sont le plus grand nombre dans tout le pais."

54 Castañeda Vielakamen and Toguchi Kayo, "Imagen de la mujer afroperuana en el teatro del siglo XIX: 'El deseo de figurar' de Juana Manuela Laso de Eléspuru," 295. The original Spanish reads: "La negra es lo opuesto a la belleza y blancura de la tapada limeña; esa es la travesura de Amor, dar gato por liebre. La negra es la sorpresa no deseada."

55 See, for example, AAL, Nulidades, L 52, 11 de Diciembre 1730, which concerned an enslaved woman's marriage to a Spanish tailor. References to enslaved women as concubines can be found in AAL, Causas de Negros, L 33, E 3, 1792, "Autos seguidos por Natividad, esclava del licenciado don Juan de la Reinaga, presbiterio domicilario del arzobispado, sobre que le reconozca su libertad por el concubinato que tuvo con su amo;" and AAL, Causas de Negros, L 33, E 9, 1792, "Autos seguidos por Maria Mercedes Olvide contra su amo el licenciado don Pablo Barron y Perez, presbiterio,

sobre que le reconozca su libertad cumpliendo lo prometido durante el tiempo que fueron concubinas. See also Michelle A. McKinley, "Illicit Intimacies: Virtuous Concubinage in Colonial Lima," *Journal of Family History* 39, no. 3 (2014): 204–21.

56 Particularly detailed accounts of royal *exequias* (in honor of Philip IV in 1666) can be found in Josephe de Mugaburu, *Diario de Lima (1640–1694) crónica de la época colonial, por Josephe de Mugaburu y Francisco de Mugaburu (hijo). Publícanlo por primera vez, tomándolo del manuscrito original.* Horacio H. Urteaga y Carlos A. Romero (Lima: 1918); and Osorio, *Inventing Lima: Baroque Modernity in Peru's South Sea Metropolis*, 89–93.

57 *Gaceta de Lima*, No. 4, 17 de Junio hasta 1 de Agosto de 1758. The original text reads, "Fallecio en esta Capital la Señora Dona Rosa de Ilardy y Sabedra. Ha sido muy sentida su falta; y la sumptuosa pompa del Funeral correspondió al mérito de su calidad, y afables prendas."

58 AML, CL, CE, XXII, "*Bando sobre la forma de los lutos y funerales*," (1740), foja.342.

59 AML, CL, CE, XXII, "*Bando del Gobierno sobre la moderacion de lutos y funciones*" (1771).

60 AML, CL, CE, XXIV, "*Bando sobre lutos*" (1786).

61 BNP, EJ, C 3640, 1798, "Cuenta de los gastos impendidos en el vestuario de los cinco negros esclavos de Su Majestad existentes en la Real Sala de Armas, correspondiente al presente año."

NOTES FOR CHAPTER 2

1 AGN, RA, CCR, L 5, C 39, 1732, "Causa seguida contra Juan Ramos, esclavo de Doña Clara Manrique por hurto cometido en perjuicio del Hospital del Espíritu Santo."

2 Ann Pollard Rowe, *Costume and History in Highland Ecuador* (Austin: University of Texas Press, 2012), 99, describes the cloth as "by far Quito's most important textile."

3 See, for example, Hünefeldt, *Paying the Price of Freedom*, 109.

4 For an overview of lawsuits filed by slaves protesting *sevicia*, blocked marriages, sales to owners outside of the city, and separation from their children (primarily in the eighteenth century), see Barrantes, *Replanteando la Esclavitud*, 57–72. On manumission claims in the

seventeenth and eighteenth centuries, respectively, see Michelle A. McKinley, "Till Death Do Us Part: Testamentary Manumission in Seventeenth-Century Lima, Peru," *Slavery & Abolition: A Journal of Slave and Post-Slave Studies* 33, no. 3 (May 2012): 381–401; and Bianca Premo, "An Equity against the Law: Slave Rights and Creole Jurisprudence in Spanish America," *Slavery & Abolition* 32, no. 4 (2011): 495–517; and Hünefeldt, *Paying the Price of Freedom*, 167–98.

5 For a discussion of confraternity lawsuits, see Ciro Corilla Melchor, "Cofradías en la ciudad de Lima, siglos XVI y XVII: Racismo y conflictos étnicos," in *Etnicidad y discriminación racial en la historia del Perú*, eds. Elisa Dasso et al. (Lima: Pontificia Universidad Católica del Perú, 2002), 11–34; Roberto Rivas Aliaga, "Danzantes negros en el Corpus Christi de Lima, 1756: 'Vos estis Corpus Christi,'" in *Etnicidad y discriminación racial en la historia del Perú* (Lima: Pontificia Universidad Católica del Perú, 2002), 35–63; and Karen Graubart, "'So color de una cofradía': Catholic Confraternities and the Development of Afro-Peruvian Ethnicities in Early Colonial Peru," *Slavery & Abolition* 33, no. 1 (2012): 43–64.

6 Michelle A. McKinley, "Fractional Freedoms: Slavery, Legal Activism, and Ecclesiastical Courts in Colonial Lima, 1593–1689," *Law & History Review* 28, no. 3 (August 2010): 749–90.

7 For a classic study of the relationship between literacy, social status, and power in the colonial Spanish-American city, see Angel Rama, *The Lettered City* (Durham: Duke University Press, 1996).

8 Martín, *Esclavos de la Ciudad Letrada*.

9 See, for example, Rebecca J. Scott and Michael Zeuske, "Le 'droit d'avoir des droits': les revendications des ex-esclaves a Cuba (1872–1909)," *Annales: Histoire, Sciences Sociales* 59, no. 3 (2004): 521–45; and Alejandro de la Fuente, "Slave Law and Claims-Making in Cuba: The Tannenbaum Debate Revisited," *Law and History Review* 22, no. 2 (2004): 339–69.

10 Hünefeldt, *Paying the Price of Freedom*, 170, describes how slaves' relatives, friends, and religious confraternities served as guarantors when the claimants could not afford to pay for their own lawyers.

11 Barrantes, *Replanteando la Esclavitud*, 59, shows that for the period between 1760 and 1820, 123 enslaved women filed lawsuits over *sevicia* and the right to marry, and to prevent the sale of their children (among

other cases) in the *Real Audiencia* and *Tribunal Eclesiástico*, compared to sixty enslaved men.

12 See, for instance, Barrantes, *Replanteando la Esclavitud*, 70–3; McKinley, "Till Death Do Us Part," 381–401; and Hünefeldt, *Paying the Price of Freedom*, 130–9.

13 For an analysis of traditionally masculine forms of rebellion in colonial Peru, see Carlos Aguirre and Charles Walker, eds. *Bandoleros, Abigeos y Montoneros: Criminalidad y violencia en el Perú, siglos XVIII–XX* (Lima: Instituto de Apoyo Agrario, 1990). On the subject of slave rebellion, see Wilfredo E. Kapsoli, *Sublevaciones de Esclavos en el Perú: siglo XVIII* (Lima: Universidad Ricardo Palma, 1975); Carlos Flores, "Crisis agraria y revuelta de esclavos: Nepeña, 1767–1790," in *Etnicidad y discriminación racial en la historia del Perú*, Vol. 2, eds. José Luis Carrillo Mendoza et al. (Lima: Instituto Riva Agüero, 2003), 43–58; and Maria Ángela Morales Polar, "El espacio del esclavo negro en las haciendas del valle de Cañete, 1747–1821," *Investigaciones Sociales* 12, no. 21 (July 2008): 161–83.

14 To gather this sampling of *Real Audiencia* records, I used the search terms *hurto* (theft) and *robo* (robbery).

15 Stephanie M.H. Camp, *Closer to Freedom: Enslaved Women and Everyday Resistance in the Plantation South* (Chapel Hill: University of North Carolina Press, 2004), 60–92.

16 Camp, *Closer to Freedom*, 92.

17 Bronner, "Elite Formation in Seventeenth-Century Peru," 26.

18 Maribel Arrelucea Barrantes, "Conducta y Control Social Colonial. Estudio de las Panaderías Limeñas en el Siglo XVIII," in *Revista del Archivo General de la Nación*, Vol. 13 (Lima: Ministerio de Justicia, 1996), 133–51.

19 For example, when a man named Don Francisco Antonio Solórzano accused a free *bozal* named Maria Mercedes of hiding a diamond-encrusted cross stolen by his *bozal* slave, Tomasa, the language of the complaint reflected Solórzano's profound preoccupation with the question of status. His claim stated that he had taken Tomasa to a local slave prison with the intention of inflicting harm or threatening the woman "so that she would confess to the theft." See, AGN, RA, CCR, L 67, C 84, 1790.

20 Hünefeldt, *Paying the Price of Freedom*, 188–93.

21 AGN, RA, CCR, L 5, C 39, 1732, "Causa seguida contra Juan Ramos."

22 AGN, RA, CCR, L 5, C 39, 1732, "Causa seguida contra Juan Ramos."

23 Indeed, throughout Spanish America, certain punishments were meted out along color lines. For example, William Taylor, *Drinking, Homicide, & Rebellion in Colonial Mexican Villages* (Stanford: Stanford University Press, 1979) notes that public whippings were nearly exclusively reserved for persons of African and indigenous ancestry, even when Spaniards were accused and convicted of the same crimes.

24 See, for example, John Hope Franklin and Loren Schweninger, *Runaway Slaves: Rebels on the Plantation* (Oxford: Oxford University Press, 2000), which describes the many brandings and scars and the "mark of the whip" that marred the bodies of runaways.

25 Barrantes, *Replanteando La Esclavitud*, which places particular focus on enslaved women's social networks and strategies for negotiating their status.

26 Jean-Pierre Tardieu, *Los negros y la Iglesia en el Perú: siglos XVI–XVII* (Quito: Centro Cultural Afroecuatoriano, 1997); Michelle A. McKinley, "'Such Unsightly Unions Could Never Result in Holy Matrimony': Mixed-Status Marriages in Seventeenth-Century Colonial Lima," *Yale Journal of Law & The Humanities* 22, no. 2 (Spring 2010): 217–55, which examines annulment petitions by free husbands seeking to dissolve unions with enslaved wives on grounds of mistaken identity.

27 Bowser, *The African Slave in Colonial Peru*, 222–71.

28 This was particularly true in cases involving cross-caste marriages, such as those between slaves and Indians. See, for example, Jesus Cosamalón Aguilar, *Indios detrás de la muralla: Matrimonios indígenas y convivencia interacial en Santa Ana (Lima, 1795–1820)* (Lima: Pontificia Universidad Catolica del Peru, 1999).

29 For discussions of the rates and importance of slave marriage in the eighteenth century, see Barrantes, *Replanteando el Esclavitud*, 64–5. For the nineteenth century, see Hünefeldt, *Paying the Price of Freedom*, 129–66.

30 See, for example, Nancy Van Deusen, *Between the Sacred and the Worldly: The Institutional and Cultural Practice of Recogimiento in Spanish America* (Palo Alto: Stanford University Press, 2002); and Alexander L. Wisnosky, "'It Is Unjust for the Law of Marriage to Be Broken by the Law of Slavery': Married Slaves and Their Masters in Early Colonial Lima," *Slavery & Abolition* 35, no. 2 (June 2014): 234–52. For comparison to other slaveholding societies in Spanish America, see Bennett,

"Christian Matrimony and African Self-Fashioning," in *Africans in Colonial Mexico*; and Sherwin Bryant, "Enslaved Rebels, Fugitives, and Litigants: The Resistance Continuum in Colonial Quito," *Colonial Latin American Review* 13, no. 1 (June 2004): 7–46.

31 The term refers to an individual of mixed African and indigenous ancestry. Given Alvarado's status as a slave, it is most likely that his mother was enslaved (with her son following in her condition due to the law of maternal descent) and that his father was of indigenous ancestry.

32 AGN, RA, CCR, L 8, C 69, 1740, "Autos seguidos por Pedro de Vargas Machuca contra José Alvarado, esclavo de Don Sebastián de Alvarado y Merino sobre la restitución de su esclava, María Dominga de Loayza y su complicidad en el hurto de especies varias."

33 AGN, RA, CCR, L 8, C 69, 1740, "Autos seguidos por Pedro de Vargas Machuca contra José Alvarado, esclavo de Don Sebastián de Alvarado y Merino sobre la restitución de su esclava, María Dominga de Loayza y su complicidad en el hurto de especies varias."

34 AGN, RA, CCR, L 8, C 69, 1740, "Autos seguidos por Pedro de Vargas Machuca contra José Alvarado."

35 Elite Spanish women engaged in various forms of face-covering, the most popular of which involved the use of a large *manto*, or veil, which covered all but one of the wearer's eyes. Known as *tapadas*, or veiled women, they were a source of admiration, mystery, and even scorn from the sixteenth to the nineteenth centuries. Other forms of covering were more simple, involving the use of a small cloth similar to the kind in Loayza's case, which kept both eyes unveiled to better expose one's face. For a discussion of the origins and dissemination of these practices, see Bass and Wunder, "The Veiled Ladies of the Early Modern Spanish World," 97–144.

36 See, for example, Verena Martínez Alier, *Marriage, Class and Colour in Nineteenth-Century Cuba* (New York: Cambridge University Press, 1974); Silvia Marina Arrom, *The Women of Mexico City, 1790–1857* (Stanford: Stanford University Press, 1985); Richard Boyer, *The Lives of the Bigamists: Marriage, Family and Community in Colonial Mexico* (Albuquerque: University of New Mexico Press, 1995), 61–100; Ramón Gutiérrez, *When Jesus Came, the Corn Mothers Went Away: Marriage, Sexuality and Power in New Mexico, 1500–1846* (Stanford: Stanford University Press, 1991); and Ann Twinam, "Honor, Sexuality and Illegitimacy in Colonial Spanish America," in *Sexuality and Marriage in*

Colonial Latin America, ed. Asunción Lavrin (Lincoln: University of Nebraska Press, 1989), 118–55.

37 Bryant, "Enslaved Rebels, Fugitives, and Litigants," 7–46. For a discussion of how slaves in coastal Peru used marriage as a means of securing "multigenerational alliances," see O'Toole, *Bound Lives*, 35–63.

38 Sandra Lauderdale Graham, "Honor among Slaves," in *The Faces of Honor: Sex, Shame, and Violence in Colonial Latin America* (Albuquerque: University of New Mexico Press, 1998), 201–228. Similarly, R. Douglas Cope, *The Limits of Racial Domination: Plebian Society in Colonial Mexico City, 1660–1720* (Madison: University of Wisconsin Press, 1994) shows that many *castas* derived their beliefs in their reputations from their peers and took great care to offer mutual assistance and friendship to ensure their so-called reputational standing.

39 AGN, RA, CCR, L 17, C 192, 1755, "Autos seguidos por D. Juan Bautista Angel contra Francisco Calvo, negro criollo [esclavo], por hurto."

40 AGN, RA, CCR, L 17, C 192, 1755.

41 AGN, CA, JO, 2, 205, 375, "Estefanía Guerrero, vecina de Lima, contra José Orrantía, negro, sobre robo de ropa y objetos de uso de su casa."

42 AGN, RA, CCR, L 27, C 322, 1766, "Autos seguidos por Juan Antonio Súarez contra Domingo Calderón esclavo del convento de Santo Domingo por robo."

43 For a discussion of the way in which *castas* could make use of specific taverns to signal their membership in certain social groups, see Rachel Sarah O'Toole, "Castas y representación en Trujillo Colonial," in *Más allá de la dominación y la resistencia: Estudios de historia peruana, siglos xvi–xx*, eds. Paulo Driniot and Leo Garofalo (Lima: Instituto de Estudios Peruanos, 2005), 48–76.

44 *Diario de Lima*, "Se vende un negro bozal por no pagar a su ama los jornales," December 4, 1790.

45 Slave owners could be especially vindictive toward slaves who failed to pay *jornales*. In a case from 1781, an African-descent father filed a lawsuit against his enslaved daughter's former owner for listing her as a runaway in a "for sale" advertisement following one such failure. According to the father, the label was making it exceedingly difficult for his daughter to find a new owner, leaving her to languish in prison in the meantime. See AGN, CA, JO, 2, 197, 195, 1781, "Autos seguidos por Pedro Nolasco Boller contra

Don Fernando Jose Salvatierra sobre que se tache la palabra 'cimarrona' en la escritura de venta de su hija Hipolita."

46 The field owes a great debt to Marcel Mauss, *The Gift: The Form and Reason for Exchange in Archaic Societies*, trans. W.D. Halls (New York: W.W. Norton, 1990). Originally published in 1925, this study argues that "prestations" and "counter-prestations" (including the exchange of ceremonies and feasts), particularly in societies and cultures without formal economic markets, formed complete social systems in their own rights.

47 Mark Osteen, "Introduction: Questions of the Gift," in *The Question of the Gift: Essays across Disciplines*, ed. Mark Osteen (New York: Routledge, 2002), 2–43.

48 See, for example, Sophie White, "'Wearing Three or Four Handkerchiefs Around His Collar, and Elsewhere about Him': Slaves' Constructions of Masculinity and Ethnicity in French Colonial New Orleans," in *Dialogues of Dispersal: Gender, Sexuality, and African Diasporas*, eds. Sandra Gunning, Tera W. Hunter, and Michele Mitchell (Oxford: Blackwell Publishing, 2004), 132–53. In this study (based on an analysis of eighteenth-century criminal cases), White argues that for male slaves in New Orleans, clothing theft provided access to desirable material goods as well as the opportunity to curry social favor among contemporaries, especially women.

49 On internal divisions among slaves, see Bowser, *The African Slave in Colonial Peru*, 147–86, who argues that such divisions precluded the possibility of collective rebellion. Nicholas P. Cushner, "Slave Mortality and Reproduction on Jesuit Haciendas in Colonial Peru," *Hispanic American Historical Review* 55, no. 2 (May 1975): 186, likewise states that slaves were too focused on securing minor privileges from their owners to form a coherent social class. For a discussion of conflicts between free people of African descent, see Bowser, *The African Slave in Colonial Peru*, 302–23, who argues that "[a]ny sense of community the free coloreds possessed was constantly eroded by their recognition of the value of having ties to those who were lighter or wealthier or better connected than themselves." Free blacks, "[t]orn by values and ambitions imposed upon them by the larger society ... were anxious to forget their racial origins or at least to whiten themselves as much as possible." Bowser cites as evidence a Jesuit-sponsored *cofradía* that "fragmented on precisely the

question of racial and cultural whiteness." The question of how fragmentations within religious organizations exposed divisions along legal and color lines is explored in Karen Graubart, "'So color de una cofradía': Catholic Confraternities and the Development of Afro-Peruvian Ethnicities in Early Colonial Peru," 50–51, and Hünefeldt, *Paying the Price of Freedom*, 98–106, which detail the degree of internal conflict that characterized many of these organizations, where intraracial hierarchies tended to prevail. "Slave and free black populations," Hünefeldt asserts, "developed hierarchies and perceptions that differentiated darker-skinned blacks from lighter individuals, poorer from richer, and free blacks from slaves."

50 Hünefeldt, *Paying the Price of Freedom*, 98–9.
51 Ibid., 102.
52 AGN, RA, CCR, L 73, C 898, 1792, "Segundo cuaderno de la causa seguida por Doña María Dolores de Iturrigaray contra Juana María Lobatón, su esclava, por robo."
53 Hünefeldt, *Paying the Price of Freedom*, 247, describes a *cholo* as a "darker skinned person without clearly defined racial, cultural, or economic features (usually a pejorative term)." For his part, David Cahill, "Colour by Numbers: Racial and Ethnic Categories in the Viceroyalty of Peru, 1532–1824," *Journal of Latin American Studies* 26, no. 2 (May, 1994): 325–46, defines a *cholo* as the child born to an Indian and a mestizo/a. Davila and Lobatón's child, according to their testimonies, died shortly after birth.
54 The man's status as a member of a militia likely instilled a significant measure of pride, both for him and his female companion, given that the late-eighteenth and early-nineteenth centuries marked a period during which the Spanish Crown sought to improve both the organization and effectiveness of its colonial armed forces, which resulted in the elevation of military service to an honorable profession in Lima. See, for example, Monica Ricketts, "The Rise of the Bourbon Military in Peru, 1768–1820," *Colonial Latin American Review* 21 (2012), 413–39.
55 AGN, RA, CCR, L 73, C 898, 1792.
56 AGN, RA, CCR, L 76, C 919, 1792.
57 Lyman L. Johnson, "Dangerous Words, Provocative Gestures, and Violent Acts: The Disputed Hierarchies of Plebeian Life in Colonial Buenos Aires," in *The Faces of Honor: Sex, Shame, and Violence in Colonial Latin*

America, eds. Lyman L. Johnson and Sonya Lipsett-Rivera (Albuquerque: University of New Mexico Press, 1998), 152–178.

58 Rachel O'Toole, "From the Rivers of Guinea to the Valleys of Peru: Becoming a *Bran* Diaspora within Spanish Slavery," *Social Text* 25, no. 3 (Fall 2007): 19–36.

59 AGN, PN, Notario Teodoro Ayllon Salazar, Protocolo 94, March 13, 1781, "Libertad Graciosa: La hermana Juana Foronda a un mulato nombrado Joséf Foronda ... para que desde hoy día de la fecha en adelante goce de su libertad sin con que ni gravamento alguno, y en su virtud pueda hacer su testamento, dar y donar sus bienes que tuviere y adquiere, trabajar y contratar, residir en las partes y lugares que por bien tuviere, y practicar todas las operaciones que pueden hacer y hacen las personas libres de su nacimiento." This definition of freedom was not unique to Peru. For a discussion of the formalization of the Spanish-American notary office, see Kathryn Burns, "Notaries, Truth, and Consequences," *American Historical Review* 220, no. 2 (2005): 350–80, who describes the circulation of manuals that guided practitioners through American notarial forms.

60 AGN, RA, CCR, L 17, C 192, 1755.

61 For a discussion of the different meanings that public and private spaces contained for masters and servants in Brazil, see Sandra Lauderdale Graham, *House and Street: The Domestic World of Servants and Masters in Nineteenth-Century Rio de Janeiro* (Cambridge: Cambridge University Press, 1988). Graham argues that between 1860 and 1910, the house was a place of safety and security for masters, a setting both literally and figuratively removed from the dangers, contagions, threats, and temptations of the street. For domestic workers, especially water carriers and laundresses, the street provided a certain degree of autonomy, especially when the nature and duration of their tasks placed them at a healthy remove from the watchful eyes of their masters. Graham argues that given their reliance on domestic labor, however, masters were forced to bring the world of the streets into the perceived sanctity of their homes.

62 AGN, RA, CCR, L 28, C 339, 1767.

63 Foucault, *Discipline and Punish: The Birth of the Prison*, 201.

64 Ibid., 205–9.

65 Lacan, *The Four Fundamental Concepts of Psychoanalysis*, 84.

66 Ibid., 74.

67 Ibid., 101.

68 Kathryn Burns, *Into the Archive: Writing and Power in Colonial Peru* (Durham: Duke University Press, 2010), provides compelling insight into the kinds of motivations that guided these various actors, as well as the collaboration and conflict that went into the documents they collectively produced. Because of its focus on the process of creating what we consider to be the "historical record," it offers tremendous insight into the relationship between writing and power.

NOTES FOR CHAPTER 3

1 AAL, Nulidades, L 53, 18 de Septiembre de 1741, "Doña María Cayetana de Escobar y Barrantes contra Joseph de Ypinsa."
2 AAL, Nulidades, L 53, 18 de Septiembre de 1741, "Doña María Cayetana de Escobar y Barrantes contra Joseph de Ypinsa," foja.13.
3 See, for example, El derecho de antiguedad del Colegio Real de San Martin de la Ciudad de los Reyes en el Piru (1619). https://archive.org/details/elderechodeantig00cole. For more on Lima's Jesuit colleges, see Nicolas Kushner, *Lords of the Land*.
4 AAL, Nulidades, L 53, 18 de Septiembre de 1741, "Doña María Cayetana de Escobar y Barrantes contra Joseph de Ypinsa," foja.24 (first quote) and foja.19 (second quote).
5 Ibid., fojas.19–20.
6 Ibid., foja.20–1.
7 Ibid., foja.5.
8 Ibid., foja.42.
9 For a particularly insightful discussion of the myriad processes by which Spaniards marked Africans as inferior subjects, see Sherwin Bryant, *Rivers of Gold, Lives of Bondage: Governing through Slavery in Colonial Quito* (Chapel Hill: University of North Carolina Press, 2014), 46–83; and for a discussion of the vocabulary Spaniards produced to constitute indigenous alterity and inferiority, see Nancy E. van Deusen, "Seeing Indios in Sixteenth-Century Castile," *William and Mary Quarterly* 69, no. 2 (April 2012): 205–34.
10 A discussion of this case appears in Chapter 6.
11 See, for example, Tamara J. Walker, "'*Blanconas Sucias and Putas Putonas*': Women, Social Conflict, and the Power of Words in Late-Colonial Lima, Peru" *Gender & History* 27, no. 1 (April 2015): 131–150.

12 For a particularly useful discussion of the concept of "calidad" in colonial Spanish America, see Joan Bristol, *Christians, Blasphemers and Witches*, 1–22.
13 Joanne Rappaport, *The Disappearing Mestizo*, 24.
14 AAL, Testamentos, Ana de Ariola, L 140, C 2, 1710.
15 AAL, Testamentos, Petronila Cortes, Legajo (L) 46, Cuaderno (C) 10, 1720.
16 AAL, Testamentos, Ana de Ariola, L 140, C 2, 1710.
17 AAL, Testamentos, E 2, L 175, 1766.
18 The term "Pinchbeck" refers to a copper and zinc alloy used to imitate gold in jewelry.
19 AGN, PN, Teodoro Ayllon Salazar, Protocolo, March 24, 1792.
20 For example, of the hundreds of extant wills in the Archivo Arzobispal de Lima for the eighteenth century, approximately twenty of them were recorded by persons of African descent (who were marked in the documents by such terms as *negro/a, moreno/a, pardo/a*, and *cuarteron/a*). This figure is based on a survey of AAL, Testamentos, Legajos 140–81. In the case of the wills housed in the Archivo General de la Nacion, my analysis is based primarily on a study of the following records: AGN, PN, Notario Orencio de Ascarrunz, Protocolos 74 (1739–46), 75 (1747–8), 76 (1749–50), 77 (1751–2), 78 (1753–4), 79 (1755–6), 80 (1757–8), 81 (1759–60), 82 (1761–3), 83 (1764–8), 84 (1769–71), 85 (1772–3), 86 (1774–5), 87 (1776–9), 88 (1780–2), 89 (1788–93); AGN, PN, Notario Silvestre Bravo, Protocolo 148 (1769–86); AGN, PN, Notario Fernando J. de la Hermosa, Protocolos 523 (1754), 524 (1764–8), 525 (1769–81); 526 (1770–2), 527 (1774–7), 528 (1778–80), 529 (1780–1); 530 (1782–3), 531 (1784–6), 532 (1787–9), 533 (1789–91), 534 (1790–3); AGN, PN, Notario Teodoro Ayllon Salazar, Protocolos 93 (1773–80), 94 (1780–3), 95 (1784–9), and 96 (1790–5); and AAL, Testamentos (1723–1854).
21 "Reflexiones históricas y políticas sobre estado de la población de esta Capital,"*Mercurio Peruano*, February 3, 1791.
22 See also AGN, PN, Notario Silvestre Bravo, Protocolo 148, foja.40, October 20, 1770, "Testamento de Marcela Farfán morena criolla," whose will did not list any conventional property. But she did note that she had seven letters of confraternity membership in her possession. Her reasons for mentioning these letters were clear, for she wanted to ensure that "upon my death [the confraternities] will pay for my funeral and burial and ensure the protection of my soul." See also AGN, PN, Notario Orencio de

Ascarrunz, Protocolo 88, January 27, 1781, "Delcaración final de Josefa Cueto morena libre." Josefa noted that she was a humble woman who would die poor, with "no other goods besides a *sambito* named Javier."
23. AGN, PN, Notario Silvestre Bravo, Protocolo 148, November 18, 1781, "Testamento de Buena Ventura Pastrana, parda libre."
24. AGN, PN, Notario Silvestre Bravo, Protocolo 148, December 22, 1775, "Testamento de Maria Javiera Ramires."
25. AAL, Testamentos, E 12, L 180, 1784, "Testamento de Maria Josefa Pintado."
26. AGN, PN, Notario Orencio de Ascarrunz, Protocolo 74, April 15, 1744.
27. AGN, PN, Notario Orencio de Ascarrunz, Protocolo 74, February 1, 1741, "Testamento de Doña Francisca Casal."
28. AGN, PN, Notario Orencio de Ascarrunz, Protocolo 74, November 3, 1744. "Testamento de Doña Juana de Rivas."
29. Amanda Vickery, "Women and the World of Goods," 274–301.
30. AGN, PN, Notario Orencio de Ascarrunz, Protocolo 74, February 1, 1741, "Testamento de Doña Francisca Casal."
31. AGN, PN, Notario Orencio de Ascarrunz, Protocolo 83, March 6, 1758. See also AGN, PN, Notario Orencio de Ascarrunz, Protocolo 83, March 6, 1758, in which Don Miguel Gomendio made provisions for Juana Garníca, a *quarterona*, to be given her freedom along with 500 pesos.
32. Nancy E. van Deusen, "The 'Alienated' Body," 12.
33. van Deusen, "The 'Alienated' Body."
34. AGN, PN, Orencio de Ascarrunz, Protocolo 74, April 5, 1741, "Testamento de Doña Narsisa de Espinosa." Male testators acknowledged similar types of bonds, as when Don Josef de Mais y Arcas recorded his will in 1772, he stipulated that María Rosa, a 40-year-old *negra de casta conga*, be given her freedom upon his death. According to his executor, Don Juan Manuel de Elcorobarrutia, the testator wanted to acknowledge María Rosa "for having raised [his] children." See AGN, PN, Orencio de Ascarrunz, Protocolo 85, April 22, 1772, "Libertad graciosa Don Juan Manuel de Elcorobarrutia albacea tenedor de bienes de Don Josef de Mais y Arcas."
35. Sandra Lauderdale Graham, *Caetana Says No*, 122.
36. Ibid., 122.
37. Elizabeth Fox-Genovese, *Within the Plantation Household*, 140.
38. The most notable example of this type of scenario concerns a Brazilian *mulato* named Antonio de Lisboa, better known as *O Aleijadinho*

("the crippled one") who was born to a Portuguese father and his African slave, granted freedom at birth, trained as an artist, and created baroque sculptures and structures in the mining region of Minas Gerais. See Tania Costa Tribe, "The Mulatto as Artist and Image in Colonial Brazil," *Oxford Art Journal* 19, no. 1 (1996): 67–79.
39 AGN, PN, Notario Orencio de Ascarrunz, Protocolo 74, April 15, 1744. "Testamento de Doña Theresa Catalina de Espinosa."
40 AAL, Testamentos, E 2, L 175, 1766.
41 BPR, II, 2861, "Plan demonstrativo de la poblacion comprendida en el recinto de la Ciudad de Lima." The census counted a total of 47,796 inhabitants, of whom 22,438 were of African descent (including *negros, mulatos, quarterones, quinterones, zambos,* and *chinos*); 17,215 were Spaniards; and 8,143 were Indians and mestizos.
42 Esteban de Terralla y Landa, *Lima por dentro y fuera,* 158.
43 Ibid.
44 Ibid., 42–3.

NOTES FOR CHAPTER 4

1 AGI, Lima 652, N. 57, 1770-05-13; also cited in Natalia Majluf, ed. *Los cuadros de mestizaje del Virrey Amat: la representación etnográfica en el Perú colonial* (Lima: Museo de Arte de Lima, 1999).
2 In retaining the original orthography, syntax, and punctuation (or, in some instances, the lack thereof), I wish to draw attention to the idiosyncratic nature of the images' captions. Most notable is the way some captions, like *Mulata. con Español. Produsen. Quarteron de mulato* (image 11 in the series), include punctuation marks between each racial "type" (as well as after the verb "to produce"), while others, such as *Español Quarterona de Mulato. Produce Quinteróna de Mulato* (image 12 in the series), do not. There are also differences in spelling, with alternations between "produce" and "produse" and "Indio" and "Yndio." Still other captions in the series eschew the use of the verb "to produce" in any form and, instead, read as *Mestizo. Mestiza. Mestizo.* and *Quinterona de Mulato Requinterona de Mulato. Español* (images 4 and 13 in the series, respectively). Such inconsistencies suggest that the captions – and by extension the paintings – were drawn by different hands, at different times, or both. Nonetheless, they retain a narrative cohesion.

3 AGI, Lima 652, N. 57, 1770-05-13.
4 See, for example, J. David Archibald, *Aristotle's Ladder, Darwin's Tree: The Evolution of Visual Metaphors for Biological Order* (New York: Columbia University Press, 2014).
5 For a discussion of the colonial origins of these and other artifacts on board the ship, see Fermín del Pino Díaz, "Historia natural y razas humanas en los "cuadros de castas: Hispano-Americanas," in *Frutas y castas ilustradas*, ed. Pilar Romero de Tejada (Madrid: Museo Nacional de Antropología, 2004), 48–62.
6 Mercurio Peruano, "Reflexiones históricas y políticas sobre estado de la población de esta Capital," February 3, 1791.
7 Magali Carrera, *Imagining Identity in New Spain: Race, Lineage, and the Colonial Body in Portraiture and Casta Paintings* (Austin: University of Texas Press, 2003); Ilona Katzew, *Casta Painting: Images of Race in Eighteenth-Century Mexico* (New Haven and London: Yale University Press, 2004); Susan Deans-Smith, "Creating the Colonial Subject: Casta Paintings, Collectors, and Critics in Eighteenth-Century Mexico and Spain," *Colonial Latin American Review* 14, no. 2 (2005): 169–204; Ilona Katzew and Susan Deans-Smith, eds. *Race and Classification: The Case of Mexican America* (Stanford: Stanford University Press, 2009); and Evelina Guzauskyte, "Fragmented Borders, Fallen Men, Bestial Women: Violence in the Casta Paintings of Eighteenth-Century New Spain," *Bulletin of Spanish Studies: Hispanic Studies Researches on Spain, Portugal, and Latin America* 18, no. 2 (2009): 175–204.
8 Katzew, *Casta Painting*, 1.
9 Deans-Smith, "Creating the Colonial Subject," 182–9.
10 Ibid., 184.
11 Ibid., 189–91.
12 Katzew, *Casta Painting*, 42.
13 Ann Twinam, *Public Lives, Private Secrets: Gender, Honor, Sexuality, and Illegitimacy in Colonial Spanish America* (Stanford: Stanford University Press, 1999), 7.
14 Joanne Rappaport, "'Asi lo paresçe por su aspeto': Physiognomy and the Construction of Difference in Colonial Bogotá," *HAHR* 91, no. 4 (2011): 631.
15 Katzew, *Casta Painting*, 114.
16 Del Pino Díaz, "Historia natural y razas humanas en los cuadros de castas: Hispano-Americanas," 64.

17 The marks are especially reminiscent of the black *chiquedoras,* or beauty marks, that Magali Carrera observed on the faces of elite Spanish women in eighteenth-century New Spain. See Carrera, *Imagining Identity in New Spain,* 24.

18 Del Pino Díaz, "Historia natural y razas humanas en los cuadros de castas: Hispano-Americanas," 64.

19 Juan and Ulloa, *Relación histórica del viaje à la América Meridional,* 82. "A. Limeña en el trage de Saya de montar; B. [Limeña] En el trage Casero; C. Español en trage del Peru; D. Mulata; E. Negro criado; F. Mulata a l modo que andan a Caballo; G. Calesa al modo de Lima; H. Vicuña; I. Huanaco ó taruga; J. Llama ó carnero de la tiera."

20 For a discussion of Spain's broader efforts to contribute to the field of natural history, see, for example, Emily Berquist, "Bishop Martínez Compañón's Practical Utopia in Enlightenment Peru," *The Americas* 64, no. 3 (January 2008): 377–408; and Daniela Bleichmar, "Visible Empire: Scientific Expeditions and Visual Culture in the Hispanic Enlightenment," *Postcolonial Studies* 12, no. 4 (2009): 441–66.

21 On the tribute obligations imposed on Indo-Africans to discourage this kind of race mixing, see Bowser, *The African Slave in Colonial Peru,* 303; and Berta Ares Queija, "Mestizos, mulatos y zambaigos (Virrenato del Perú, siglo XVI)," 75–88. For a discussion of the intimate and sexual relationships that nonetheless continued to produce Indo-Africans, see Jesus Cosamalón Aguilar, *Indios detrás de la muralla.* Finally, for a more comprehensive treatment of the relative status of Africans and Indians in Peru, see Jean-Pierre Tardieu, *Noirs et Indiens au Pérou.*

22 It is important to note that just because Antonia was labeled in the record as *de casta conga,* we should not assume that notarial classifications neatly mapped onto precise geographic locations in Africa, or that they referenced specific ethno-linguistic heritages, since they appeared in the archive following complex trade processes that made it difficult to trace individual arrivals' exact points of origin. Terms like "Congo" and "Guinea" (the latter of which referenced arrivals from the region between the Senegal and Niger rivers in West Africa), in fact, were *inscriptions* rather than descriptions. But because they also formed part of an extensive set of labels that Spaniards used to constitute Africans, Indians, and their descendants as distinct and subordinate groups, the terms also carried profound meaning in Lima as well as in other parts of the Americas, where

they served to signal both difference and belonging. For a particularly insightful discussion of the myriad processes by which Spaniards marked Africans as inferior subjects, see Sherwin Bryant, *Rivers of Gold, Lives of Bondage: Governing through Slavery in Colonial Quito* (Chapel Hill: University of North Carolina Press, 2014), 46–83.

23 AGN, PN, Notario Orencio de Ascarrunz, Protocolo 83, October 7, 1766.
24 AGN, Colección Francisco Moreyra y Matute, D1. 9-255. "Padrón General de 1771." "Calle derecha desde la esquina de Santa Ana, hasta la muralla mano izquierda ... Casa no. 16."
25 Ibid., Casa no. 21.
26 AGN, Colección Francisco Moreyra y Matute, D1. 9-255. "Padrón General Comprensibo de todas las personas de ambos sexos aun Espanoles, como morenos libres y esclavos que se hallan en la jurisdicción asignada de San Bartolome de esta ciudad de Lima, hasta la Azequia de Yzta, y de esta hasta la portada de cocharcas, con todas las calles que arrabiesan hasta la muralla, volviendo aserrar por la calle de la casa de dicho Don Pablos, hasta la referida equina de Sn Brtlme, el cuales como se sigue."
27 AGN, Colección Francisco Moreyra y Matute, D1. 9-255. "Padrón General de 1771." "Calle derecha desde la esquina de Santa Ana, hasta la muralla sobre mano derecha, Casa no. 7."
28 Ibid., Casa no. 63.
29 Twinam, *Public Lives, Private Secrets*, 307–13.
30 E.D.C. Campbell and K.S. Rice, *Before Freedom Came: African-American Life in the Antebellum South* (Charlottesville: University of Virginia Press, 1991), 10.

NOTES FOR CHAPTER 5

1 Jayme Bausate y Mesa was actually a pseudonym; the publisher's real name was Francisco Antonio Cavello y Mesa.
2 Jayme Bausate y Messa, *Representación que hace D. Jayme Bausate y Messa, Autor del Diario Curioso, Erudito, Economico y Comercial de Lima, En el Reyno del Peru a la Majestad del Senor D. Carlos IV Que Dios Guarde* (Lima: March, 1791); and Jean-Pierre Clément, "Aproximación al *Diario de Lima* (1790–1793) y a Jaime Bausate y Mesa, su autor," *El Argonauta Español* 3 (2006). Online: http://argonauta.revues.org/1001 (February 3, 2017)

3 The *Mercurio Peruano* has been the subject of slightly more extensive scholarly inquiry, including: Jean Pierre Clement, *El Mercurio Peruano, 1790–1795* (Madrid: Iberoamericana Vervuert, 1997); Juan José Saldaña, *Science in Latin America: A History* (Austin: University of Texas Press, 2006); and Augusto Salazar Bundy, ed. *Aproximación a Unanue y la Ilustración Peruana* (UNMSM, 2006).

4 *Mercurio Peruano*, "Prospecto del Papel Periodico intitulado *Mercurio Perano de Historia, Literatura y Noticias públicas*, que à nombre de una Sociedad de Amantes del Pais, y como uno de ellos promote dar à luz," January 2, 1791.

5 *Diario de Lima*, "Noticias Particulares," October 11, 1790. Although self-serving and rather dismissive in their descriptions of one another, it was true that the *Diario de Lima* was more concerned than the *Mercurio Peruano* with the city's social life (as Jacinto Calero y Moreira) in at least one sense. For the duration of its run, the *Diario* was the only one of the two papers to feature a section titled *"noticias particulares,"* which served the very utilitarian purpose of advertising people and goods for sale. It was not until the paper's demise in 1793 that the *Mercurio Peruano* endeavored to print such items, doing so only to fill the void left by the other paper and placing them on a loose page or two at the back of each issue.

6 Biblioteca del Palacio Real, II, 2861, 1790 "Plan demonstrativo de la poblacion comprendida en el recinto de la Ciudad de Lima." The census counted a total of 47,796 inhabitants, of whom 22,438 were of African descent (including *negros, mulatos, quarterones, quinterones, zambos,* and *chinos*); 17,215 were Spaniards; and 8,143 were Indians and mestizos. This data does not provide a breakdown according to legal status, but according to Alberto Flores Galindo, *Aristocracia y plebe*, 101 Lima's population totaled 52,627 by 1791. That number was estimated to include 19,986 Spaniards (including both Spanish-born *peninsulares* and native-born *criollos*, or creoles); 12,479 slaves; 10,023 *pardos*; 4,807 *mestizos*; and 4,332 Indians.

7 *Diario de Lima*, "Noticias Particulares," October 15, 1790.

8 AGN, CA JO 2, C 197, L 195, 1781, "Autos seguidos por Pedro Nolasco Boller contra D. Fernando Jose Salvatierra sobre que se tache la palabra 'cimarorona' en la escritura de venta de su hija Hipolita."

9 *Diario de Lima*, "Noticias Particulares," December 20, 1790.

10 *Diario de Lima*, "Notas Particulares," October 23, 1790. "A doña Manuela Rivera, que vive en la Calle de los Borriqueros frente a las cocheras de

Nuestro Amo de San Sebastián, se le ha huido una criada, negra, gorda, canosa, de edad de 40 años, vestida de Luto, llamada Librata; a quien diese noticia o la aprehenda se le gratificará."

11 *Diario de Lima*, "Huido," January 5, 1791.
12 Shane White and Graham White, "Slave Clothing and African American Culture in the Eighteenth and Nineteenth Centuries," *Past and Present* 148 (August 1995): 149–86. Elsewhere, Shane White and Graham White, "Slave Hair and African American Culture in the Eighteenth and Nineteenth Centuries," *Journal of Southern History* 61, no. 1 (February 1995): 45–76, examine the descriptions those notices contained of slave men's and women's (often fashionable) hairstyles, which runaways frequently changed with the help of wigs to avoid detection.
13 David Waldstreicher, "Reading the Runaways: Self-Fashioning, Print Culture, and Confidence in Slavery in the Eighteenth-Century Mid-Atlantic," *William and Mary Quarterly* 56, no. 2 (April 1999): 243–72.
14 *Diario de Lima*, "Huido" March 12, 1791.
15 With few exceptions, each of the dozens of notices that were published during the paper's 1790–3 run appeared only once, which on its own is only evidence that owners in these cases decided against reissuing their calls for help.
16 AGN, RA, CCR, L 5, C 39, 1732, "Causa seguida contra Juan Ramos."
17 Jayme Bausate y Messa, *Representación que hace D. Jayme Bausate y Messa, Autor del Diario Curioso, Erudito, Economico y Comercial de Lima, En el Reyno del Peru a la Majestad del Senor D. Carlos IV Que Dios Guarde* (Lima: 1791).
18 Premo, *Children of the Father King: Youth, Authority, and Legal Minority in Colonial Lima*, 142.
19 Mariselle Meléndez, "Patria, *Criollos* and Blacks: Imagining the Nation in the Mercurio Peruano, 1791–1795," *Colonial Latin American Review* 15, no. 2 (December 2006): 207–27.
20 Manuel Lucena Samoral, *Los Códigos Negros de la América Española*, 279.
21 Manuel Lucena Samoral, *Los Códigos Negros de la América Española*, 279–284.
22 *Diario de Lima*, "Apoyo de nuestro rasgo, sobre la introduccion perniciosa de Negros, con la practica actual de Chile, Concepcion, Potosi, la Paz, Oruro, Cuzco, y otras Provincias," April 13, 1790.

23 *Diario de Lima*, "Reflexiones critico-fisicas y economicas," April 14, 1792.
24 *Mercurio Peruano*, "Carta sobre amas de leche," January 27, 1791.
25 *Mercurio Peruano*, "Idea de las congregaciones publicas de los negros bozales," June 16, 1791.
26 Ibid.
27 See, for example, AGN, Cabildo, Gobierno de la Ciudad, C 31, D 3, 1785. "Alberto Chosop, procurador general de los naturales, solicita se notifique a los mayordomos de cofradías para que no permitan que sus fieles roben ocultándose bajo las máscaras y disfraces que usan en las festividades de Cuasimodo y Corpus Christi;" and AML, CL-CE-XXIV, "Decreto Prohibiendo Danzas Y Diablillos En Las Procesiones De Cuasimodo" (1789), foja.125.
28 *Diario de Lima*, "Reflexiones critico-fisicas y economicas," April 14, 1792.
29 Ibid.
30 *Diario de Lima*, "Venta," April 13, 1792.
31 Ibid., October 4, 1790.
32 *Diario de Lima*, "Huido" March 12, 1791.
33 *Diario de Lima*, "Reflexiones critico-fisicas y economicas," April 14, 1792.
34 Ibid., April 15, 1792.
35 See, for example, Maribel Arrelucea Barrantes, *Replanteando La Esclavitud: estudios de etnicidad y género en Lima Borbónica* (Lima: CEDET Centro de Desarollo Étnico, 2009).

NOTES FOR CHAPTER 6

1 Christine Hünefeldt, *A Brief History of Peru*, 99.
2 Quoted in Basil Hall, Extracts from a *Journal*, Vol. 1, 256.
3 For two classic studies of the events surrounding the independence proclamation in Peru, see Basadre, *Historia de la república del Perú, 1822–1933*; Timothy E. Anna, "The Peruvian Declaration of Independence."
4 For a useful overview, see Claire Brewster, "Women and the Spanish-American Wars of Independence."
5 John R. Fisher, "The Royalist Regime in the Viceroyalty of Peru, 1820–1824," 56–7, sees this outsized focus on Lima as a consequence of "the traditional preoccupation with the metropolis and its elite groups" but notes that scholars have given increased attention over the past few

decades to the role of Peru's interior, and its indigenous and rural populations, in shaping the independence era. For a classic study of Peruvian independence that looks beyond Lima and centers on indigenous actors, see Charles Walker, *Smoldering Ashes*. For more recent examinations of Cusco's role in the independence era, see David Cahill, "New Viceroyalty, New Nation, New Empire: A Transnational Imaginary for Peruvian Independence," 203–35, which examines the Cuzco Revolution of 1814–1815 to draw attention to how the architects of the revolution articulated a political vision of a postcolonial state that would consist of the viceroyalties of both Peru and Charcas; and Sergio Serulnikov, *Revolution in the Andes: The Age of Túpac Amaru*.

6 Peter Blanchard, *Slavery & Abolition in Early Republican Peru*, 11.
7 Peter Blanchard, "The Slave Soldiers of Spanish South America: From Independence to Abolition," in Christopher Leslie Brown and Philip D. Morgan, *Arming Slaves: From Classical Times to the Modern Age* (New Haven: Yale University Press, 2006), 261.
8 Dawn Ades, *Art in Latin America: The Modern Era* (New Haven: Yale University Press, 1989), 17.
9 Blanchard, *Slavery & Abolition in Early Republican Peru*, 11.
10 Blanchard, "The Slave Soldiers of Spanish South America," 266.
11 For analyses of the simultaneous (and often conflicting) currents of anti-colonialism and anti-racism in times of war, see George Reid Andrews, "The Black Legions," *Problems in Modern Latin American History: A Reader*, eds. John Charles Chasteen and Joseph S. Tulchin (Wilmington: Scholarly Resources, 1994), 29–34; Laurent Dubois, *Les Esclaves de la Republique: L'histoire oubliée de la Première émancipation, 1789–1794* (Calmann-Lévy, 1998); Ada Ferrer, *Insurgent Cuba: Race, Nation, and Revolution, 1868–1898* (Chapel Hill: University of North Carolina Press, 1999); and Michele Mitchell, "'The Black Man's Burden': African Americans, Imperialism, and Notions of Racial Manhood 1890–1910," *International Review of Social History*, 44 (1999): 77–99.
12 Peter Blanchard, *Under the Flags of Freedom*, 117.
13 Ibid., 117–19.
14 For a detailed discussion of enslaved women's participation in Spanish America's Wars of Independence, see ibid., 141–59.
15 "Solo es grande el que es útil a la Patria," *La Abeja Republicana* 1, no. 19 (October 6, 1822): 173.

16. Ibid., 177.
17. "Rasgo patriotico," *La Abeja Republicana* 1, no. 21 (October 13, 1822): 202.
18. "Señor Editor," *La Abeja Republicana* 1, no. 32 (November 21, 1822): 288.
19. See, for example, Sara Castro-Klarén and John Charles Chasteen, eds. *Beyond Imagined Communities* (especially the Introduction and chapters by Guerra, Sarah C. Chambers, and Andrew Kirkendall); and Victor Uribe Urán, ed. *State and Society in Spanish America during the Age of Revolution*. For a discussion of the role of pulperías and other public spaces during the debates and struggles that comprised Peru's transition from colony to republic, see Sarah Chambers, *From Subjects to Citizens*.
20. AGN, Superior Gobierno, L 36, C 1268, 1818 "Expediente promovido ante el Superior Gobierno por Doña Maria del Carmen Gómez, mujer legítima de Pedro Rosas, soldado de la Primera Compañía de Morenos de esta capital, uno de los primeros que se ofreció voluntariamente a la Expedición del Desaguadero, en donde se dio la primera batalla a los insurgentes de Buenos Aires. La recurrente solicite se le abonen los sueldos y pensiones que se le adeudan."
21. For an analysis of the social meanings the titles "Don" and "Doña" contained for the men and women who carried – and aspired to carry – them in colonial Spanish America, see Ann Twinam, *Public Lives, Private Secrets*.
22. Ibid., 25.
23. AGN, Signatura Colección Moreyra, Impresos, Reales Cédulas (1763–1845), D1, 98-2224.
24. "Remitido," *La Abeja Republicana* 2, no. 15 (March 29, 1823): 259.
25. See, for example, Marixa Lasso: *Myths of Harmony*.
26. Blanchard, "The Slave Soldiers of Spanish South America," 270.
27. Flora Tristan, *Peregrinations of a Pariah*, 254.
28. Ibid., 258.
29. Ibid., 259. In his analysis of the Algerian revolution, Franz Fanon, *A Dying Colonialism*, translated by Haakon Chevalier (New York: Grove Press, 1965), argued that French occupation forces sought to unveil Algerian women not as a gesture of liberation, but out of a "will to bring this woman within his reach, to make her a possible object of possession. This woman who sees without being seen," Fanon continues, "frustrates the colonizer. There is no reciprocity. She does not yield herself, does not give

herself, does not offer herself. ... The European faced with an Algerian woman wants to see. He reacts in an aggressive way before this limitation of his perception." Given the similarities between the *saya y manto* costume worn by women in eighteenth- and nineteenth-century Lima and the veils worn by women in the Arab world, that European male visitors noted the city's *tapadas* with some of the same frustration later expressed by Fanon's European observers is particularly striking.

30 Helene E. Roberts, "The Exquisite Slave: The Role of Clothes in the Making of the Victorian Woman," *Signs: Journal of Women in Culture and Society* 2, no. 3 (1977): 554.

31 For a discussion of the role of the black servant in the work of eighteenth-century writer and illustrator William Hogarth, see Catherine Molineux, "Hogarth's Fashionable Slaves: Moral Corruption in Eighteenth-Century London," *ELH*, 72, no. 2 (2005): 497. "Hogarth's contribution to this iconography and display of blacks," she writes, "is satirical and subversive of the civility, politeness, and Christian virtue that slave owners hoped to convey by affiliating themselves with the fashioning of an exotic black savage into a domestic servant." For a discussion of the black female body as an indicator of white female sexuality, see Sander L. Gilman, "Black Bodies, White Bodies: Toward an Iconography of Female Sexuality in Late Nineteenth-Century Art, Medicine, and Literature," *Critical Inquiry* 12 (Autumn 1985): 204–42, who argues that the black female attendant in such images as Edouard Manet's *Olympia* (1863) "indicates the covert sexuality of the white woman." Some scholars have also argued that child servants functioned as stand-ins for children and pets in nineteenth-century visual imagery. For a discussion of the iconography of child servants, see Molineaux, "Hogarth's Fashionable Slaves."

32 AGN, Protocolos Notariales, Escribano Jose Simeon Ayllon Salazar, Protocolo 68, 1847.

33 Biographers generally disagree on the subject of Fierro's exact date of birth. According to Angelica Palma, *Pancho Fierro: Acuarelista Limeño* (Lima: San Martín y CIA, S.A, 1935), Fierro was born in 1803. For his part, Manuel Cisneros Sanchez, *Pancho Fierro y la Lima del 800* (Lima: Importadora, Exportadora, y Librería García Ribeyros, S.C.R.L, 1975), argues that since Fierro's 1879 death certificate showed that he died at age seventy, he had to have been born in 1809. More recently, Gustavo León y León Duran, *Apuntes histórico-genealógicos de Francisco Fierro: Pancho Fierro* (Lima:

Biblioteca Nacional del Perú, Fondo Editorial, 2004), points to an October 5, 1807, birth date. He bases his argument on an examination of Fierro's February 5, 1809, baptism record, which shows that Fierro was baptized at sixteen months of age. I have also examined the document AAL, Libros Parroquiales, Libro no. 6 de Bautismos de Indios y Esclavos. "Partida del Bautismo de Francisco Rodríguez del Fierro," and believe that Fierro's 1879 death certificate most likely conflated his baptism date with his birth date.

34 Gustavo León y León Duran, *Apuntes histórico-genealógicos de Francisco Fierro*, 113.
35 Angelica Palma, *Pancho Fierro*, xv.
36 *El Capeador*. Lithograph. A.A. Bonnaffé, 1855. Instituto Riva Agüero. Also cited in Raul Porras Barrenechea and Jaime Bayly, *Pancho Fierro* (Lima: Instituto de Arte Contemporáneo, 1960), 67–68.
37 *Esteban Arredondo*. Watercolor. Francisco Fierro, undated. Municipalidad de Lima. I have found no biographical details about Arredondo, but according to Barrenechea and Bayly, *Pancho Fierro*, 67, Arredondo and Manuel Monteblanco (who Fierro paints as strikingly similar in dress and color) were the most popular bullfighters in nineteenth-century Lima. The two men, or composites thereof, appear in several other artistic renderings from the period, wearing the same style of suit and hat, carrying capes, and smoking cigars.
38 Barrenechea and Bayly, *Pancho Fierro*, 67–8. According to Palma, *Pancho Fierro*, xv, Fierro did not date his own work. When her father Ricardo Palma began to organize the image collection after Fierro's death (which he received as a gift from a collector and later bequeathed to his daughter), he assigned dates to many of the images himself. This makes it difficult for contemporary scholars to trace Fierro's artistic development over time or to definitively ascertain whether and how Fierro's work influenced that of his contemporaries and vice versa.
39 Alicia del Águila, *Los velos y los pieles: cuerpo, género y reordenamento social en el Perú republicano (Lima, 1822–1872)* (Lima: Instituto de Estudios Peruanos, 2003).
40 Ida Pfeiffer *A Lady's Second Journey Round the World: From London to the Cape of Good Hope, Borneo, Java, Sumatra, Celebes, Ceram, the Moluccas, etc., California, Panama, Peru, Ecuador, and the United States* (New York: Harper & Brothers, 1856), 350.

41 Juan Manuel Ugarte Elespuru, "Prólogo," in Manuel Cisneros Sanchez, *Pancho Fierro y la Lima del 800* (Lima: Importadora, Exportadora, y Librería García Ribeyros, S.C.R.L, 1975), xxiii. "Segun las referencias, Fierro era muy atilado en el vestir, con lujo mulato, vistoso y colorinero."
42 Cisneros Sanchez, *Pancho Fierro y la Lima del 800*, 25.
43 *Puesto de chicha y picante*. Watercolor. Francisco Fierro, undated. Galería de la Municipalidad de Lima.

NOTES FOR EPILOGUE

1 *El Negro*, Vol. 1, 15 May 15, 1858.
2 Ibid., "Episodio Crinolino."
3 *El Negro*, Vol. 2, May 28, 1858, "Bufonadas."
4 Ibid.
5 Peter Blanchard, *Slavery & Abolition in Early Republican Peru* (Delaware: Scholarly Resources Inc., 1992), 222.
6 Jill Lane, *Blackface Cuba, 1840–1895* (Philadelphia: University of Pennsylvania Press, 2005).
7 Grand Bobalition of Slavery: Grand and most helligunt Selebrashum of the Bobalition of Slabery in de Nited Tate ob Neu Englunt, and commonwet of Bosson in de country of Massa-chuse-it. Boston: s.n., ca. 1819.
8 For more on the circulation of "Bobalition" broadsides in the United States, see White and White, *Stylin'*, 114.
9 For a discussion of the origins and early iterations of the Jacobs text, as well as a biography of Jacobs herself, see Jean Fagan Yellin, *Harriet Jacobs: A Life* (New York: Basic Civitas Books, 2005).
10 Edward William Clay (1799–1857), "Life in Philadelphia. 'Whut you tink of my new poke bonnet...?'" ca. 1830. Library Company of Philadelphia. For more on Clay's series, see Gary B. Nash, *First City: Philadelphia and the Forging of Historical Memory* (Philadelphia: University of Pennsylvania Press, 2011), 200–1.
11 Tannenbaum, *Slave and Citizen*.
12 A comprehensive overview of the challenges to the Tannenbaum Thesis can be found in Michelle A. McKinley, "Fractional Freedoms: Slavery, Legal Activism, and Ecclesiastical Courts in Colonial Lima, 1593–1689," *Law & History Review* 28, no. 3 (August 2010): 749–90. For a discussion of the Spanish America's black codes, see Manuel Lucena Salmoral, *Los*

Códigos Negros de la América Española (Universidad Alcalá: Ediciones Unesco, 1996).

13 See, for example, Alejandro de la Fuente, "Slave Law and Claims-Making in Cuba: The Tannenbaum Debate Revisited," *Law and History Review* 22, no. 2 (2004): 339–69; and Bianca Premo, "An Equity against the Law: Slave Rights and Creole Jurisprudence in Spanish America," *Slavery & Abolition* 32, no. 4 (2011): 495–551.

14 Herman L. Bennett, *Colonial Blackness: A History of Afro-Mexico* (Bloomington: Indiana University Press, 2009), 7–8.

15 See, for example, Michael Hanchard, *Orpheus and Power: The Movimento Negro of Rio de Janeiro* (Princeton: Princeton University Press, 1994); Aline Helg, "Race in Argentina and Cuba, 1880–1930: Theory, Policies, and Popular Reaction," in *The Idea of Race in Latin America, 1870–1940*, ed. Richard Graham (Austin: University of Texas Press, 1997), 37–70; Butler, *Freedoms Given, Freedoms Won*; and George Reid Andrews, *Afro-Latin America, 1800–2000* (Oxford: Oxford University Press, 2004), 85–152.

16 See, for example, Christine Hünefeldt, *Liberalism in the Bedroom: Quarreling Spouses in Nineteenth-Century Lima* (University Park: Penn State University, 2000), 17–60.

Bibliography

ARCHIVES

Peru

Archivo Arzobispal de Lima (AAL)

    Causas Civiles
    Causas de Negros
    Estadística Lima
    Testamentos

Archivo General de la Nación (AGN)
Protocolos Notariales

    Orencio de Ascarrunz, Protocolos 74–89 (1739–1793)
    Silvestre Bravo, Protocolo 148 (1769–1786)
    Andrés Calero, Protocolo 136 (1804–1826)
    José Cardenas, Protocolos 132–135 (1804–1821)
    Fernando J. de la Hermosa, Protocolos 523–534 (1754–1793), 264 (1800–1805)
        Jose Simeon Ayllon Salazar, Protocolos 60–70 (1828–1852)
    Teodoro Ayllon Salazar, Protocolos 93–96 (1773–1795)
    Gerónimo de Villafuerte, Protocolos 1020–1028 (1820–1854)

Sección Colonial

    Justicia Ordinaria
    Causas Civiles
    Causas Criminales
    Real Audiencia
    Causas Civiles
    Causas Criminales
    Signatura Colección Moreyra
    Superior Gobierno

Sección Republicana

    Corte Superior de Justicia
    Depositivos Legales

Archivo de la Municipalidad de Lima (AML)
    Cabildo
    Cedulas
    Superior Gobierno

Biblioteca Nacional del Perú (BNP)

    Manuscritos Virreynato
    Esclavitud, Cacicazgos, Indios, Bienes, Judiciales
    Vida Social, Hospitales, Colegios

Spain

    Archivo General de las Indias, Seville (AGI)
    Archivo General de la Nación, Madrid (AGNM)
    Bibliteca del Palacio Royal, Madrid (BNP)

The United States

    The Clements Library, Ann Arbor, MI
    The John Carter Brown Library, Providence, RI
    The Library of Congress, Washington, DC

GALLERIES AND EXHIBITIONS

    Galería de la Municipalidad de Lima
    Museo de Arte de Lima
    Museo del Banco Central de Reserva del Perú

NEWSPAPERS AND PERIODICALS

    Abeja Republicana
    Comercio del Perú
    Diario de Lima
    Gaceta de Lima

Gaceta del Gobierno
Mercurio Peruano
El Negro
El Peruano

PUBLISHED PRIMARY SOURCES AND HISTORICAL ACCOUNTS

Betagh, William. *A Voyage Round the World: Being an Account of a Remarkable Enterprise, Begun in the Year 1719, Chiefly to Cruise on the Spaniards in the Great South Ocean* (London: T. Combes, 1728).

Burns, Robert I., ed. *Las Siete Partidas del muy noble rey Don Alfonso el Sabio, glosadas por el Lic. Gregorio Lopez, del Consejo Real de Indias de S.M*, Vol. 2, Part 4, Tit. 22, Law 7 (Madrid: Compañia General de Impresores y Libreros del Reino, 1844), translated by Samuel Parsons Scott.

Concolorcorvo. *El Lazarillo de ciegos caminantes desde Buenos Ayres hasta Lima con sus itinerarios según la más puntual observación, con algunas noticias útiles á los nuevos comerciantes que tratan en mulas; y otras históricas. Sacado de las memorias que hizo Don Alonso Carrió de la Vandera en este dilatado viage, y comisión que tuvo por la corte para el arreglo de correos, y estafetas, situación, y ajute de postas, desde Montevideo, por Don Calixto Bustamante Carlos Inca, alias Concolorcorvo, natural del Cuzco, que acompaño al referido ecomisionado en dicho viage, y escribió sus extractos* (Lima: Imprenta de la Rovada, 1773).

Frezier, Amédée. *Relation du voyage de la mer du sud aux côtes du Chili, du Pérou, et du Brésil, fait pendant les années 1712, 1713, & 1714* (Amsterdam: Chez Pierre Hubert, 1717).

Gage, Thomas. *Travels in the New World* (Norman: University of Oklahoma Press, 1958).

Hall, Basil. *Extracts from a Journal, Written on the Coasts of Chili, Peru, and Mexico, in the Years 1820, 1821, 1822, by Captain Basil Hall*, Vols. 1 and 2 (Edinburgh: A. Constable and Co., 1824).

Konetzke, Richard. *Colección de Documentos para la Historia de la Formación Social de Hispanoamerica, 1493–1810, v. 3 pt. 1* (Madrid: Colección Superior de Investigaciones Científicas, 1962).

Lucena Salmoral, Manuel. *Los Códigos Negros de la América Española.* (Universidad Alcalá: Ediciones Unesco, 1996).

Mugaburu, Josephe de. *Diario de Lima (1640–1694) crónica de la época colonial, por Josephe de Mugaburu y Francisco de Mugaburu (hijo): Publícanlo por primera vez, tomándolo del manuscrito original.* Horacio H. Urteaga y Carlos A. Romero (Lima: 1918).

Parsons Scott, Samuel (translator) and Robert I. Burns, ed. "In What Way a Slave Can Obtain His Freedom by Lapse of Time," in *Las Siete Partidas* Part 4, Tit. 22, Law 7 (Philadelphia: University of Pennsylvania Press, 2001), 983.

Peralta Barnuevo y Rocha, Pedro de. *Júbilos de Lima y fiestas reales, que hizo esta muy Noble y Leal Ciudad, Capital y Emporio de la America Austral, en celebración de los augustos casamientos del Serenísimo Señor Don Luis Fernando, Principe de las Asturias, N. Señor, con la Serenísima Señora Princesa de Orleáns, y del Señor Rey Cristianísimo Luis Decimo Quinto con la Serenísima Señora Doña Maria Anna Victoria, Infanta de España, Ordenadas, y Dirigidas por el Exmo Sr. Don Fr. Diego Morcillo Rubio de Auñon, Arzobispo de la Plata, Virrey, Governador, y Capitan General de los Reynos del Peru, Tierra firme, y Chile* (Lima: en la Imprenta de la Calle de Palacio, por Ignacio de Luna y Bohorques, 1723).

Pfeiffer, Ida. *A Lady's Second Journey Round the World: From London to the Cape of Good Hope, Borneo, Java, Sumatra, Celebes, Ceram, the Moluccas, etc., California, Panama, Peru, Ecuador, and the United States* (New York: Harper & Brothers, 1856).

Terralla y Landa, Esteban de. *Lima por dentro y fuera en consejos económicos, saludables, políticos y morales que da un amigo a otro con motivo de querer dejar la ciudad de México por pasar a la de Lima* (Madrid: Imprenta de Villalpando, 1798).

Tristan, Flora. *Mémoires et pérégrinations d'une paria* (London: Virago Press, 1838).

SECONDARY SOURCES

Books

Adelman, Jeremy, ed. *Colonial Legacies: The Problem of Persistence in Latin American History* (New York: Routledge, 1999).

Águila, Alicia del. *Los velos y los pieles: cuerpo, género y reordenamento social en el Perú republicano (Lima, 1822–1872)* (Lima: Instituto de Estudios Peruanos, 2003).

Aguirre, Carlos. *Agentes de su Propia Libertad: los esclavos de Lima y la desintegración de la esclavitud, 1821–1854* (Lima: Pontifica Universidad Católica del Perú, Fondo Editorial, 1993).

Aguirre, Carlos. *Breve historia de la esclavitud en el Perú: Una herida que no deja de sangrar* (Lima: Fondo Editorial del Congreso del Perú, 2005).

Aguirre, Carlos and Charles Walker, eds. *Bandoleros, Abigeos y Montoneros: Criminalidad y violencia en el Perú, siglos XVIII–XX* (Lima: Instituto de Apoyo Agrario, 1990).

Aguirre, Carlos and Robert Buffington, eds. *Reconstructing Criminality in Latin America* (Wilmington: Jaguar Books on Latin America, 2000).

Andrews, George Reid. "The Black Legions," in *Problems in Modern Latin American History: A Reader*, John Charles Chasteen and Joseph S. Tulchin, eds. (Wilmington: Scholarly Resources, 1994), 29–34.

Ares Quejia, Berta and Alessandro Stella, coordinadores. *Negros, Mulatos, Zambaigos: Derroteros africanos en los mundos ibéricos* (Sevilla: Escuela de Estudios Hispano-Americanos, 2000).

Bakewell, Peter. *A History of Latin America: Empires and Sequels, 1450–1930* (Oxford: Blackwell Publishing, 2002).

Basadre, Jorge. *Historia de la república del Perú, 1822–1933* (Lima: Ediciones "História," 1968).

Bauer, Arnold J. *Goods, Power, History: Latin America's Material Culture* (Cambridge: Cambridge University Press, 2001).

Berlin, Ira. *Many Thousands Gone: The First Two Centuries of Slavery in North America* (Cambridge: Harvard University Press, 1998).

Berlin, Ira. *Generations of Captivity: A History of African-American Slaves* (Cambridge: Belknap Press of Harvard University Press, 2003).

Bernales Ballesteros, Jorge. *Lima: la ciudad y sus monumentos* (Seville: Escuela de Estudios Hispano-americanos de Sevilla, 1972).

Bernand, Carmen. "Amos y esclavos en la ciudad," in *Colonización, resistencia, y mestizaje en las américas (siglos XVI–XX)*, Boccara Guillaume, ed. (Quito: Ediciones Abya-Yala, 2002), 83–104.

Blanchard, Peter. *Markham in Peru: The Travels of Clements R. Markham, 1852–1853* (Austin: University of Texas Press, 1991).

Blanchard, Peter. *Slavery & Abolition in Early Republican Peru* (Delaware: Scholarly Resources Inc., 1992).

Blanchard, Peter. *Under the Flags of Freedom: Slave Soldiers and the Wars of Independence in Spanish South America* (Pittsburgh: Pitt Latin American Studies, 2008).

Bonilla, Heraclio and Karen Spalding. *La independencia en el Perú* (Lima: Instituto de Estudios Peruanos, 1972).

Boskin, Joseph. *Sambo: The Rise & Demise of an American Jester* (Oxford: Oxford University Press, 1988).

Bowser, Frederick. *The African Slave in Colonial Peru, 1524–1650* (Stanford: Stanford University Press, 1974).

Boyer, Richard E. *Lives of the Bigamists: Marriage, Family, and Community in Colonial Mexico* (Albuquerque: University of New Mexico Press, 1995).

Brading, D.A. "Civic Ceremonies in Colonial Spanish America," in *Europa Triumphans: Court and Civic Festivals in Early Modern Europe, Vol. II*, J.R. Mulryne, ed. (Hampshire: Ashgate Publishing, 2004), 350–7.

Brion Davis, David. *The Problem of Slavery in Western Culture* (Ithaca, NY: Cornell University Press, 1966).

Brown, Christopher Leslie and Philip D. Morgan, eds. *Arming Slaves: From Classical Times to the Modern Age* (New Haven: Yale University Press, 2006).

Brown, Vincent. *The Reaper's Garden: Death and Power in the World of Atlantic Slavery* (Cambridge: Harvard University Press, 2008).

Buckridge, Steeve O. *The Language of Dress: Resistance and Accommodation in Jamaica, 1760–1890* (Kingston: University of the West Indies Press, 2004).

Burns, Kathryn. *Colonial Habits: Convents and the Spiritual Economy of Cuzco, Peru* (Durham: Duke University Press, 1999).

Burns, Kathryn. "Unfixing Race," in *Rereading the Black Legend: The Discourses of Religious and Racial Difference in the Renaissance Empires*, Margaret R. Greer, Walter D. Mignolo, and Maureen Quilligan, eds. (Chicago: University of Chicago Press, 2007), 188–202.

Burns, Kathryn. *Into the Archive: Writing and Power in Colonial Peru* (Durham: Duke University Press, 2010).

Butler, Kim. *Freedoms Given, Freedoms Won: Afro-Brazilians in Post-Abolition São Paulo and Salvador* (New Brunswick, NJ: Rutgers University Press, 1998).

Camp, Stephanie M.H. *Closer to Freedom: Enslaved Women and Everyday Resistance in the Plantation South* (Chapel Hill: University of North Carolina Press, 2004).

Campbell, E.D.C. and K.S. Rice. *Before Freedom Came: African-American Life in the Antebellum South* (Charlottesville: University of Virginia Press, 1991).

Campbell, Leon G. "Racism without Race: Ethnic Group Relations in Late Colonial Peru," in *Studies in Eighteenth Century Culture: Racism in the Eighteenth Century*, Harold E. Pagliaro, ed. (Cleveland: Case Western Reserve University, 1973), 326–8.

Carrillo Mendoza, José Luis, ed. *Etnicidad y discriminación racial en la historia del Perú, Tomo II* (Lima: Instituto Riva Agüero, 2003).

Castañeda Vielakamen, Esther and Elizabeth Toguchi Kayo, "Imagen de la mujer afroperuana en el teatro del siglo XIX: 'El deseo de figurar' de Juana Manuela Laso de Eléspuru," in *Mujeres y género en la historia del Perú*, Margarita Zegarra, ed. (Lima: Cendo-Mujer, 1999), 287–304.

Castro-Klarén, Sara and John Charles Chasteen, eds. *Beyond Imagined Communities: Reading and Writing the Nation in Nineteenth-Century Latin America* (Baltimore: Johns Hopkins University Press, 2004).

BIBLIOGRAPHY 215

Chambers, Sarah. *From Subjects to Citizens: Honor, Gender, and Politics in Arequipa, Peru, 1780–1854* (University Park: Pennsylvania State University Press, 1999).

Clark, Emily. *The Strange History of the American Quadroon: Free Women of Color in the Revolutionary Atlantic World* (Chapel Hill: The University of North Carolina Press, 2013).

Cisneros Sanchez, Manuel. *Pancho Fierro y la Lima del 800* (Lima: Importadora, Exportadora, y Librería García Ribeyros, S.C.R.L, 1975).

Cohen, David W. and Jack Greene. *Neither Slave Nor Free: The Freedman of African Descent in the Slave Societies of the New World* (Baltimore: Johns Hopkins University Press, 1972).

Cooper, Frederick, Thomas C. Holt, and Rebecca J. Scott. *Beyond Slavery: Explorations of Race, Labor, and Citizenship in Postemancipation Societies* (Chapel Hill: University of North Carolina Press, 2000).

Corilla Melchor, Ciro. "Cofradías en la ciudad de Lima, siglos XVI y XVII: Racismo y conflictos étnicos," in *Etnicidad y discriminación racial en la historia del Perú*, Elizabeth Dasso, ed. (Lima: Pontificia Universidad Católica del Perú, 2002), 11–34.

Cosamalón Aguilar, Jesus. *Indios detrás de la muralla: Matrimonios indígenas y convivencia interacial en Santa Ana (Lima, 1795–1820)* (Lima: Pontificia Universidad Catolica del Peru, 1999).

Drinot, Paulo and Leo Garofalo, eds. *Más allá de la dominación y la resistencia: Estudios de historia peruana, siglos xvi–xx* (Lima: Instituto de Estudios Peruanos, 2005).

Dubois, Laurent. *Les Esclaves de la Republique: L'histoire oubliée de la Première émancipation, 1789–1794* (Calmann-Lévy, 1998).

Duncan, Barbara and Theresa Gisbert, eds. *Gloria in Excelsis: The Virgin and Angels in Viceregal Painting of Peru and Bolivia* (New York: Center for Inter-American Relations, 1986).

Elkins, Stanley M. *Slavery: A Problem in American Institutional and Intellectual Life* (Chicago: University of Chicago Press, 1959).

Farge, Arlette. *Subversive Words: Public Opinion in Eighteenth-Century France*, translated by Rosemary Morris (University Park: Pennsylvania State University Press, 1994).

Feldman, Heidi Carolyn. *Black Rhythms of Peru: Reviving African Musical Heritage in the Black Pacific* (Middletown: Wesleyan University Press, 2006).

Ferrer, Ada. *Insurgent Cuba: Race, Nation, and Revolution, 1868–1898* (Chapel Hill: University of North Carolina Press, 1999).

Fisher, John. *Commercial Relations between Spain and Spanish America in the Era of Free trade, 1778–1796* (Liverpool: Centre For Latin-American Studies, University of Liverpool, 1985).

Fisher, John. *Trade, War, and Revolution: Exports from Spain to Spanish America, 1797–1820* (Liverpool: Institute for Latin American Studies, University of Liverpool, 1992).

Fisher, John. *Bourbon Peru: 1750–1824* (Liverpool: Liverpool University Press, 2003).

Flores Galindo, Alberto. *Aristocracia y plebe: Lima, 1760–1830* (Lima: Mosca Azul Editores, 1984).

Foner, Laura and Eugene Genovese, eds. *Slavery in the New World: A Reader in Comparative History* (Englewood Cliffs, NJ: Prentice-Hall, 1969).

Fox-Genovese, Elizabeth and Eugene Genovese. "Foreword," in Allen Kaufman, *Capitalism, Slavery, and Republican Values: American Political Economists, 1819–1848* (Austin: University of Texas Press, 1982).

França Paiva, Eduardo. *Escravidao e universo cultural na colonia Minas Gerais, 1716–1789* (Belo Horizonte: Editora UFMG, 2001).

Fraser, Valerie. *The Architecture of Conquest: Building in the Viceroyalty of Peru, 1535–1635* (Cambridge: Cambridge University Press, 1990).

Genovese, Eugene. "Foreword: Ulrich Bonnell Phillips and His Critics," in *American Negro Slavery: A Survey of the Supply, Employment, and Control of Negro Labor as Determined by the Plantation Regime* (Baton Rouge: Louisiana State University 1918, First Paperback Edition, 1966).

Genovese, Eugene. *Roll, Jordan, Roll: The World the Slaves Made* (New York: Pantheon Books, 1974).

Gibson, Charles. *Spain in America* (New York: Harper & Row, 1966).

Graubart, Karen. *With Our Labor and Sweat: Indigenous Women and the Formation of Colonial Society, Peru 1550–1700* (2008).

Gray White, Deborah. *Ar'n't I a Woman? Female Slaves in the Plantation South* (New York: W.W. Norton & Company, 1985).

Gross, Ariela. "The Law and the Culture of Slavery: Natchez, Mississippi," in *Local Matters: Race, Crime, and Justice in the Nineteenth Century South*, Christopher Waldrep and Donald G. Nieman eds. (Athens: University of Georgia Press, 2001), 92–124.

Harth-Terré, Emilio. *Presencia del negro en el virreinato del Perú* (Lima: Editorial Universitaria, 1971).

Holguín Callo, Oswaldo. "Literatura y cultura material: El mobilario doméstico en Lima (1840–1870)," in *Familia y vida cotidiana en América Latina, siglos XVIII–XX*, Scarlett O'Phelan Godoy, Ramón Muñoz, and Ricketts, eds. (Lima: Instito Riva-Agüero, 2003).

Huebner, Timothy S. "The Roots of Fairness: *State v. Caesar* and Slave Justice in Antebellum North Carolina," in *Local Matters: Race, Crime, and Justice in the*

Nineteenth Century South, Christopher Waldrep and Donald G. Nieman, eds. (Athens: University of Georgia Press, 2001), 29–52.

Hünefeldt, Christine. Paying the Price of Freedom: Family and Labor among Lima's Slaves, 1800–1854 (Berkeley: University of California Press, 1994).

Hünefeldt, Christine. Liberalism in the Bedroom: Quarreling Spouses in Nineteenth-Century Lima (University Park: Penn State University, 2000).

Hunt, Alfred. Governance of the Consuming Passions: A History of Sumptuary Law (New York: St. Martin's Press, 1996).

Hunt, Alfred N. Haiti's Influence on Antebellum America: Slumbering Volcano in the Caribbean (Baton Rouge: Louisiana State University Press, 1988).

Hunt, Patricia K. "Clothing as an Expression of History: The Dress of African-American Women in Georgia, 1880–1915," in "We Specialize in the Wholly Impossible": A Reader in Black Women's History, Darlene Clark Hine, King, and Reed, eds. (New York: Carlson, 1995).

James, C.L.R. The Black Jacobins; Toussaint L'Ouverture and the San Domingo Revolution (New York: Vintage Books, 1963).

Johnson, Walter. Soul by Soul: Life inside the Antebellum Slave Market (Cambridge: Harvard University Press, 1999).

Jones, Jacqueline. Labor of Love, Labor of Sorrow: Black Women, Work, and the Family, from Slavery to the Present (New York: Basic Books, 1985).

Jouve Martín, José Ramón. Esclavos de la Ciudad Letrada: Esclavitud, escritura y colonialismo en Lima (1650–1700) (Lima: Instituto de Estudios Peruanos, 2005).

Juan, Jorge and Antonio de Ulloa, Relación histórica del viage à la América Meridional (Madrid: Antonio Marín, 1748).

Juan, Jorge and Antonio de Ulloa. A Voyage to South America, translated by John Adams (New York: Knopf, 1964).

Kapsoli, Wilfredo. Rebeliones de Esclavos en el Perú (Lima: Ediciones Purej, 1990).

Katzew, Ilona. Casta Painting: Images of Race in Eighteenth-Century Mexico (New Haven and London: Yale University Press, 2004).

Katzew, Ilona and Susan Deans-Smith, eds., Race and Classification: The Case of Mexican America (Stanford: Stanford University Press, 2009).

Keane, Webb. "The Hazards of New Clothes: What Signs Make Possible," in The Art of Clothing: A Pacific Experience, Susanne Küchler and Graeme Were, eds. (London: UCL Press, 2005), 1–16.

Kelemen, Pál. Baroque and Rococo in Latin America (New York: Macmillan, 1951).

Kellogg, Susan and Matthew Restall, eds. Dead Giveaways: Indigenous Testaments of Colonial Mesoamerica and the Andes (Salt Lake City: University of Utah Press, 1998).

Klein, Herbert. *Slavery in the Americas: A Comparative Study of Virginia and Cuba* (Chicago, 1967).

Kraay, Hendrik. "Urban Slavery in Salvador, Bahia, Brazil: The Wills of Captain Joaquim Félix de Santana, Colonel Manoel Pereira da Silva, and Rosa Maria da Conceição," in *Colonial Lives: Documents on Latin American History, 1550–1850*, Richard Boyer and Geoffrey Spurling, eds. (Oxford: Oxford University Press, 2000).

Lauderdale Graham, Sandra. *House and Street: The Domestic World of Servants and Masters in Nineteenth-Century Rio de Janeiro* (Austin: University of Texas Press, 1998).

Lauderdale Graham, Sandra. *Caetana Says No: Women's Stories from a Brazilian Slave Society* (Cambridge: Cambridge University Press, 2002).

Lavrin, Asunción. "Cofradías Novohispanas: economías material y spiritual," in *Cofradías, capellanias y obras pías en la América colonial*, Pilar Martínez Lopez-Cano, Gisela VonWobeser and Juan Guillermo Muñoz, eds. (Mexico City: Universidad Autónoma Nacional, 1998), 49–64.

León y León Duran, Gustavo. *Apuntes histórico-genealógicos de Francisco Fierro: Pancho Fierro* (Lima: Biblioteca Nacional del Perú, Fondo Editorial, 2004).

Lipsett-Rivera, Sonya. "Scandal at the Church: José de Alfaro Accuses Dona Theresa Bravo and Others of Insulting and Beating His Castiza Wife, Josefa Cadena (Mexico, 1782)," in Richard Boyer and Jeffrey Spurling, *Colonial Lives: Documents on Latin American History, 1550–1850* (Oxford: Oxford University Press, 1999), 216–23.

Lockhart, James. *Spanish Peru, 1532–1560: A Colonial Society* (Madison: University of Wisconsin Press, 1968).

Lockhart, James. *Spanish Peru, 1532–1560: A Social History* (Madison: University of Wisconsin Press, 1994).

Lockhart, James and Stuart B. Schwartz. *Early Latin America: A History of Colonial Spanish America and Brazil* (Cambridge: Cambridge University Press, 1983).

Lucena Salmoral, Manuel. *Los Códigos Negros de la América Española* (Universidad Alcalá: Ediciones Unesco, 1996).

Luqui Lagleyze, Julio. *Los cuerpos militares en la historia Argentina: organizacion y uniformes; 1550–1950* (Rosario, Argentina: Instituto Nacional Sanmartiano, 1995).

Majluf, Natalia, ed. *Los cuadros de mestizaje del virrey Amat* (Lima: Museo de Arte, 2004).

McKnight, Katherine Joy and Leo J. Garofalo, eds. *Afro-Latino Voices: Narratives from the Early Modern Ibero-Atlantic World, 1550–1812* (Indianapolis: Hackett, 2009).

Meillassoux, Claude. *The Anthropology of Slavery: The Womb of Iron and Gold* (Chicago: University of Chicago Press, 1991).

Merrim, Stephanie. *The Spectacular City, Mexico, and Colonial Hispanic Literary Culture* (Austin: University of Texas Press, 2010).

Merriman, John. "The Rise of the Atlantic Economy: Spain and England," in *A History of Modern Europe, Vol. 1* (New York: W.W. Norton and Company, 1996).

Miers, Suzanne and Igor Kopytoff, eds. *Slavery in Africa: Historical and Anthropological Perspectives* (Madison: University of Wisconsin Press, 1977).

Miller, Joseph. *Way of Death: Merchant Capitalism in the Angola Slave Trade, 1730–1830* (Madison: University of Wisconsin Press, 1988).

Miller, Monica. *Slaves to Fashion: Black Dandyism and the Styling of Black Diasporic Identity* (Durham: Duke University Press, 2009).

Miller, Rory. *Britain and Latin America in the Nineteenth and Twentieth Centuries* (London: Longman Press, 1993).

Mills, Kenneth and William B. Taylor, eds. *Colonial Spanish America: A Documentary History* (Scholarly Resources, 1998).

Mintz, Sidney. *Sweetness and Power: The Place of Sugar in Modern History* (New York: Penguin Books, 1985).

Mintz, Sidney. *Tasting Food, Tasting Freedom: Excursions into Eating, Culture, and the Past* (Boston: Beacon Press, 1996).

Mintz, Sidney and Richard Price. *The Birth of African-American Culture: An Anthropological Perspective* (Boston: Beacon Press, 1976).

Moore, Robin. *Nationalizing Blackness: Afrocubanismo and Artistic Revolution in Havana, 1920–1940* (Pittsburgh: University of Pittsburgh Press, 1997).

Mörner, Magnus. *European Travelogues as Sources to Latin American History from the Late Eighteenth Century until 1870* (Stockholm, 1981).

Morris, Thomas D. *Southern Slavery and the Law, 1619–1860* (Chapel Hill: University of North Carolina Press, 1996).

Morrison, Samuel E. *Admiral of the Ocean Sea: A Life of Christopher Columbus* (Boston: Little Brown Co., 1942).

O'Neal, Gwendolyn S. "The African American Church, Its Sacred Cosmos and Dress," in *Religion, Dress and the Body*, Linda B. Arthur, ed. (Oxford: Berg Press, 1999).

O'Phelan Godoy, Scarlett "El vestido como identidad étnica e indicador social de una cultura material," in *El Barroco Peruano*, Ramón Mujica Pinilla et al., eds. (Lima: Banco de Crédito, 2002), 99–133.

O'Toole, Rachel. *Bound Lives: Africans, Indians, and the Making of Race in Colonial Peru* (Pittsburgh: University of Pittsburgh Press, 2012).

Painter, Nell. *Sojourner Truth: A Life, a Symbol* (New York: W.W. Norton, 1996).

Palma, Angelica. *Pancho Fierro: Acuarelista Limeño* (Lima: San Martín y CIA, S.A, 1935).

Pastor de la Torre, Celso and Luis Enrique Todd, eds. *Peru: fe y arte en el Virreynato* (Cordoba: Publicaciones Obra Social y Cultural CajaSur, 1999).

Patterson, Orlando. *Slavery and Social Death: A Comparative Study* (Cambridge: Harvard University Press, 1982).

Paz, Octavio. "Will for Form," in *Mexico: Splendors of Thirty Centuries*, translated by Edith Grossman et al. (New York: Metropolitan Museum of Art; Boston: Little, Brown, 1990).

Phillips, Ulrich Bonnell. *Life and Labor in the Old South* (Boston: Little, Brown & Company, 1929).

Poole, Deborah. *Vision, Race, and Modernity: A Visual Economy of the Andean Image* World (Princeton: Princeton University Press, 1997).

Pratt, Mary Louise. *Imperial Eyes: Travel Writing and Transculturation* (New York: Routledge, 1992).

Rabi Chara, Miguel. *El Hospital de San Bartolome de Lima (1646–2000): La protección y asistencia de la gente de color* (Lima: Grahuer Editores, 2001).

Ramos, Frances. *Identity, Ritual, and Power in Colonial Puebla* (Tuscon: University of Arizona Press, 2012).

Reis, João José. *A Morte é uma Festa: Ritos Fúnebres e Revolta Popular no Brasil do Século XIX* (São Paulo: Companhia das Letras, 1991).

Reis, João José. *Slave Rebellion in Brazil: The Muslim Uprising of 1835 in Bahia* (Baltimore: Johns Hopkins University Press, 1993).

Ribeiro, Aileen. *Dress in Eighteenth Century Europe, 1715–1789* (London: Batsford, 1984).

Ribeiro, Aileen. *Dress and Morality* (New York: Holmes & Meier, 1986).

Romero, Fernando. *Quimba, Fa, Malambo, Ñeque: Afronegrismos en el Perú* (Lima: Instituto de Estudios Peruanos, 1988).

Rowe, Ann Pollard. *Costume and History in Highland Ecuador* (Austin: University of Texas Press, 2012).

Safier, Neil. *Measuring the New World: Enlightenment Science and South America* (Chicago: University of Chicago Press, 2008).

Sauer, Carl Ortwin. *The Early Spanish Main*. New foreword by Anthony Pagden (Berkeley: University of California Press, 1992).

Schafer, Judith Kelleher. "Slaves and Crime: New Orleans, 1846–1862," in *Local Matters: Race, Crime, and Justice in the Nineteenth Century South*, Christopher Waldrep and Donald G. Nieman, eds. (Athens: University of Georgia Press, 2001), 53–91.

BIBLIOGRAPHY 221

Schenone, Héctor H. *Iconografía del Arte Colonial, Vol. 3* (Argentina: Fundación Tarea, 1998).

Scott, Julius. "Crisscrossing Empire: Ships, Sailors, and Resistance in the Lesser Antilles in the Eighteenth Century," in *The Lesser Antilles in the Age of European Expansion*, Robert Paquete and Stanley Engerman, eds., 128–43.

Scott, Rebecca J. *Slave Emancipation in Cuba: The Transition to Free Labor, 1860–1899* (Pittsburgh: University of Pittsburgh Press, 1985).

Schurz, William Lytle. *The Manila Galleon* (New York: E.P. Dutton & Co., 1939).

Serulnikov, Sergio. *Revolution in the Andes: The Age of Túpac Amaru* (Durham: Duke University Press, 2013).

Smallwood, Stephanie. *Saltwater Slavery: A Middle Passage from Africa to American Diaspora* (Cambridge: Harvard University Press, 2007).

Socolow, Susan. *The Women of Colonial Latin America* (Cambridge: Cambridge University Press, 2000).

Spalding, Karen. "The Human Landscape," in *Huarochirí: An Andean Society under Inca and Spanish Rule* (Stanford: Stanford University Press, 1984).

Stampp, Kenneth. *The Peculiar Institution: Slavery in the Ante-Bellum South* (New York: Alfred Knopf, 1956).

Stein, Stanley J. and Barbara H. Stein. *The Colonial Heritage of Latin America: Essays on Economic Dependence in Perspective* (New York: Oxford University Press, 1970).

Stern, Steve J. *Resistance, Rebellion, and Consciousness in the Andean Peasant World, 18th to 20th Centuries* (Madison: University of Wisconsin Press, 1987).

Sweet, David and Gary B. Nash, eds. *Struggle and Survival in Colonial America* (Berkeley: University of California Press, 1981).

Tannenbaum, Frank. *Slave and Citizen* (Boston: Beacon Press, 1992).

Tardieu, Jean-Pierre. *Noirs et Indiens au Pérou: Histoire d'une politique ségrégationniste, XVI–XVII siècles* (Paris: Éditions L'Harattan, 1990).

Tardieu, Jean-Pierre. *Los negros y la Iglesia en el Perú: siglos XVI–XVII* (Quito: Centro Cultural Afroecuatoriano, 1997).

Tardieu, Jean-Pierre. *El decreto de Huancayo* (Lima: Instituto de Estudios Peruanos, 2004).

Tauro, Alberto. *Viajeros en el Perú republicano* (Lima: Universidad Nacional Mayor de San Marcos, 1967).

Thornton, John. *Africa and Africans in the Making of the Atlantic World, 1400–1800* (New York: Cambridge University Press, 1998).

Todorov, Tzvetan. *The Conquest of America: The Question of the Other* (New York: Harper and Row, 1985).

Twinam, Ann. *Public Lives, Private Secrets: Gender, Honor, Sexuality, and Illegitimacy in Colonial Spanish America* (Stanford: Stanford University Press, 1999).

Van Deusen, Nancy, ed. *Souls of Purgatory: The Spiritual Diary of a Seventeenth-Century Afro-Peruvian Mystic, Ursula de Jesús* (Albuquerque: University of New Mexico Press, 2004).

Vickery, Amanda. "Women and the World of Goods: A Lancashire Consumer and her Possessions, 1751–1781," in *Consumption and the World of Goods*, John Brewer and Roy Porter, eds. (London and New York: Routledge, 1993), 274–301.

Vinson, Ben. *Bearing Arms for His Majesty: The Free-Colored Militia in Colonial Mexico* (Stanford: Stanford University Press, 2001).

Vinson, Ben. "'The Lord Walks among the Pots and Pans': Religious Servants of Colonial Lima," in *Africans to Spanish America: Expanding the Diaspora*, Sherwin K. Brywant, Ben Vinson III, and Rachel Sarah O'Toole, eds. (Chicago: University of Illinois Press, New Black Studies Series, 2012), 136–60.

Walker, Charles. *Smoldering Ashes: Cuzco and the Creation of Republican Peru: 1780–1840* (Durham: Duke University Press, 1999).

Watson, Alan. *Slave Law in the Americas* (Athens: University of Georgia Press, 1989).

White, Sophie. "'Wearing Three or Four Handkerchiefs around His collar, and Else-Where about Him': Slaves' Constructions of Masculinity and Ethnicity in French Colonial New Orleans," in *Dialogues of Dispersal: Gender, Sexuality, and African Diasporas*, Sandra Gunning, Tera W. Hunter and Michele Mitchell, eds. (Oxford: Blackwell Publishing, 2004), 132–53.

Zemon Davis, Natalie. *Fiction in the Archives: Pardon Tales and Their Tellers in Sixteenth-Century France* (Stanford: Stanford University Press, 1987).

Journals

Anna, Timothy E. "The Peruvian Declaration of Independence: Freedom by Coercion," *Journal of Latin American Studies* 7, no. 2 (November 1975): 221–48.

Blassingame, John. "Using the Testimony of Ex-Slaves: Approaches and Problems," *Journal of Southern History* 41, no. 4 (November 1975).

Bleichmar, Daniela. "Visible Empire: Scientific Expeditions and Visual Culture in the Hispanic Enlightenment," *Postcolonial Studies* 12, no. 4 (2009): 441–66.

Brett, Guy. "Being Drawn to an Image," *Oxford Art Journal* 14, no. 1 (1991): 3–9.

Brewster, Claire, "Women and the Spanish-American Wars of Independence: An Overview," *Feminist Review* 79, Latin America: History, War, and Independence (2005): 20–35.

Bromley, Juan. "Recibimiento de los virreyes en Lima," *Revista Histórica* 20 (1953): 1–108.

Bryant, Sherwin. "Enslaved Rebels, Fugitives, and Litigants: The Resistance Continuum in Colonial Quito," *Colonial Latin American Review*, 13, no. 1 (2004): 7–46.

Buschiazzo, Mario J. "Exotic Influences in American Colonial Art," *Journal of the Society of Architectural Historians* 5, Latin American Architecture (1945): 21–3.

Cahill, David. "Colour by Numbers: Racial and Ethnic Categories in the Viceroyalty of Peru, 1532–1824," *Journal of Latin American Studies* 26, no. 2 (May 1994): 325–46.

Cahill, David. "New Viceroyalty, New Nation, New Empire: A Transnational Imaginary for Peruvian Independence," *Hispanic American Historical Review* 91, no. 2 (2011): 203–35.

Charney, Paul. "A Sense of Belonging: Colonial Indian *Cofradías* and Ethnicity in the Valley of Lima, Peru," *The Americas* 54, no. 3 (January 1998): 379–407.

Cobb, Gwendolin B. "Supply and Transportation for the Potosí Mines, 1545–1640," *Hispanic American Historical Review* 29, no. 1 (February 1949): 25–45.

Degler, Carl. "Slavery and the Genesis of American Race Prejudice," *Comparative Studies in Society and History* 2 (October 1959).

Fisher, John R. "The Royalist Regime in the Viceroyalty of Peru, 1820–1824," *Journal of Latin American Studies* 32, no. 1 (2000): 55–84.

Foner, Laura. "The Free People of Color in Louisiana and St. Domingue: A Comparative Portrait of Two Three-Caste Slave Societies," *Journal of Social History*, III (1970): 406–30.

Garner, Richard L. "Long-term Silver Mining Trends in Spanish America: A Comparative Analysis of Peru and Mexico," *American Historical Review* 93, no. 4 (1988): 898–935.

Gilman, Sander L. "Black Bodies, White Bodies: Toward an Iconography of Female Sexuality in Late Nineteenth-Century Art, Medicine, and Literature," *Critical Inquiry* 12 (Autumn 1985): 204–2.

Gómez Acuña, Luis. "Las cofradías de negros en Lima (siglos XVII): estado de la cuestión y análisis de caso," *Páginas* 129 (October 1994): 28–39.

Graubart, Karen B. "The Creolization of the New World: Local Forms of Identification in Urban Colonial Peru, 1560–1640," *Hispanic American Historical Review* 89, no. 3 (2009): 471–99.

Handlin, Oscar and Mary F. Handlin. "Origins of the Southern Labor System," *William and Mary Quarterly*, 7, no. 2 (April 1950): 199–222.

Harth-Terré, Emilio. "El esclavo negro en la sociedad indoperuano," *Journal of Inter-American Studies* 3, no. 3. (July 1961): 297–340.

Ingersoll, Thomas N. "Free Blacks in a Slave Society: New Orleans, 1718–1812," *William and Mary Quarterly*, 3rd Ser., 48, no. 2 (April 1991): 173–200.

Ingersoll, Thomas N. "Slave Codes and Judicial Practice in New Orleans, 1718–1807" *Law & History Review* 13, no. 1 (Spring 1995): 23–62.

Jouve Martín, José Ramon. "Public Ceremonies and Mulatto Identity in Viceregal Lima: A Colonial Reenactment of the Fall of Troy (1631)," *Colonial Latin American Review* 16, no. 2 (2007): 179–201.

Lane, Kris. "Captivity and Redemption: Aspects of Slave Life in Early Colonial Quito and Popayán," *The Americas* 57, no. 2 (October 2000): 225–46.

Lara, Silvia. "The Signs of Color: Women's Dress and Racial Relations in Salvador and Rio de Janeiro, ca. 1750–1815," *Colonial Latin American Review* 6, no. 2 (1997): 205–24.

Lara, Silvia. "Customs and Costumes: Carlos Julião and the Image of Black Slaves in Late Eighteenth-Century Brazil," *Slavery & Abolition: A Journal of Slave and Post-slave Societies* 23, no. 2, (2002): 125–46.

Lévano Medina, Diego. "Organización y funcionalidad de las cofradías urbanas: Lima, siglo XVII," *Revista del Archivo General de la Nación* 24 (May 2002).

Mathé, Allain, "Slave Policies in French Louisiana," *Louisiana History*, XXI (1980): 127–37.

McKinley, Michelle A. "'Such Unsightly Unions Could Never Result in Holy Matrimony': Mixed-Status Marriages in Seventeenth-Century Colonial Lima," *Yale Journal of Law & the Humanities* 22, no. 2 (Spring 2010): 217–55.

McKinley, Michelle A. "Fractional Freedoms: Slavery, Legal Activism, and Ecclesiastical Courts in Colonial Lima, 1593–1689," *Law & History Review* 28, no. 3 (August 2010): 749–90.

Mitchell, Michele. "'The Black Man's Burden': African Americans, Imperialism, and Notions of Racial Manhood 1890–1910," *International Review of Social History*, 44 (1999, Supplement): 77–99.

Morales Polar, Maria Ángela. "El espacio del esclavo negro en las haciendas del valle de Cañete, 1747–1821," *Investigaciones Sociales* 12, no. 21 (July 2008): 161–83.

Morgan, Jennifer L. "'Some Could Suckle over Their Shoulder': Male Travelers, Females' Bodies, and the Gendering of Racial Ideology, 1500–1770," *William and Mary Quarterly*, 3rd Ser., 54, no. 1. (January 1997): 167–92.

O'Toole, Rachel. "From the Rivers of Guinea to the Valleys of Peru: Becoming a *Bran* Diaspora within Spanish Slavery," *Social Text* 92, no. 3 (Fall 2007): 19–36.

Premo, Bianca. "An Equity against the Law: Slave Rights and Creole Jurisprudence in Spanish America," *Slavery & Abolition* 32, no. 4 (2011): 495–51.

Rankin, David C. "The Tannenbaum Thesis Reconsidered: Slavery and Race Relations in Antebellum Louisiana," *Southern Studies*, XVIII (1979): 5–31.

Ricketts, Monica. "The Rise of the Bourbon Military in Peru, 1768–1820," *Colonial Latin American Review* 21 (2012): 413–39.

Rivas Aliaga, Roberto. "Danzantes negros en el Corpus Christi de Lima, 1756: 'Vos estis Corpus Christi,'" *Etnicidad y discriminación racial en la historia del Perú*: 35–63.

Rizo-Patrón, Paul. "La nobleza de Lima en tiempos de los Borbones," *Bulletin de L'Institut Français D'Études Andines* 19, no. 1 (1990): 129–63.

Scott, Rebecca J. "Reclaiming Gregoria's Mule: The Meanings of Freedom in the Arimao and Caunao Valleys, Cienfuegos, Cuba, 1880–1899," *Past and Present* 170 (February 2001): 181–216.

Scott, Rebecca J., and Michael Zeuske, "Le droit d'avoir des droits: l'oral et l'ecrit dans les revendications legales des ex-esclaves à Cuba, 1872–1909," *Annales, Histoire, Sciences Sociales* 59, no. 3 (2004): 521–45.

Schurz, William Lytle. "Mexico, Peru, and the Manila Galleon," *Hispanic American Historical Review* 1, no. 4 (November 1918): 389–402.

Stampp, Kenneth. "The Historian and Southern Negro Slavery," *American Historical Review* 57, no. 3 (April 1952): 613–24.

Waldstreicher, David. "Reading the Runaways: Self-Fashioning, Print Culture, and Confidence in Slavery in the Eighteenth-Century Mid-Atlantic," *William and Mary Quarterly* 56, no. 2 (April 1999): 243–72.

Walker, Charles. "The Upper Classes and Their Upper Stories: Architecture and the Aftermath of the Lima Earthquake of 1746," *Hispanic American Historical Review* 3, no. 1 (2003): 53–82.

Walker, Tamara J. "'He Outfitted His Family in Notable Decency'": Slavery, Honour, and Dress in Eighteenth-Century Lima, Peru," *Slavery & Abolition* 30, no. 3 (September 2009): 383–402.

White, Shane and Graham White. "Slave Hair and African American Culture in the Eighteenth and Nineteenth Centuries," *Journal of Southern History* 61, no. 1 (February 1995): 45–76.

White, Shane and Graham White. "Slave Clothing and African-American Culture in the Eighteenth and Nineteenth Centuries," *Past and Present*, 0, no. 148 (August 1995): 149–86.

Index

criollos. *See* Spain and Spaniards
El Comercio (newspaper), 12
Lima por dentro y fuera (poem), 94
calidad, 2, 40
    socio-racial marker, 81–2
casta paintings, New Spain
    Diceño de Mulata yja de negra y español en la Ciudad de Mexico, 101
    Gabinete de Historia Natural, 103
    Indios Barbaros, 102
    contextual details in, 105
    financed by wealthy patrons, 103
    race-mixing process in, 105
    zoology-inspired terminology, 104
casta paintings, Peruvian, 11, 13, 16, 100–1, 106–20, 126–7
    "Chichimec" Indians, 101
    distinction between casta painting genres, 127
    facial features and dress in, 106
    imaginings for alternate future possibilities, 126
    importance of, 100–1
    inventory of, 98–9
    pseudoscientific labels, 104
    race-mixing process, absent Spanish women, 105
    transformation from African origins to almost pure, 113
    white marks on women's temples, 110–12
casta paintings, Peruvian examples
    Español Quarterona de Mulato. Produce Quinterona de Mulato, 109
    Español. China. produce Quarterón de Chino, 119
    Español. Requinterona de Mulato. Produce Genteblanca, 112
    Mulata. con Español. Produsen. Quarteron de mulato, 108
    Mulata. Y Mulato producen Mulato, 108
    Negra de Guinea o criolla. Español. Producen Mulatos, 106

Negro. con Mulata Produce Sambo, 117
Negros bozales de Guinea. Yden, 106, 117
Quinterona de Mulato Requinterona de Mulato. Español, 110
Español. Genteblanca. Quasi limpio de su Orígen, 113–14
Mestizo. con Yndia. Producen Cholo, 117
castas (Indians, Africans, and their mixed-race offspring), 2, 82 *See also* artwork, *See also* sumptuary laws and regulations
    attire and weapons of, 32–3
    lawsuits, 45
    ownership of slaves, 32
    shared housing, 67
cofradías (religious brotherhoods), 45
    status conflicts within, 66
criado/a (servant), 130, 132, 142
Diario de Lima (newspaper), 12, 127–8
    articles on owners of slaves, 139–40
    articles on slavery, 17, 135–7
    criticism of lazy slaves, Spaniards as passive victims, 142–4
    runaway slave notices, 129, 131–4
El Amor Duende (saynete, Monforte y Vera), 35–7
    "*la sorpresa no deseada*" the unwanted surprise, 39
El Negro (newspaper), 165
    "Bufonadas", Afro-Peruvians in embarrassing situations, 166
    "La Esclava Americana", 170
    Afro-Peruvian characters, 166–7
    anecdote of Dominga and *portero*, 166–7
    denigration and discrimination of Afro-Peruvians, 166–7
    Rimac River anecdote, 166
Escuela de Bellas Artes de San Fernando, 114
exequias (funerary rites in honor of deceased monarchs), 40
Gabinete de Historia Natural, 103

Gaceta de Lima (monthly newspaper), 12
    funeral of Señora Doña Rosa de Ilardy y Sabedra, 40
Incidents in the Life of a Slave Girl (Jacobs), 170
La Abeja Republicana (newspaper)
    appeal to women to "provide an example of virtue", 148
    Spaniards as "casta maldita,", 152
Life in Philadelphia series, Harper's Weekly, 170
Mercurio Peruano (newspaper), 143
    articles on slavery, 17, 135–6
    black as an epitome of disorder, 136
    letter complaining holiday of Corpus Christi costumes, 138–9
    letter detailing bond between his slave and child, 137–8
    Spaniards as passive victims of slaves' sexual and social predations, 143
New York Tribune, 170
Real Gabinete de Historia Natural (Royal Cabinet of Natural History), 98, 126
Slave and Citizen (Tannenbaum), 171–2
Systema Naturae (Linnaeus), 99

abolition, 3, 6, 146, 164, *See also* slaves and slavery
    "bobalition", 169–70
Acapulco, 23
African descendents. *See also El Negro* (newspaper)
    cuarterona libre, will of, 83, 86–7
    morena libre, will of, 83, 87
    Jim Crow laws and segregation, 172
    mocked in poem by Terralla y Landa, 94–6
    women's attire, 17, 33–4, 39
Aguirre, Carlos, 3
Aguirre, Joseph, mestizo, 124
Alba, María de, 67
Alvarado, José, zambo, theft for wife's clothing, 55–60
Alvarado, Sebastian de, 56
Amat y Junyient, Manuel de, 16, 98–9, 120–2
    casta paintings and racial purity, 144
    Gabinete de Historia Natural, 103
    patron of Peruvian *casta* paintings, 103
    restrictions on mourning dress, 41
Angrand, Leonce, 154

Antonio Suárez, Juan, 65
Arellano, Manuel, 101
    "Chichimec" Indians, 101
    Diceño de Mulata yja de negra y español en la Ciudad de Mexico, 101
    focus on wealth of the colony, 102
Ariola, Ana de, morena libre, 83–5, 87
Armendaríz, José de, 20, 35, 37
artistic tradition
    costumbrismo, 18
    depiction of color and status in early-republican era, 156
    dressed slaves identically to masters, 153
    monochrome engraving, 11
    watercolors, 11
    watercolors of daily life in Lima, 159
artwork. *See also casta* paintings
    "A Merry Company on the Banks of the Rimac River", 127–8
    "Convite al coliseo de gallos", 162–3
    "El Capeador", 158
    "En Amancaes", 159–60
    "En día de fiesta", 164
    "Esteban Arredondo", 158
    Tapada limeña, 159
Ascarrunz, Orencio de (notary), 9, 86, 124
Asempción, María, zamba, 124
Aspertía, Manuela, parda libre, 86
attire, 114, *See also casta* paintings, Peruvian examples, *See also* sumptuary laws and regulations, *See also* status and attire
    saya y manto, 35–7, 95
    tapada, 35, 38–9, 95, 157
    extravagant dress of lower class women, 160
    Gil de Castro, army uniform designer, 146
    headscarf, 112
    headscarf,*(tignon)* influence on Louisiana, 106, 109, 114, 116–17, 126
    livery, noblemen and slaves, 26–7, 31, 34, 38–9
    military uniforms, 12, 17, 26, 38, 148, 152
    plain shirt (unbuttoned) and cape, 117
    ponchos of plantation slavery, 106
    shoes, indication of labor and status, 59–60
    Spanish men's sartorial splendor, 117, 120
    Victorian England, 156

Balcazar, Agustina, parda libre, 85–7
Bautista Angel, Juan, Spaniard, 62–3, 70–2
Bayly, Jaime, 158
Beluzo, Antonio, 41
Bennett, Herman, 4, 32
Bentham, Jeremy, 74
Berlin, Ira, 4
Bernardo de Tagle, José, 151
Betagh, William, 1–2
Blanchard, Peter, 3, 148–9
blood mending. *See* whitening
Blumenthal, Debra, 25
Bolaños, Manuela, 62, 69
Bonnaffé, André Auguste, 154
 "El Capeador", 158
Bowser, Frederick, 3, 6, 24
Brazil
 divorce proceedings and slave reputation, 60
 slave rebellion, 8
Burns, Kathryn, 8

Cabrera, Miguel, 102
Calderón, Domingo (jornalero), theft for leisure and friends' use, 65–6, 69–70
Callao, 56–7, 61
 port near Lima, 22–4
Calvo, Francisco, negro, 62–5, 69–72
Camp, Stephanie M.H., 5, 48–9
Canal, Joachin, *mulato*, 124
Carabaya, gold mines of, 23
Carmen, Clementina del, 73
Carrera, Magali, 101
Cartagena, 24
Casal, Francisca, will of, 87
 and manumission of slave Enferma, 89
Castro, Gil de, "Primer Pintor del Gobierno del Perú", 146
Catalina de Espinosa, Theresa, will of, 87
Cavello y Mesa, Antonio, Spaniard, 129
Cayetana de Escobar y Barrantes, María, 82
census groups. *See also* racial identity
 Español/a, 104
 indios and *pardos*, 104
 mestizo/a, 104
 negros, 104
Cervantes Saavedra, Miguel de, 160
Chachapoyas, gold mines of, 23
Charles III (king), 16, 21, 98
Cisneros Sanchez, Manuel, 161

City of Kings. *See* Lima
Clay, Edward W., *Life in Philadelphia* series, 170
Cobo, Bernabé, 32–3
Colegio Real de San Martin, school's uniform casaca, 78
color classifications, 13–15, *See also* racial identity
Cortes, Petrona, cuarterona libre, 83, 87
court records, civil and criminal, 6–10, *See also* divorce and annulment proceedings
 cofradías (religious brotherhoods) suits against, 45
 cruel and excessive punishment suits, 45
 slaves and marriage issues, 55
 stealing, motivation for, 10
 use and barriers of litigation, 46
 witnesses under duress, 53
crimes. *See also* court records, civil and criminal, *See also* Ramos, Juan, *See also* Calvo, Francisco
 cimarronaje (running away) by male slaves, 47
 excuse for imposition of restrictive laws, 75
 José Alvarado theft case, 55–60
 José Orrantía theft case, 63
 Juana Maria Lobatón case, 67–9
 motivation for stealing, 76
 sentences of exile, 33–5, 68, 134
 theft, 43, 47–9, 54
Croix, Teodoro de, 41
cultural bricolage, 5

Dávila, Cayetano, cholo, 67–8
Davis, Natalie Zemon, 8
Daza, Francisca Xavier, quinterona de mestizo, 124–5
Daza, Josepha, 124–5
Deans-Smith, Susan, 101, 103
divorce and annulment proceedings
 deception based on dress and racial identity, 78–83
 scrutiny of alleged *chino*, 94
Dolores de Iturrigaray, María, Spaniard, 67
Dominga de Loayza, María, 55–7, 60, 62–4

Echave y Roxas, Pedro Antonio de, 20
Espinosa, Narsisa de, will of, 90

families. See also *casta* paintings, See also
    Romano, Joseph, See also Xavier
    Daza, Francisca
  annulment based on racial identity, 94
  influence of slavery on, 143
  kinship networks, 61–5, 67
  mixed racial status in, 123–5
  mixed slave and free, 121–3, 125
  Pragmatic Sanctions on Marriage law,
    126
  whitening as generational progress, 113,
    123
Farfán, Marcela, morena, 124
Farge, Arlette, 9
Ferrer, Ada, 13
Fierro, Francisco "Pancho", 11, 18, 158–9,
    164
  "Convite al coliseo de gallos", 162–3
  "En Amancaes", 159–60
  "En día de fiesta", 164
  "Esteban Arredondo", 158
  elegant dresser, "lujo mulato", 161
  fashionable dark-hued men and women,
    160
  granted freedom as a baby, 157
  self-taught, 158
Foronda, Joséf (*mulato*)
  manumission of, 69
Foronda, Juana, 69
Foucault, Michel, 74
Frézier, Amedée, 1–2, 38

Gage, Thomas, 32
gentleman, 49–51, 75, 134
Gómez, Maria del Carmen, *negra* slave,
    150
Graham, Sandra Lauderdale, 7, 60, 89, 91
Granados, Santiago, 75
Guerrero, Estefanía, *mulata*, 63

Hall, Kim, 28
Herboso, Natividad, 67
Hünefeldt, Christine, 3, 66

Ignacia de Vargas, María, 67
independence (1821), declaration, 17, 145
independence, war of
  Battle of Ayacucho (1824), 146
  declaration (1821), 145–6
Islas, Andrés de, 102

Jacobs, Harriet, 170
Javiera Ramires, Maria, quarterona, 87
jornaleros (hired out slaves), 3, 24, 44–5, 49,
    65
José de Asco y Arostegui, Martin, 68
José de Sucre, Antonio, 146
Juan, Jorge, 1–2, 11, 37, 114–17

Katzew, Ilona, 101–2
Keane, Webb, 37
Koyo, Elizabeth Toguchi, 39

Lacan, Jacque, 75
Lane, Jill, 169
lawsuits. See crimes, See court records, civil
    and criminal
Lazaro, Petrona de, negra, 58
legislation. See also sumptuary laws and
    regulations, See also Pragmatic
    Sanctions on Marriage law
  "free-womb" legislation, freeing
    newborn children of slaves, 147
  funerary practices, restrictions on, 41
  headscarf, (*tignon*) influence on
    Louisiana, 126
  restrictions on Spaniards' dress and
    weapons, 152
Lima. See also Spain and Spaniards
  mining wealth in, 22–3
  naming of (1535), 22
  population of, 3
  Real Audiencia (appellate court), 20, 47
  slaves armed with weapons, 29–32
  Viceroyalty of Peru (1542), 22, 25
Linnaeus, Carl, 99
literacy, 16, 149
Lobatón, Juana Maria, 67–9
Lozano, Cristobal, 16, 98

Madrid, 26, See also Gabinete de Historia
    Natural
Manrique, Clara, 49–50
Manso de Velasco, José, 41
Manuel, Juan (*mulato*), runaway slave, 131–2
manumission
  definition of, 69
  Enferma, slave, 89
  Joséf Foronda, 69
  Joseph Nazaro, letter documenting
    freedom, 121

manumission (cont.)
　Maria Josefa de la Soto, 89
　records, 6, 45, 69
　to sick slaves, 89
　will of Juana de Rivas, 89
María, Ignacia, 50
Mariano Rodríguez del Fierro y Robina, Nicolás, 157
Martínez, Feliciana, blanca, 123
Medrano, Mercedes, 157
Meléndez, Mariselle, 136
Melís, Mateo, Spaniard, 62, 70
Mena, Isabel de, 124
Mendoza y Madero, Victoria, 124
Mexico City. *See also* casta paintings, New Spain
　capital of New Spain, 22
　slave attire in, 4, 32
military service
　Primera Compañía de Morenos, 150
　portrayal in "En Amancaes", 159–60
　slave to soldier and freedom, 151
mines and mining
　Cerro Rico ("Rich Hill") of Potosí, 22–3
　gold mines of Carabaya and Chachapoyas, 23
　silver, 23
Mintz, Sidney, 5
Miró, Esteban, 126
Mörner, Magnus, 10

Nazaro, Joseph, *negrito*, 121–3
New Spain. *See* Mexico City, *See* casta paintings, New Spain
newspapers. *See also Diario de Lima* (newspaper), *See also Mercurio Peruano* (newspaper), *See also La Abeja Republicana* (newspaper), *See also El Negro* (newspaper), *See also Gaceta de Lima* (monthly newspaper)
　readership, 135
　slaves and Africans target of racial hatred, 144
Nieto, Francisco, 124
notaries, 8–9, 12, 69, 81

O'Higgins, Ambrosio, 12, 41
Orrantía, José, *negro*, 63
Ortega, Nicolasa, *quarterona* , 124
O'Toole, Rachel, 3
Oyaque, Jacoba, 67

Panopticon, 74
Peralta y Barnuevo, Pedro de, 2
Peresbuelta, Isabel, 62
Philippine-Spanish American commerce, 23
Pino Díaz, Fermín del, 107, 113
Pintado, Maria Josefa, *morena libre de casta chala*, 87
Pizarro, Francisco, 22
Porras Barrenechea, Raul, 158
Portugal, African slave trade in, 25
Potosi, 3
　Cerro Rico ("Rich Hill"), 22
Pragmatic Sanctions on Marriage law, 126
Premo, Bianca, 136
Price, Richard, 5
Prince of Asturias 21, 98, 121

Quiroz, Gabriel de, *negro libre*, 84–5, 87, 93

racial terms, 82, *See also* castas, *See also casta* paintings
　blanco/a, 82–3, 123–4
　bozales (African-born blacks), 66, 138–9
　chino/a, 13, 80–2, 94
　cuarterona libre, 83, 86
　Español/a, 81–2
　indios, 15, 20, 35, 81–3, 97–8, 104
　mestizo/a, 13, 15, 20, 35, 81–3, 97, 104–5, 124–5, 143
　moreno/a, 83, 87, 104, 124–5
　mulato/a, 2, 14, 35, 69, 81, 97, 101, 104–5, 121, 123–4, 132, 139
　negro/a de casta congo, 82, 121
　negro/a libre, 84, 86
　pardo/a, 15, 66, 82, 85–6, 104, 123
　quarteron/a, 13, 66, 104, 121, 123–4
　quinteron/a, 13, 66, 104, 121, 124
　requinterona de mulato, 104
　sacalagua, 104
　sambo/a (or *zambo/a*), 13, 55, 82, 89, 104, 123
Spaniards as "casta maldita", 152
subjective and shifting process, 81, 94, 151
Ramón Jouve Martín, José, 45
Ramos, Juan, 43, 51–4, 72, 75
　sent to *panadería*, 50
　Camparón, "the distinguished one", 43
　attire of a gentleman, 134
Rappaport, Joanne, 83, 104
Reina, Josepha de, *blanca*, 124
Reis, João José, 8

INDEX

Rimac River, 22, 62, 140
Risco, Ilario, 150
Rivas, Gregoria de, 89
Rivas, Juana de, 89
Roberts, Helene E., 156
Rodríguez del Fierro, Mariana, 157
Rodríguez Juárez, Juan, *Indios Barbaros*, 102
Romano, Joseph, *quarterón libre*, 123–4
Rosas, María Antonia, 150
Rosas, Pedro, *negro de casta congo*, 150
royalty. *See also* Charles III (king)
    exequias (funerary rites in honor of deceased monarchs), 40
    ceremonies honoring, 32
    colonial officials as representatives, 29
    Pragmatic Sanctions on Marriage law, 126
runaway slaves
    appearance changes, 132
    Juan Manuel, 132
    newspaper description details, 130, 132
    passing as free, 93, 134

Salaverde, Josepha de, 73
San Martín, José de, 145–6
Sanchez, Maria, 63–4
shipping
    Manila Galleons, 23
    Philippine-Spanish American commerce, 23
    trade routes, 24
slaveholders
    jornaleros (day laborers), income from, 3, 24
    complicated intimacies shown in wills, 90–3
    dressed slaves identically to masters, 37–8
    ignoring sumptuary laws, 21, 30–2, 34–5
    obligations to feed and clothes slaves, 58–60
    purchases for domestic and other uses, 24
    Sumba (South Pacific) dressed slaves for status, 37
    will of Francisca Casal and manumission, 89
    will of Francisco de la Sota and manumission, 89
    will of Juana de Rivas and manumission, 89–90
slaves and slavery. *See also* mines and mining, *See also* military service, *See also* newspapers
    "free-womb" legislation, 147
    panadería (slave prison and bakery), 50
    abolition (1854), 3, 6, 146, 164
    African slaves, symbolic uses of, 23–5
    behavior scrutinized, 72–6, 93
    connections throughout Americas, 169–71
    families and, 62–4
    female slaveholder and female slaves, 27–8, 39
    gift giving and, 66–7
    literacy, forms of, 45
    marriage and, 55–6, 60–1, 67
    newspaper articles blaming slaves for poor behavior, 137
    presumptions about laziness, 71, 142
    role in fight for independence, 146–8
    roles in Lima, 3
    secret parties, 48
    women's role in war for independence, 148–50
slaves and slavery, attire. *See also* sumptuary laws and regulations
    á la Turque, 27
    elegant self-presentation, 2, 5, 16, 32, 42, 49–50, 54, 69, 75–6, 146
    identical to slaveholder, 37, 141
    passing as free, 93
    restrictions on mourning dress, 41
    secret parties, women's efforts for, 48–9
    slaves as discerning customers, 64
    status based on attire, 59
    status symbol, finery and, 21, 25–9, 31–2
social criticism, "A Merry Company on the Banks of the Rimac River", 142
social hierarchy. *See also* status and attire, *See also calidad* (quality)
    cofradías restricted to free blacks only, 66
    attire of gentleman and, 50
    relations between enslaved and free African descendents, 66
social networks, 49
    access to litigation and, 46
    runaway slaves and, 134
    sharing resources, 69–70
Sota, Francisco de la, and manumission of slave Maria Josefa, 89
Spain and Spaniards
    peninsulares and *criollos*, 2, 15
    quinto real, paid to Spanish crown, 23

232 INDEX

Spain and Spaniards (cont.)
    influence on New World, 25–8
    post-independence shift in to political term, 152
    slaves as symbols of masculine power, 25
    slaves used in public spectacles, 26–7
status and attire, 37, 61
    El Amor Duende as morality play, 37
    dressed slaves identically to masters in Lima, 37–9
    failure to legislate social hierarchy, 42
    slaves as symbols of masculine power, 38
    Sumba (South Pacific) dressed slaves for status, 37
Steen, Jan, 142
sumptuary laws and regulations, 37
    dress of African descendent women (1631), 33
    dress of mulatto or Negro women (1665), 33
    dress of mulatto or Negro women (1667), 33
    dress of negros, mulatos, indios, and mestizos (1723), 21, 35
    dress of negros, mulatos, indios, and mestizos (1725), 15, 20
    failure of, 83–4, 97

Tadeo Acuña, José, 67
Tagle, Brigida, 63–4
Taller, Pedro, Spaniard, 124
Tannenbaum, Frank, 171–2
Tardieu, Jean-Pierre, 3
Terralla y Landa, Esteban de, 94
Theresa de Solís, María, 89
Thoribio, 51
Tristan, Flora, 165, 167
Twinam, Ann, 104, 151

Ugarte Elespuru, Juan Manuel, 161
Ulloa, Antonio de, 1–2, 11, 37, 114–17
United States
    "outlaw parties", 5
    comparison to Lima slaves, 49
    WPA slave testimonies, 8–9

Valencia, 25
Van Deusen, Nancy, 89
Vargas Machuca, Pedro de, 55–60

Ventura Pastrana, Buena, parta libre, 87
Vickery, Amanda, 89
Vidal, E.E., *Tapada limeña*, 153–4
Vielakamen, Esther Castañeda, 39
Villa-Fuerte, Marques de, 139
Villanueva, Diego de, 11, 114, 116–17
    engraving based on Juan and Ulloa's journey, 114–16

Waldstreicher, David, 132
weapons
    all African descendents prohibited from carrying (1538, 1549), 30–2
    free *castas* arming themselves, 32
    military service and manumission for slaves, 148
white marks on their temples. *See casta* paintings, Peruvian examples
White, Graham, 5, 132
White, Shane, 5, 132
whitening, 113, 117, 124
wills, 9–10
    African-descent testators, 86–7
    Catalina de Espinosa, Theresa, 87
    Cortes, Petrona, *cuarterona libre*, 83
    inventory of possessions, 84–5, 88–9
    Josefa Pintado, *morena libre de casta chala*, 87
    manumission, motives for, 90
    manumissions granted, 89–90
    Medrano, Mercedes, 157
    Narsisa de Espinosa, 90
    wardrobe and jewels, 83, 93
women. *See also* sumptuary laws and regulations, *See also casta* paintings
    African descendents attire, 17, 33–4, 39
    African-descent wives of Spaniards, 34–5
    Africans portrayed as less attractive, 157
    appeal to "provide an example of virtue" in war of independence, 148
    census and, 125
    census data for, 125
    complex status of enslaved, 39
    secret parties, women's efforts for, 48–9

Ypinsa, Joseph de, 82–3, 94

Zaya, Margarita, 43, 51–2, 54
Zevallos Guerra, José, 20–1, 35
Zorilla, Magdalena, parda libre, 56, 61

Milton Keynes UK
Ingram Content Group UK Ltd.
UKHW030812101024
2102UKWH00041BB/224